from Waiting *to* Wonder

A Journey Through Infertility,
Perseverance, and Miracles

by
Naomi Franchetti

FOR AVERY, ALIANA, AND DECLAN

∞

I LOVE YOU

INFINITY

AND MORE

3,000

Cover & Layout Design: Mel Wise
Portrait Photo: Catherine Dean Photography

From Waiting to Wonder: A Journey Through Infertility, Perseverance, and Miracles

Hardcover ISBN: 979-8-9944077-0-7 Paperback ISBN: 979-8-9944077-1-4
eBook ISBN: 979-8-9944077-2-1

Table of Contents

Preface

As I sit here writing, I'm fresh out of the fourth trimester. This week, our baby boy turned three months old. His squishy cheeks dominate my photo reel.

While I'm eager to get things done and find my way back to myself, I also want to soak in this fleeting newborn phase. It's a strange dichotomy. I miss the wellness rituals that helped me feel grounded. I miss being able to do, and teach, 90 minutes of hot yoga without needing to plan around feeding or pumping.

But I don't regret the time I have with him. He's our last baby. I am, after all, considered to be of "advanced maternal age." Or, dare I say… *geriatric.*

Infertility affects one in six people, and increasingly, friends and family are turning to fertility treatments to achieve the families they yearn for. I never intended to write this book, but I couldn't ignore the call from within to share my story. Countless people ask me, "How did you manage to have a healthy baby at 45?" The answer is even more incredulous when I reveal that my husband and I relied on IVF to conceive our first two children. This book captures our journey and the practices that led to the arrival of our unexpected "bonus baby."

I'm sharing this story to offer insight, encouragement, and hope to those navigating infertility, those hoping to protect their fertility and longevity, or anyone simply seeking to understand the path.

This book is for anyone holding onto hope and exploring what's possible. Though I write specifically from the lens of infertility, the heart of this story is perseverance. It's about learning to step past your doubts and move forward—one day, one decision, one moment of courage at a time.

Every story has a hero, a person who embarks on a journey filled with challenges, growth, and transformation. As I stand at the beginning of this narrative, I realize that the hero in this story is not a warrior or a mythical figure but an ordinary person, someone like me. My journey is not to slay dragons or conquer distant lands, but to face the trials of infertility, a battle fought in the quiet moments of hope, despair, and everything in between.

You may have heard of the "Hero's Journey." It's a storytelling framework from mythology, popularized by Joseph Campbell, that outlines a path we intuitively recognize: the hero receives a call to adventure, faces trials and challenges, descends into a dark place, and ultimately returns transformed. It's powerful because it reflects something true about the emotional and psychological paths we all walk.

For me, the call came when my husband and I decided to start a family. It began with excitement and hope but we had no idea how difficult the road would be.

The trials weren't mythical monsters, but they were just as brutal. They came as fertility treatments, endless doctor's visits, and the emotional rollercoaster of each cycle. Month after month, we poured ourselves into trying, hoping, and bracing for heartbreak. Each time brought fresh disappointment and deeper doubt. I often felt like a shadow of myself.

The darkest part, what Campbell calls the "abyss," came with every negative test result. After weeks of waiting, hoping, and praying, I'd stare at that blank space where a positive should have been. It was devastating. I questioned everything: my body, my choices, my future. Each loss chipped away at my sense of self.

But like any true Hero's Journey, the abyss was not the end.

My husband and I emerged from those years with two beautiful children through IVFs...gifts that brought joy beyond words. Still, our journey didn't feel finished. We attempted one final embryo transfer and when it failed, it felt like the closing of a chapter. We grieved. We accepted. We let go.

During that time, we explored everything we could to support our health and fertility: mindfulness, nutrition, mindset work, and intentional lifestyle changes. We leaned into research, resilience, and self-care. This approach is often referred to as biohacking: changing the environment outside and inside of you so you can have full control of your biology.[1]

Eventually, we reached a kind of emotional equilibrium, not full peace, but something quieter. A settling. A sense of being okay with the unknown, and with the shape our family had taken. And then life surprised us.

At 44 years old, I became pregnant naturally. At 45, I delivered our healthy baby boy. No medical intervention. Just a gift.

That's why I wrote this book.

It's divided into two parts.

Part I is our story: raw, personal, and real. It's the emotional heart of this journey.

Part II is where things get a little science-heavy but stay with me. This section is a deep dive into the strategies, tools, and mindset shifts that helped support my health and fertility. It might feel like a lot but within it you might find your missing link: that one insight or approach that clicks.

It could be your $n = 1$ moment. (For the non-science crowd: $n = 1$ is a research term that means you're the experiment. It's personal data. It's figuring out what works for *you*.)

I dug into all of this because it mattered. And it made a difference. It worked.

So, if you're the kind of person who likes a little evidence with your inspiration, welcome. And if not, don't worry. I'll walk you through it like a friend would: honestly, with humor, and without pretending I have it all figured out.

This is a book about infertility, yes, but it's also about more than that. It's about what it means to hope when hope feels dangerous.

It's about the courage to keep trying. It's about healing, surrender, and the possibility of miracles. And it's about writing your story, even when you're scared, even when you've tried to walk away from it.

I'm sharing this in the hope that it might help someone. Maybe that someone is you. Because no matter where you are in your journey, you are not alone. You are already braver than you think. And sometimes when we least expect it, life delivers a twist we never saw coming and invites us to begin again.

This was my personal experience, and I will share with you some of my health data for context. If you're anything like me—Type A with a sprinkle of obsession, working through infertility struggles—you probably want to compare. I know, realistically, everyone is different, but sometimes you might wonder: How do I look in comparison to those numbers? What are my chances? What have my doctors told me about my own fertility or infertility? So, I have added some of my data in here for your reference.

This is a great time for a medical disclaimer. Everything I share here is for informational purposes only and is not meant to provide medical advice. I am not an attorney, medical professional, nutritionist, or dietician. By providing the information contained in this book, I am not diagnosing, treating, curing, mitigating, or preventing any disease or medical condition. It is always advisable to seek the advice of a licensed healthcare professional.

PART I

CHAPTER 1:

Welcome to the Detour You Never Chose

As I sit down to share my story, I'm struck by the realization that not everyone who reads this will have firsthand experience with infertility. It's a world filled with its own language, rituals, and emotional landscape that can seem foreign to those who haven't walked this path. So, before I dive into my personal journey, I feel a need to introduce some of the basics. It's like I'm about to take you on a tour of a country you've never visited, and I want to make sure you have a good map and a basic understanding of the local customs.

This isn't just about explaining medical terms or procedures; it's about conveying the emotional weight of each step, the hope that fuels us, and the resilience that keeps us going. Whether you're here because you're starting your own fertility journey, supporting a loved one, or simply curious, I hope this introduction will help you navigate the complex terrain of trying to conceive when things don't go as easily as we're led to believe they should. Let's start at the beginning, with the basics of the female menstrual cycle—a process I never thought I'd become so intimately familiar with until I found myself on this path.

The female menstrual cycle is like a monthly biological clock, ticking away with surprising precision. It all starts with the first day of your period, or as we affectionately call it on the trying-to-conceive (TTC) boards, when Aunt Flo (AF) comes to visit. This marks Cycle Day 1 (CD1), and the beginning of the follicular phase.

During this phase, your body is busy preparing for the main event: ovulation. Follicle-stimulating hormone (FSH) kicks into gear, encouraging the growth of several follicles in your ovaries. It's like a microscopic race, with each follicle vying to be the chosen one. Around CD14 (in a typical 28-day cycle), the winner emerges. Luteinizing hormone (LH) surges, triggering the release of a mature egg from the dominant follicle. This is ovulation, the star of the show in the TTC world.

It's the moment we obsess over, tracking with Ovulation Predictor Kits (OPK) and Basal Body Temperature (BBT) charts...or whatever new fertility monitor is out there! Post-ovulation, we enter the luteal phase, aka the dreaded Two Week Wait (TWW). The ruptured follicle transforms into the corpus luteum, pumping out progesterone like it's going out of style. This hormone prepares the uterine lining for a potential pregnancy, creating a cozy nest for implantation. If fertilization occurs (usually within 24 hours of ovulation), the fertilized egg begins its journey down the fallopian tube.

It takes about a week to reach the uterus, dividing and growing along the way. Around 6-10 Days Past Ovulation (DPO), implantation may occur, with the embryo nestling into the uterine lining. This is when the real nail-biting begins. Am I feeling different? Is that twinge implantation? The urge to Pee On A Stick (POAS) becomes almost irresistible. We dream of seeing that elusive Big Fat Positive (BFP) instead of another Big Fat Negative (BFN).

If pregnancy doesn't occur, the corpus luteum breaks down, progesterone levels drop, and the cycle begins anew with the arrival of AF. It's a rollercoaster of hope and disappointment, punctuated by a dizzying array of acronyms that make Trying to Conceive TTC forums look like secret code to the uninitiated. Baby Dance (BD) or Did The Deed (DTD) becomes a scheduled event, and every twinge or symptom is analyzed with the intensity of a CSI episode. Through it all, we persevere. We track, we time, we hope.

Because at the end of the day, we're all chasing that same dream, to see those two pink lines and start the next great adventure.

Common Trying To Conceive (TTC) Acronyms:

- BBT: Basal Body Temperature
- BD: Baby Dance
- BFN: Big Fat Negative
- BFP: Big Fat Positive
- CM: Cervical Mucus
- CP: Chemical Pregnancy
- DH/DW: Dear Husband/Dear Wife
- DTD: Did The Deed
- DPO: Days Past Ovulation
- EWCM: Egg White Cervical Mucus
- FET: Frozen Embryo Transfer
- hCG: Human Chorionic Gonadotropin
- HSG: Hysterosalpingogram
- IUI: Intrauterine Insemination
- IVF: In Vitro Fertilization
- LP: Luteal Phase
- MC: Miscarriage
- PIO: Progesterone in Oil
- POAS: Pee On a Stick
- RE: Reproductive Endocrinologist
- SA: Semen Analysis
- TI: Timed Intercourse

CATHOLIC GUILT AND THE COLD WAND OF TRUTH

I grew up Catholic...Catholic school, Catholic rules, and a good dose of Catholic guilt. I stayed in Catholic school until high school, mostly because that's where the road ended; there wasn't a Catholic high school nearby.

Even though I had some college scholarships, I ended up joining the Montana Air National Guard. My dad was in it, and it was a practical choice because it paid for school. I got my bachelor's degree and then applied to Active Duty Air Force Officer Training School. I was accepted as a personnel officer.

My first active-duty assignment was at Malmstrom Air Force Base, home to 150 nuclear-tipped Minuteman III Intercontinental Ballistic Missiles—basically, one of the country's strategic nuclear deterrence hubs. I was working in the missile maintenance squadron as a section commander when my squadron commander told me I should cross-train into maintenance. "You'd fit in," he said. "You'd make a difference. We'll take care of you."

I wasn't so sure. Nukes? ICBMs? Was that really *me*? There weren't any other women officers doing that job in the squadron, and I didn't exactly see myself in that world. But I respected him, and I really trusted him. So I said yes.

That "yes" ended up being one of the best decisions I ever made. The mission was high-stakes but it was also deeply meaningful. I met incredible people, and I found a sense of purpose I hadn't known I was missing.

That decision led me to F.E. Warren Air Force Base in Cheyenne, Wyoming and that's where I met my wonderful husband, Matt. He was a missileer, which meant he spent long hours underground in a launch control center, ready to send off nuclear missiles if the order ever came. We met through the Company Grade Officers Council, a professional organization for junior officers focused on leadership, networking, and service.

At first, we were just friends. Thanks to my persistence, we eventually became something more. I had been married before, though I never had children. Looking back, part of me wonders if that was by design. Maybe I wasn't meant to start a family until I met Matt. With him, for the first time, I could truly picture it—building a life together, raising children, creating something lasting. It felt right in a way it never had before.

After three short years of dating (ha), we got married en route to our next assignment: Hill Air Force Base in Utah. We weren't in a rush to have kids. I was 31, he was 29, and we figured we were healthy and had plenty of time. If only we knew what was ahead, we might have started sooner. But at that point, our careers kept us busy and mostly fulfilled. Starting a family was still on the horizon.

About a year into our marriage, we decided to give it a go. "Let's just see what happens," we said, pretty confident it would be easy. I was deep into Bikram Yoga and practicing and teaching at Higher Ground Hot Yoga in Ogden as often as I could while working full time. Matt was working out regularly too. We were healthy and ready, or so we thought.

For a year we waited while nothing happened. I tracked my cycles, and they were irregular...anything from 36 to 51 days. Surely something must be going on?

As Sherlock Holmes said, "When you have eliminated the impossible, whatever remains, however improbable, must be the truth." And the truth, unwelcome as it was, began to take shape: this might not be as simple as we'd hoped.

Ah, the journey of fertility tracking, a path I never expected would lead me to become an amateur statistician and part-time contortionist. It all started when a well-meaning friend recommended *Taking Charge of Your Fertility*. Little did I know this book would become my new bedtime reading, replacing screen time with tales of cervical mucus and ovulation predictor kits. As I dove into the pages, I had a flashback to my pre-wedding days and the Catholic Church's family planning instructions. Suddenly, those vague memories of "natural family planning" came into sharp focus. It was like the Church had given me the SparkNotes version, and now I was diving into the unabridged edition, complete with footnotes and appendices.

Determined to crack the case of my own reproductive system, I embarked on a quest to unearth the long-forgotten charts from my dusty book collection. Who knew that graph paper could evoke such excitement?

Armed with my newfound knowledge and a shiny new thermometer (because nothing says "I'm adulting" quite like a specialized thermometer), I dove headfirst into the world of "temping." Goodbye, blissful morning snooze button; hello, crack-of-dawn temperature taking...oh, what a rollercoaster it turned out to be! My temperature readings were all over the place. One day I was apparently a human furnace, the next day a walking popsicle.

The one consistent thing I noticed was that my basal body temperature (BBT) was in the 96-degree range. It was like my body had decided to permanently vacation in the cooler climates. The elusive temperature rise I was supposed to see? Nowhere to be found, at least not consistently. I couldn't figure out what was happening. Was I doing something wrong, or was my body just really committed to keeping things interesting? Despite my chart looking like a preschooler's abstract art project, good old Aunt Flo did show up, just not consistently.

As I continued this adventure in fertility awareness, I reflected on the unexpected turns my journey had taken. Here I was, a grown woman, meticulously tracking my body's every fluctuation as if I were conducting a complex research study. Who knew that "taking charge of your fertility" would require this much precision, patience, and emotional stamina? I felt like a biologist studying a rare species except the subject was my own body, and I couldn't seem to get it to follow any of the rules.

In the end, my foray into BBT tracking became an enlightening, if not sometimes frustrating, experience. Each morning, before the sun came up, I'd reach for my thermometer from the nightstand and shuffle to the bathroom in the dark, trying not to wake my husband. I'd squint at the digital reading and scribble it down, half-asleep, hoping to see what I was supposed to: a small dip just before ovulation, followed by a clear, sustained rise in temperature during the luteal phase, the biological breadcrumbs that suggested my body was cooperating.

But more often than not, my chart looked like static. Jagged lines. No clear shift. Some months, the rise never came. Other times, it came too late or jumped all over the place. I'd stare at the pattern, willing it to tell me something, anything, about what was going on inside me. There was a kind of intimacy in that daily ritual, but also a quiet ache. I wasn't just tracking numbers. I was searching for reassurance. I wanted evidence that my body could do this. That I wasn't broken. That maybe, this month, there was still a chance.

And though it wasn't always easy, I began to develop a deeper understanding of my body's rhythms and cycles. The answers weren't always clear, but I found something else: a new respect for the intricacies of human biology and for the quiet resilience it takes to keep showing up in the face of uncertainty.

After about a year of trying, I got Tricare referral from my Air Force primary care manager to see a reproductive endocrinologist (RE). On cycle day 3, armed with my irregular cycles and temperature charts, I arrived at the fertility clinic where I was poked, prodded, and introduced to the vaginal ultrasound wand. What started as a simple quest to expand my family quickly evolved into a surprisingly intimate relationship with a cold, gel-covered piece of medical equipment.

At first, I naively thought my encounters with the ultrasound wand would be few and far between. Oh, how wrong I was! It turns out, this little device and I were destined to become very close friends or perhaps frenemies is a more accurate term.

We met with the RE, who was going to reveal our results from all the testing we had done. "It looks like you have a lot of eggs left," he said. "Based on our Ovarian Assessment Report, the chances of you having a successful IVF are excellent."

For reference, I was 35 years old at this point. My antral follicle count (AFC) was 37 and my anti-Müllerian hormone (AMH) was 8.13. Antral follicle count refers to the number of small, fluid-filled follicles visible in the ovaries during a vaginal ultrasound. This provides information about a woman's ovarian reserve. AMH levels correlate with the quantity of remaining eggs and are commonly used to assess ovarian reserve. AFC and AMH levels naturally decline with age, and testing is used in fertility evaluations to help predict ovarian response to stimulation in IVF.

"What?" I cannot compute. *Who is talking about IVF here? I just need some help figuring out what is going wrong and why my cycle is inconsistent!* I look over to Matt; he also looks confused. *Why are we discussing this?*

The doctor's words hung in the air like a storm cloud, and I think he sensed it. "Well, this is not the first step, but if we're not successful, that's something to consider." I could sense the alarm bells ringing in my head, but I quickly shoved them into a mental drawer labeled "Not Gonna Happen." After all, I was completely healthy, right? This guy clearly didn't know what he was talking about. Denial, thy name is Naomi.

The only other notable result from the testing was that I had one copy of the MTHFR gene mutation, heterozygous, which roughly 30 to 40 percent of the population has. It meant I'd need to take folate instead of folic acid, and methylated B vitamins. Nothing major.

Because it seemed I was not ovulating, the doctor laid out our options like a menu of reproductive delights: Clomid or Femara, the latter being a repurposed breast cancer medication that apparently plays double agent, lowering estrogen levels while stimulating ovulation.

"Femara has fewer side effects," he explained, as if he was selling us a new car with better gas mileage. We nodded along, wide-eyed and trusting, because hey, he was the expert with the fancy degree on the wall. Decision made, prescription filled, and now all that was left was to wait for my cycle to begin.

Finally, cycle day 3 rolled around, and I popped my first Femara pill with all the optimism of a lottery ticket buyer. *This isn't so bad,* I thought, mentally patting myself on the back for being such a trooper. How naive I was. As the days went on, my body decided to throw a rebellion worthy of a medieval uprising. My bones ached like I'd run a marathon in concrete shoes. Even my beloved yoga, usually my go-to for all ailments, couldn't touch this new level of stiffness and pain. And let's not forget the bonus gifts of fatigue and brain fog—because who doesn't want to feel like they're wading through molasses while trying to remember their own name?

What the heck is happening to my body? I wondered. This medication was definitely for the birds—angry, achy birds. But I persisted, doing my best to channel my inner yoga guru. *This too shall pass, I chanted to myself. The end justifies the means. Soon, I'll be pregnant, have our baby, and this will all be a hilarious anecdote to share.*

My confidence soared when I experienced ovulation pain for the first time. *Eureka! I* thought, *My insides are working!* It felt like my body was finally getting with the program, sending up fireworks to signal its readiness. We diligently followed the Femara protocol from days 3–7, then entered the waiting game. Armed with ovulation tests and an enthusiasm that would put cheerleaders to shame, we did all the things we were supposed to do (wink, wink, nudge, nudge—DTD: Did the Deed).

To say we were optimistic would be putting it mildly. We didn't just think it might work; we were quietly confident that this was our moment. In the back of our minds, we started entertaining thoughts of parenthood, occasionally catching ourselves chatting about baby names. Small changes in my body became a point of interest, a potential sign of success. We tried not to overanalyze, but it was hard not to feel hopeful. After all the appointments, medications, and careful timing, it felt like everything was finally falling into place. This had to be our time, right? We allowed ourselves to nurture that spark of hope, cautiously excited about what the future might hold. Little did we know, our journey was far from over, and there were still many twists and turns ahead.

The Two-Week Wait after ovulation was an emotional rollercoaster I never expected. Every little sensation in my body became a source of both hope and anxiety. *Is something happening?* I'd wonder, feeling a slight twinge in my abdomen. *Is that a sign?* My mind raced constantly, analyzing every subtle change. I found myself obsessively checking my body temperature, convinced that the slightest rise could be the beacon of good news I was desperately seeking. The fear of doing too much haunted me. *Am I working out too hard?* I'd fret, scaling back my usual exercise and yoga practice. The last thing I wanted was to inadvertently interfere with conception or implantation.

Each day brought new sensations to interpret. A mild cramp would send my heart soaring with possibility. I'd rush to the bathroom, scrutinizing for the faintest hint of implantation bleeding. "This could be it," I'd whisper to myself, trying to temper my excitement with caution. The waiting felt interminable. Those two weeks stretched on like an eternity, each day a battle between hope and fear. It was mentally exhausting, my thoughts a constant swirl of 'what-ifs' and 'maybes.' But through it all, I held onto a thread of optimism. *Whatever happens, I can handle it,* I'd remind myself, drawing on an inner strength I didn't know I possessed.

When cycle day zero arrived, heralding the start of "shark week," it felt like my world came crashing down. The physical discomfort of cramps paled in comparison to the emotional tsunami that hit me. My hormone levels plummeted, leaving me feeling hollow and raw. No amount of positive thinking or reframing could penetrate the fog of disappointment that enveloped me. "This isn't fair," I sobbed, sometimes curled up on the bathroom floor. The arrival of my period wasn't just inconvenient; it was a stark reminder of failure, of hopes dashed yet again.

Normally, my default mode is relentlessly positive. I'm the one who always looks on the bright side, finding silver linings in even the darkest clouds. In tough times, my instinct is to reframe the situation, to search for the lesson or the opportunity hidden within the challenge.

But on this day, that well-honed skill deserted me entirely. There was no reasoning with my emotions, no reframing that could soften the blow. My internal dialogue, usually so quick to offer encouragement, fell silent in the face of this overwhelming disappointment. I realized that sometimes, there's no shortcut through grief. On this day, I just needed to wallow in my sorrow, to fully experience the frustration and anger that had been building up.

It felt foreign and uncomfortable to let these negative emotions take center stage, but I knew that only by acknowledging them could I eventually let them go. So, I gave myself permission to feel it all, raw and unfiltered, trusting that somewhere down the line, I'd find my way back to hope.

That day, I couldn't rally. The strength that had carried me through the Two-Week Wait was nowhere to be found. Sometimes the tears came without warning, beyond my control. In a desperate attempt to soothe myself, I ended up at the local FroYo shop, piling my cup high with strawberries and chocolate chips, shoveling spoonful after spoonful into my mouth. But the sweetness did little to mask the bitterness inside me. As I sat there, surrounded by cheerful families and carefree couples, I felt more alone than ever.

The day after the initial disappointment was always a little better. What was that mysterious force that kept propelling me forward through all the ups and downs of this fertility journey...over and over again? Maybe it was that primal, instinctive urge to reproduce, the whisper of biology telling me, "This is what you were made for." CD2 felt like emerging from a fog, my mind already shifting gears to focus on the next steps. *What's the plan this time?* I'd ask myself, a mixture of determination and cautious hope rising within me. I'd pore over books, fertility forums, and medical articles, searching for any adjustments we could make to improve our chances. As I launched myself into the new cycle, I felt a renewed sense of purpose.

CHAPTER 2:

Believing in Molecules and Miracles

As I delved deeper into my fertility journey and the mind-body-soul connection, I stumbled upon Dr. Bruce Lipton's book *The Biology of Belief*.[2] It felt like a revelation, a scientific validation of what I had intuitively believed all along. Here I was, already practicing and teaching yoga, mindfulness, and meditation, and suddenly a renowned cell biologist was confirming that my thoughts and beliefs could directly influence my health and wellness. It was as if the universe was giving me a nod of approval.

Lipton's work on epigenetics—the idea that our genes aren't fixed, but respond to signals like stress, nutrition, and even our thoughts—was both fascinating and empowering. It challenged the belief that we're simply at the mercy of our DNA. I began to see my body not as a stubborn adversary in this fertility struggle, but as a responsive partner—one I could communicate with through my beliefs and perceptions.

I started paying even more attention to my inner dialogue, catching myself when I slipped into negative self-talk about my fertility. Instead of lamenting another unsuccessful cycle, I would pause and reframe my thinking: *My body is learning and preparing*, I'd remind myself. *Each cycle brings me closer to success.*

One concept that especially resonated with me was the idea of the intelligent cell membrane. I began to imagine my cells as tiny, conscious beings, eagerly awaiting positive signals from my thoughts. During meditation, I'd visualize my cell membranes opening to receive nurturing messages—creating an optimal internal environment for conception.

Lipton's emphasis on the subconscious mind prompted me to dig deeper into my own beliefs about motherhood and fertility. I realized I was carrying limiting beliefs from childhood—stories I hadn't even known I was telling myself. With this awareness, I began using affirmations and visualization techniques to reprogram those subconscious patterns. My yoga practice took on new meaning. As I moved through each pose, I imagined I was not just stretching my muscles, but sending waves of positive intention throughout my body. After eagle pose, I'd envision blood flow delivering nutrients to my reproductive organs. In savasana, I'd picture my reproductive system bathed in healing light, my cells dancing with vitality.

Lipton's work also reinforced the importance of managing stress. I was practicing yoga, praying, and meditating, but the truth is, my military obligations and Type A drive to excel often overwhelmed those efforts. Eventually it dawned on me: the pressure to *do it all*—career, treatments, inner peace—may have been working against me more than I realized.

I was attempting to cultivate a sense of calm and surrender through mindfulness practices. The cognitive dissonance was palpable. I can't help but chuckle at the image of myself rushing from a high-stress work meeting to a yoga class, my mind still buzzing with tasks and to-do lists as I tried to quiet my thoughts on the mat.

In hindsight, this constant switching between high-stress mode and forced relaxation probably didn't do me any favors in my fertility journey.

No wonder my body was confused—was it supposed to fight or surrender? Push forward or let go? That push-and-pull left me exhausted.

Still, despite moments of doubt and frustration, Lipton's insights provided a framework for hope. They reminded me that I wasn't powerless in this process. Every thought, every belief, every moment of mindfulness was potentially contributing to my fertility journey. As I continued on this path, I felt a sense of alignment between my spiritual practices and the scientific understanding of cellular biology. It was comforting to know that my intuitive approach to wellness had a basis in cutting-edge science.

FUEL AS MEDICINE

On the physical front, our diet became another focus of this effort. We went dairy-free and gluten-free, embraced raw foods, and started juicing. I never thought I'd become one of those people who obsessed over food, but there I was, standing in front of my refrigerator, staring down a pile of green vegetables like they were plotting against me. The journey to parenthood had led us down a rabbit hole of alternative therapies and dietary changes.

Our kitchen had transformed into a makeshift laboratory. Gone (well, mostly) were the days of carefree nacho dinners and ice cream indulgences, though the occasional froyo still slipped through! Instead, a juicer claimed prime real estate on the counter, humming with the promise of vitality. I'd sip on my latest green concoction—one that tasted suspiciously like lawn clippings, thanks to the wheatgrass—and wonder how we'd gotten here. But we were determined, and if that meant turning our digestive systems into temples of health, so be it.

Surprisingly, this journey brought unexpected joys. We stumbled upon foods we genuinely liked (who knew cashew cheese could be so delicious?) and found ourselves laughing at the ridiculous situations we got into. Take raw cinnamon rolls, for instance: one of my all-time favorite discoveries. Sure, they were made of nuts and flaxseeds and required an afternoon of effort and a small fortune, but the payoff was worth it. Did they have the pillowy texture of a real cinnamon roll? Not even close. But they became a household legend, a small victory and reminder that joy could be found in nut and flaxseed packages.

Beyond the recipes, we discovered new habits and lessons that stuck with us. We learned to be more creative in the kitchen, discovered how food could nourish not just our bodies but our minds, and came to value slowing down and enjoying the process. It wasn't just about what we restricted but it was about what we gained, the small wins that made us better and lasted long after the cinnamon rolls disappeared.

Of course, I'm sure our friends (well, not our yoga friends) and family thought we were quite crazy...and perhaps they still do, but we were willing to try anything to get us closer to success. At the time, it felt like if we just dieted enough, prayed enough, exercised enough, did *enough* of anything, we could finally overcome the challenge. We would be deserving. So, we threw ourselves into every possible solution, clinging to the hope that one of them would finally work.

BENDING WITHOUT BREAKING

Alongside these dietary changes, we also continued to utilize Bikram yoga, otherwise known as the 26/2. The intense, heated sessions were already a crucial part of our routine, not just for physical fitness but as a form of moving meditation. I had been teaching Bikram Yoga for at least a year at this point and practicing for six years, so I was committed. The 26 postures, practiced in the heat, demanded my full concentration, pushing my body to the limits while quieting the noise in my mind. For 90 minutes, the moving meditation forced us to set aside the fear and frustration of our fertility journey. It became a sanctuary, a place to quiet the chaos in my head and reconnect with a sense of calm and purpose.

Every once in a while, as I moved through the poses, emotions I'd stuffed away would bubble to the surface, usually during the spine-strengthening series, because apparently backbends are where my feelings like to hide. I was so grateful the sweat helped camouflage the silent tears streaming down my face, so at least there was that small mercy. By the time we hit savasana, the final resting pose, it was like someone had flipped a release valve. I felt the weight of it all lift—if only for a moment. In those fleeting minutes of stillness, I wasn't just surviving the struggle; I was finding peace.

In my never-ending quest to find things that might support our journey, I also became aware of a concern rooted in Eastern medicine. According to traditional Chinese beliefs, practices like hot yoga, while beneficial in many ways, can potentially drain the body's vital energy, or *Qi*. More specifically, excessive internal or external heat is thought to deplete *Yin*, the cooling, nourishing energy essential for hormonal balance and reproductive health. A depletion of Yin is believed to impact estrogen levels, potentially disrupting the body's natural cycles. Practicing too intensely or too frequently could, in theory, throw off that delicate balance.

And it wasn't just about me, heat can also affect male fertility. Prolonged exposure to high temperatures is known to impair sperm production, adding another layer to our battle.

This understanding made us more cautious, reminding us of the fine balance between pushing our physical limits and preserving our overall energy and well-being. I could not—would not—give up yoga; it was the only thing that truly settled me at this point. But I decided to scale back, especially during the Two-Week Wait, and opt for gentler, more restorative practices when my body needed support rather than challenge.

NEEDLES, HERBS, AND HOPE

After reading *The Infertility Cure: The Ancient Chinese Wellness Program for Getting Pregnant and Having Healthy Babies*,[3] one of the things that stuck with me was the recommendation to try acupuncture. I was at a point where I was willing to try anything—no stone left unturned. If this ancient practice had worked for others, why not me? I made an appointment with a fertility specialist who was also an acupuncturist. She came highly recommended, and I figured if I were going to do this, I'd do it right with someone who understood fertility treatment on a deeper level.

Preparing for my first appointment felt a little surreal. I scheduled it during my lunch break, the only time she had available. Between the demands of my military career and the emotional weight of our fertility journey, finding time for anything extra felt like a feat in itself. But I was committed. I walked into her office in full military uniform, ready to embrace this new approach. *Let's get this started,* I said to myself, not quite knowing what to expect.

The acupuncturist explained that for the treatment to be effective, I would need to come regularly—at least once a week—and that it wasn't just the needles that would make a difference. I would also need to take Chinese herbs tailored to balance my body's energy and promote fertility. My initial reaction was one of hesitation. *Herbs?* I thought to myself. *Is this really going to work? How would that interfere with the fertility meds?* But at that point, I had tried so many other things, and I knew people had found success with it, so I told myself, *Why not?*

As I sat down in her cozy room, the contrast between the rigid structure of my military uniform and the peaceful, natural atmosphere of the acupuncture clinic wasn't lost on me. I was stepping into a world far removed from the discipline of military life. She asked me to take off my boots and socks so she could access specific fertility points on my legs and feet: Spleen 6 (*San Yin Jiao*), Kidney 3 (*Tai Xi*), and Liver 3 (*Tai Chong*)—which are said to stimulate the reproductive system and help regulate the menstrual cycle. I stretched out on the table, feeling oddly vulnerable in this setting, but I was determined to stay open-minded.

As the needles went in, I felt a strange combination of discomfort and relief—not physically, but mentally. This was something completely out of my comfort zone, but in a way, it felt good to be trying something different. Something proactive. It wasn't about instant results; it was about taking a step, however small, in the direction of hope.

THE WEIGHT OF HOPE

Over the course of several weeks, still nothing happened, but I started to look forward to these lunchtime acupuncture sessions. At first, I would rush in from work, my mind still spinning from the demands of the day, struggling to settle into the quiet space. Often, I was so drained, from the fertility drugs, from the stress of work, from everything, that I'd fall asleep almost as soon as the needles were placed. Those naps were the best part, brief moments of peace where, for just a little while, I wasn't carrying the weight of our fertility journey.

Other times, though, my mind refused to rest. I'd lie there, staring at the ceiling, my thoughts racing. *What if this is the month I finally get pregnant? What if it changes everything? What if it means I can't attend Air Command and Staff College in residence or pursue the other dreams I've worked so hard for?* It was the classic monkey mind I often talk about in yoga—thoughts swinging wildly like a monkey swinging from branch to branch, never settling, never stopping.

We didn't know many people who struggled like we did. It felt as if we were isolated in our pain, living in a world where everyone else seemed to have it all figured out. But even in those moments of isolation, there was a small, persistent voice within us that refused to be silenced—a voice that whispered, "Keep going." Every time we saw a family laughing together in the park or heard the joyful announcement of a new pregnancy, it stung, yes, but it also ignited a flicker of hope. Maybe, just maybe, our time was coming.

And in the quiet moments, when the house was still, we often found ourselves shedding silent tears: tears that held the weight of our longing, frustration, and the belief that tomorrow might be different.

CHAPTER 3:

Trying Again (And Again...and Again)

Despite our efforts, with each passing month, we experienced failure after failure. The disappointment was relentless. Each negative test result was a setback, but it didn't extinguish the faith we held onto. It also fueled a deeper determination to keep trying, to keep believing that the next time could be different.

With each failure, the tears came, exacerbated by the roller-coaster of hormones, I'm sure: tears of disbelief, of weariness, and sometimes, tears of anger at a body that seemed to betray us month after month. We did not understand why this was happening to us, but we clung to the belief that there was a reason, a purpose that we couldn't yet see. Perhaps we were being tested to see if we could be good parents, if we could handle the stress of it all. So many questions.

Throughout this journey, I had been so focused on my own body, on all the tests, the symptoms, the cycles, that I'd almost forgotten the other half of the equation: my husband. In my mind, the infertility was mine to bear. But as he began his own round of tests, we learned his numbers weren't perfect either, low motility and count meant his sperm needed a little attention, too.

His solution? Add *Fertile Aid* to the already absurd lineup of fifteen supplements he was taking, bringing his daily pill count to about twenty-four. He adjusted his exercise routine, cleaned up his diet, and did everything he could. His numbers held steady, not awesome but not worse. Compared to the unpredictability of my body, his side of the "fix" felt almost...straightforward. I couldn't shake the feeling that the heavier weight of this struggle still rested on my shoulders.

We pressed on, completing four medicated cycles with Femara. By the fourth round, the emotional toll was crushing. It had been nearly two years of trying. I needed a break, a moment to breathe, to recenter myself before plunging back into the fertility fray.

In the middle of this break, we scheduled an HSG (hysterosalpingogram) to check if my fallopian tubes were clear. It's a procedure where they inject dye into the uterus and use an X-ray to see if the tubes are open, allowing eggs to pass through freely. One of the silver linings of the HSG is that sometimes the dye itself can help clear minor blockages, almost like giving the body a little nudge. My doctor assured me he was skilled at this, mentioning I'd likely feel only minor cramping.

I tried to focus on that reassurance as I walked into the exam room, putting my feet in the stirrups yet again, a now too-familiar routine. As the procedure began, I watched the screen, waiting anxiously to see the results unfold. Would this be the moment something finally clicked? I held my breath, hoping for clear tubes and a sign that we were one step closer.

Thankfully, my tubes were clear. This was good news! Finally, something was working in our favor! The doctor confirmed it, and I felt a wave of optimism wash over me. With nothing physically holding us back, it seemed like we were on the right track. I clung to that small victory, telling myself, *This should work. We should be successful.* It was one less hurdle in what had felt like an endless series of obstacles, and for the first time in a while, I felt a glimmer of hope that maybe, just maybe, we were moving closer to the outcome we had been fighting for.

When we picked up the gauntlet a month later for cycle #5, we added progesterone and an hCG trigger to stimulate ovulation. Surely between the Femara, the hCG shot, and the progesterone to support the luteal phase, this would do the trick, right? Wrong. Another negative.

For a long time, we kept our struggles a secret from most people. I felt a deep sense of shame about what I was going through. It seemed like everyone around me was either happily child-free or able to conceive without difficulty. I didn't know anyone else experiencing this rollercoaster of hope and disappointment, which only intensified my feelings of isolation. The last thing I wanted was for people to feel sorry for me—or to be seen as the "infertile one."

Still, we pressed forward. By cycle #6, we escalated to gonadotropins, FSH injectables like Follistim and Menopur. Apparently, popping pills wasn't quite enough of a challenge. Femara, FSH or FSH/GH shots, and an hCG trigger were added to our growing arsenal. I felt like a walking pharmacy, but if it gave us the best chance, we were all in.

And then there was the Menopur. Oh, the Menopur. No one warned me it would sting like liquid fire going in, a slow burn that made me clench my jaw every time the needle touched skin. I'd ice the spot beforehand, try to distract myself, go slow, but nothing really dulled it. It was like punishment in a syringe. The irony of enduring that kind of pain in the name of creating life wasn't lost on me.

This was also when we hit the Tricare wall. The military's version of insurance treated advanced fertility treatments like luxury services. FSH combined with IUI? Not covered. The costs added up fast: gonadotropins ($1,000–$4,000), hCG trigger shots ($200 each), and IUI procedures ($1,500). I half-joked about selling a kidney.

Thankfully, our nurse helped when she could, slipping us leftover injectable meds like Follistim or Menopur from successful IVF cycles to help stimulate my ovaries. It felt like we were part of a secret underground fertility network. But even with these quiet kindnesses, the emotional and financial burden mounted. Welcome to the wild world of military infertility treatments, where the fight to conceive starts long before the baby.

Each new cycle meant more ultrasounds, more awkward exam table shuffles, more intrusive wand dates. For cycle #6, I had four promising follicles. I dared to hope again. But it wasn't just the physical effects of the meds—it was the bloating, the needle bruises, the emotional volatility.

And then? Another negative.

By cycle #7, we upped the Femara to 5 mg and the FSH to 150 units. My ovaries responded in kind, producing eight hopeful follicles that were the right size to turn into eggs. A hCG trigger shot, timed intercourse, and the infamous Two-Week Wait followed.

Eleven days post-trigger, I found myself squinting at yet another pregnancy test. But wait—was that a line? Was it real or an evaporation line? A faint whisper of hope, barely visible? "Matt!" I called, practically vibrating with excitement. "Take a look at this! Does it look positive to you?"

We huddled over the test, tilting it this way and that, as if the right angle would make our dreams materialize. My mind raced. Surely the hCG trigger shot was out of my system by now, right? Since pregnancy tests detect hCG, it could still be a false positive...but this had to be real. This tiny, maybe-there line was our ticket to parenthood. I could barely contain myself. I wanted to tell someone.

Sleep that night? Forget about it. My brain went into overdrive, planning a future that was still far from certain. The due date, work arrangements, pregnancy symptoms—you name it, I thought about it. The night stretched on, filled with equal parts hope and anxiety.

Morning couldn't come fast enough. I bolted to the bathroom, ready to POAS (Pee On A Stick). "If I'm really pregnant, the line will be darker now, right?" I muttered to myself, unwrapping the test with shaking hands. Then came the wait. Three minutes. An eternity compressed into 180 seconds.

As I reached for the test, my heart pounding so loud I was sure the neighbors could hear it, I wondered, *Is this finally our moment? Or am I about to come crashing back to earth?*

With trembling hands, I picked up the test. My eyes frantically searched for that second line, the one I'd convinced myself I'd seen yesterday. But there was nothing. Just one stark, solitary line staring back at me, as if mocking my hopes and dreams.

Negative. Again.

It hit me like a physical blow, knocking the air from my lungs. I stood there, frozen, staring at the test as if I could will a second line into existence through sheer force. But reality doesn't bend to our wishes, no matter how desperately we want it to.

Cycle #8 came next. We increased the FSH dose to 225 units, aiming to stimulate even more follicles. It felt like a high-stakes game of reproductive roulette. This time, we had 8–10 follicles that looked promising. Surely this time, with this response, we were on the verge of success.

The trigger shot was in, we'd done the deed (DTD), and now came the agonizing wait. This was our best shot yet. Eleven days post-trigger, I tested again.

Another negative.

Disappointment hit like a tidal wave. My heart sank deeper with each cycle, each evaporation line, each lost dream. And yet, somehow, I kept going.

On the military front, we were running out of time in Utah. Our next assignment loomed—Air Command and Staff College in Montgomery, Alabama. We had just one more shot, one final cycle before the move.

This has to be it, I silently willed, clinging to the hope that we'd saved the best for last. Our doctor, ever optimistic, prescribed the same protocol as before. After all, my body had responded beautifully last time, producing follicles like a champ. But as we'd learned over and over, doing everything "right" didn't guarantee success.

When the negative result came back, it felt like a punch to the gut. Again.

But we didn't have the luxury of wallowing. Our move was approaching fast, and we threw ourselves into the turbulence of packing and goodbyes. It was easier to focus on what was working—our successful Air Force careers, the friends we'd made, the growth we'd experienced. Utah had been good to us in many ways, and leaving was bittersweet.

CLOSURE IS A MYTH

As I stated previously, throughout this journey, we'd kept our struggles mostly to ourselves. The shame I felt about our infertility was a heavy burden; one I didn't want coloring people's last impressions of us as we left Utah. It was easier to paste on a smile and talk about our exciting new adventure in Alabama than to explain the heartache we were carrying.

As part of our pre-move checklist, we met with our doctor one last time. His recommendation was clear: IVF. "You've done everything else," he explained. "If you want the best chance of success, IVF is the next step. I recommend ICSI to deal with any unknown male factors, and I estimate a 40 percent pregnancy rate each cycle."

I explained that I thought it had to be stress causing this infertility. I was healthy. I worked out. I ate reasonably well!

But even as I clung to this theory, a nagging voice in the back of my mind whispered doubts. If it was just stress, why hadn't any of our treatments worked? Why had our doctor recommended IVF? Still, I pushed those thoughts aside. It was easier to believe a change of scenery would be the solution.

I casually asked the nurse for her opinion as I requested copies of my medical records. That's when she mentioned something that completely blindsided me: "Your ovaries are polycystic, like someone with PCOS."

I immediately freaked out. *What the heck is she talking about?* No one had ever mentioned PCOS to me before, and it wasn't listed anywhere in my paperwork. All this time, I could have been researching ways to manage it, but instead, I had been obsessing over simply being regular. For those who have been through this, you'll understand. Every time you peel back another layer of the fertility onion, you uncover something new, a fresh revelation, another challenge to explore and optimize.

I was, for lack of a better term, angry. How could they keep this from me?

I went home and combed through my blood work. As far as I could see, nothing definitively pointed to PCOS except my high AMH, AFC, and irregular ovulation. According to the Rotterdam criteria, a diagnosis of PCOS requires at least two of the following: irregular or absent ovulation, high androgen levels, and polycystic ovaries visible on an ultrasound. My blood tests showed no elevated androgens that I could find. My fasting glucose was 90, HbA1C was 5.4, LH was 4.6, and FSH was 6.2—all within normal ranges. I had no other physical signs of excess androgens.

According to the Rotterdam criteria, I had PCOS.

And yet no one had ever explained that to me.

Why would she say that? It felt careless, as if she was throwing around a label without considering what it would mean to me. Her comment left me questioning everything, diving into research, and second-guessing our entire treatment plan. Had I known earlier, I could have started addressing this and potentially made progress. Instead, I was blindsided.

I couldn't shake the unease that had settled in. I made a mental note to investigate further. If PCOS, or something like it, was affecting my fertility, I needed to know for sure. I wasn't going to accept an offhand comment or brush it aside. If there was anything I had learned from this journey, it was that I had to be my own strongest advocate, especially when navigating something as complex and personal as fertility.

Note: Later, when I finally saw a functional medicine doctor, someone who looks at root causes and how different systems in the body interact, we realized something surprising: no one had ever checked my testosterone or DHEA-S in the initial fertility workup. DHEA-S is the stable, storage form of DHEA produced by the adrenal glands, and it's one of the best markers for androgen status. When we ran a full panel, both my testosterone and DHEA-S came back very *low*... not high.

It was a lot to process as we prepared to uproot our lives. But it gave us a new goal to focus on in Alabama. As we drove away from Utah, our car packed to the brim, I felt a mix of emotions. We were leaving behind the place where our fertility journey had begun, where we'd experienced so many highs and lows. But ahead of us lay a new chapter, a new state, and potentially a new approach to building our family.

The road to Montgomery stretched out before us, filled with uncertainty but also possibility.

CHAPTER 4:

Faith and Frustration in Alabama

After leaving Utah and struggling with fertility, I can almost hear the question now: *If you wanted kids so badly, why not just attempt IVF earlier?* The truth is, it wasn't that simple. It was a tangled knot of denial, timing, finances, and faith. And at the center of it all was a hope I wasn't ready to let go of.

As we drove toward Montgomery, I kept thinking: *This will be the reset. This move will fix everything.*

I found myself mentally listing all the stress-reducing habits we'd try in our new home. More yoga (with less heat), more meditation, long quiet walks through our new neighborhood. Surely one of these would be the key to unlocking our fertility issues. A little calmer and a little less cortisol would flip the switch.

At the time, I had no idea our journey was far from over or that the real cause of our struggle was more complex than I could have imagined.

What I didn't understand was this: Denial doesn't always look like avoidance. Sometimes it looks like hope dressed in determination.

It wasn't that we didn't want to try IVF. We just weren't ready to let go of the belief that maybe we wouldn't have to. That maybe next month would be *the* month. That we were one supplement, one acupuncture session, one perfectly timed cycle away from a miracle.

Then there was the timing.

Timing moves.

Timing school.

Timing command.

The Air Force does not schedule life around ovulation windows, and we were constantly trying to thread the needle between career expectations and the dream of becoming parents. It felt like trying to plant a seed during a hurricane.

And of course, IVF isn't something you casually attempt. It's a $15,000–$20,000 gamble, per round, with zero guarantees. After years of diagnostics, supplements, failed IUIs, and co-pays, we were already emotionally and financially depleted. When decisions get this heavy, I've always turned to faith but this time, faith complicated everything.

Specifically, our Catholic faith.

The Catholic Church doesn't condone IVF, a stance formalized in a 1992 declaration that already felt outdated by the time we were wrestling with it. I mean, in 1992 people were still rewinding VHS tapes. Meanwhile, we were living in the HD era of 2014, trying to build a family in a world that had changed dramatically. It felt like the Church was still stuck in the Blockbuster aisle while we were navigating a Netflix reality.

I couldn't shake the feeling that the Church's position was disconnected from the lived reality of so many people walking through infertility with broken hearts and open hands. I didn't feel like I was "playing God." I felt like I was reaching for help, from medicine, from science, and from God Himself, trying to do what I believed I was biologically, emotionally, and spiritually wired to do: nurture life.

After arriving in Alabama, I spent even more months tracking my cycle with the precision of a NASA engineer. I actually felt like I had finally cracked the code of my own body. Ovulation pain? Check. Positive ovulation sticks? You bet. I was popping Woman's FertilAid like it was candy and monitoring my cycle with more dedication than an air traffic controller. *I've got this,* I'd think to myself, feeling a surge of optimism every time I felt that telltale twinge in my ovaries.

My bathroom drawer looked like a fertility supply store had exploded with ovulation predictor kits, pregnancy tests, acupuncturist herbs, and prenatals. I was ready to roll, convinced that my body was finally working the way it was supposed to. "This is it," I'd whisper to myself each month, hope blooming anew. But as more months ticked by—one, two, three, four, five—with no sign of that elusive second line on the pregnancy tests, my confidence began to waver. Each negative result felt like my body had betrayed me. *What gives?* I'd ask my reflection, as if it held the answers I was desperately seeking.

In the midst of it all, the quiet struggle I'd already been having with my faith only grew heavier as our fertility journey dragged on. Each time I went to church, a wave of emotions would wash over me. It wasn't a full-on sobfest, but I'd often find myself discreetly wiping away a tear or two during the service. The questions kept nagging at me: Why would God put us through this? What lesson was I supposed to be learning from all this heartache? I'd look around at the families filling the pews and feel a pang of longing and isolation.

Being an Air Force officer, I was trained to face challenges head-on, but this was a battle I couldn't strategize my way out of. It was humbling and frustrating to feel so powerless in this aspect of my life. I didn't always attend church regularly, but when I did, I often left with more questions than answers. The sermons on faith and God's plan felt hollow when faced with the reality of our struggles. I found myself becoming more reluctant to go, even though I still said my prayers. Those prayers became less formal over time, more like quiet conversations with God. *Hey, if you're listening, a little help would be appreciated,* I'd think to myself, trying to inject a bit of humor into each challenging situation.

One of those particularly challenging occasions was the baptism of our niece. Sitting through that service was an emotional minefield I wasn't fully prepared to navigate. I tried my best to focus on the joy of the moment, to be present for my family, but the nagging grief of what we might never have kept creeping in, uninvited and unwelcome. As I watched my sister-in-law cradle her baby, beaming with pride, I felt a complex cocktail of emotions. There was genuine happiness for them, of course, but it was mixed with a hefty dose of envy and a side of self-pity that I wasn't particularly proud of.

I kept reminding myself, *This is not about you. Be here for them.* But damn, it was difficult to stay present in that space. The symbolism of new life and new beginnings that permeated the baptism ceremony felt like a bittersweet reminder of our own struggles. Each prayer, each blessing, seemed to underscore what Matt and I were missing out on. I found myself gripping Matt's hand a little tighter, grateful for his steady presence beside me. I tried to put on my best "supportive aunt" face, smiling and cooing at the baby when appropriate. But inside, I was counting down the minutes until it was over. I'm pretty sure I set a new personal record for "number of times discreetly checking watch during a religious ceremony."

When it was finally over, I felt a mix of relief and guilt. Relief that I had made it through without breaking down, and guilt for feeling relieved at all. As we said our goodbyes, I wondered if we'd ever be on the other side of this, celebrating our own child's baptism.

Just when I was starting to feel like I was starring in my own personal version of *Groundhog Day: Fertility Edition*, we finally received another authorization for more fertility testing in Alabama. Ah, Tricare, the military insurance that treats getting pregnant like a covert operation requiring multiple levels of clearance.

But hey, at least they were covering the initial diagnostic tests, some IUIs (as long as they weren't *planned*, because heaven forbid we actually prepare for these things), and ultrasounds.

I clutched that authorization like a golden ticket. Here I was, celebrating the chance for more poking, prodding, and intimate encounters with cold medical instruments. But in the world of fertility treatments, this was progress.

Bring on the tests, I thought, ready to face whatever came next in this wild ride.

INSOMNIA AND INTROSPECTION

During this time my old nemesis, insomnia, crept back into my life like an unwelcomed shadow. Night after night, I found myself wide awake in the early hours, my mind a rush of anxieties and hopes. The soft glow of the bedside clock seemed to mock me as the minutes ticked by, each one a reminder of the sleep I wasn't getting.

In the stillness of the night, I felt the weight of stress pressing down on my chest. My heart raced, and my palms grew clammy as worries flooded my thoughts. *What about the next paper I have to write? Will it be good enough? I just turned 36, am I running out of time? What if this treatment doesn't work? What if we're putting ourselves through all this for nothing?* The questions swirled endlessly, making sleep feel like an impossible dream.

Desperate for distraction, I reached for the remote and turned on the TV, keeping the volume low. The familiar theme song of Law & Order filled the room, and I hoped it would lull me back to sleep. As the dramatic scenes unfolded, I felt my racing thoughts begin to slow, replaced by the predictable rhythm of the show's plot.

One night, from the other side of the bed, I could hear Matt stir. He rolled over, a sleepy grin on his face despite the hour. "You know," he mumbled, his voice thick with sleep, "I'm starting to have nightmares about crime scenes and courtrooms. Your late-night Law & Order marathons are becoming my own personal form of torture." I laughed, even as guilt tugged at my heart. "I'm sorry," I whispered, reaching out to touch him. "I'm just trying to quiet my mind." He pulled me closer, and I nestled into his warmth. "I know. We're in this together, remember? Even if it means I end up dreaming about being cross-examined by Sam Waterston."

IT'S NOT JUST ME

When we finally got to the new reproductive endocrinologist in Montgomery, Alabama, I felt a mix of hope and trepidation. After so many disappointments, it was hard not to be skeptical, but a part of me wondered if this time would be different. As we went through the now-familiar routine of tests and examinations, I found myself holding my breath, waiting for the other shoe to drop.

When the results came back, it wasn't my body that was the focus this time. The doctor, a kind-faced woman with steady hands, explained that Matt had been diagnosed with a varicocele. I watched my husband's face as she described the condition, a dilation of the veins in the scrotum that can affect sperm production and quality. "It's like varicose veins, but in the testicles," the doctor explained. "It can increase the temperature in the area, which isn't ideal for sperm production."

I felt a surge of emotions: a sense of clarity that we might have found an explanation, worry about what this meant for our chances, and a fierce protectiveness toward Matt, who looked a bit surprised. The doctor laid out our options: do nothing and hope for the best, try pharmaceuticals like Arimidex to lower Matt's estrogen levels, or opt for surgery to remove the varicocele. Arimidex was actually an "off-label" use of a breast cancer drug, which inhibits the aromatase enzyme that converts testosterone to estradiol. The result: increased testosterone and lower estradiol.

Each choice came with its own set of pros and cons, and I could feel the weight of the decision pressing down on us. "The drugs," the doctor continued, "would aim to optimize Matt's testosterone-to-estrogen ratio. In men, estrogen is typically converted from testosterone by an enzyme called aromatase. By lowering estrogen, we might be able to improve sperm production and quality." As she spoke, I found myself picturing Matt's hormones like a delicate balance scale, tipping one way and then the other.

It was strange to think of my husband's body in these clinical terms, to reduce our struggle to conceive to a matter of hormone levels and vein dilation. After much discussion and soul-searching, we decided to try the pharmaceutical route. The idea of Matt undergoing surgery felt too drastic at this stage but doing nothing wasn't an option for us anymore. We were too invested, too determined to give up now.

I turned to Matt. "How are you feeling about all this?" I asked, searching his face for signs of worry or doubt. He was quiet for a moment, then gave me a small smile. "It's a lot to take in," he admitted. "But if this is what we need to do to have a chance at a family, then I'm all in." I leaned into him, feeling the steady beat of his heart. As we embarked on this new phase of treatment, we felt another glimmer of hope.

PAIN IS PROGRESS?

The doctor did not think I had PCOS and she suggested a few more rounds of IUI before moving on to IVF. It wasn't what I wanted to hear. I was tired: physically, emotionally, spiritually. The IUIs weren't covered by Tricare. Again. Every round felt like rolling loaded dice and still, we kept playing.

When the next IUI cycle failed, I developed ovarian cysts, which only made everything worse. The pain was sharp and persistent, a constant reminder of what we were putting my body through. An ultrasound confirmed the cysts, and the doctor mentioned something we hadn't heard before: endometriosis. She suspected I had it and recommended laparoscopic surgery to find out for sure and possibly remove any lesions. I nodded, but inside, I felt like I was crumbling.

Another procedure. Another hope. Another hurdle.

I remember walking out to the car after the appointment, closing the door, and finally letting the tears fall. I gripped the steering wheel and sobbed, not just from the pain or the frustration, but from the sheer exhaustion of it all. I didn't want to be brave anymore. I wanted this to be over. I wanted a baby.

At home, I dove into research about endometriosis and laparoscopic surgery. Blog posts, medical articles, forums, I read them all. The surgery sounded "routine" on paper, but nothing about this journey had ever felt routine. Still, we scheduled it.

The night before surgery was almost comical in its misery. I had to prep my bowels, which involved a lineup of laxatives that seemed more suited for medieval torture than modern medicine. I joked, tried to make light of it, even documenting my "pooping water" phase but inside, I was scared. What if they found nothing? What if they found everything?

Surgery day arrived, and with it came all the familiar sights and sounds of a hospital: antiseptic smells, beeping monitors, the soft shuffle of nurses in scrubs. Matt held my hand as I was prepped for anesthesia. I tried to stay calm, but my mind was spinning.

"You've made it this far," I whispered to myself, repeating it like a mantra as they fitted the oxygen mask over my face.

Darkness.

I woke up to pain. Not in my abdomen, surprisingly, but in my shoulders, gas pain from the procedure. They'd warned me, but it still took me off guard. Then came the nausea, which hit me like a train. I don't handle anesthesia well, and it showed. The nurse administered something, I think it was Zofran, and slowly the nausea eased.

Then came the news.

The doctor appeared, her face calm but serious. "It was everywhere," she said. "Like a shotgun blast." Endometriosis had invaded my body, even attaching itself to my bowels. They removed what they could, but some of it was too deep.

I blinked through the anesthesia haze, the words sinking in one by one. So, it wasn't just stress. It wasn't in my head. My body had been fighting a silent war, and I had no idea.

There was a quiet sense of validation in that, even amidst the pain. A sense of *finally* having some answers. A sense that I wasn't crazy all these years.

The doctor recommended a one-month recovery before we resumed treatment. She suggested trying injectable medications with IUI before jumping straight into IVF. "With most of the endometriosis removed, your body should be a more hospitable environment," she said.

Studies show pregnancy rates improve significantly in the months following laparoscopic surgery for endometriosis, sometimes by as much as 50 percent. I held onto that number like a lifeline.

But recovery was no walk in the park. The gas pain lingered for days, making even the smallest movement feel like agony. The cramping, the bleeding, it all reminded me that healing is never linear.

I recovered, and we did one more IUI. We held out the hope it would be our last. Negative again.

And just when I thought I couldn't take any more setbacks, life threw us another punch.

WHAT DOES IT TAKE TO GET A WIN?

Our time at Air Command and Staff College (ACSC), a yearlong leadership school for mid-career officers, was coming to an end. Selection for ACSC was a small percentage of officers, and it signaled you were among the Air Force's rising leaders, on track to command a squadron and for possible bigger things.

Just as I was beginning to feel hopeful for the next steps in my career, tentatively optimistic that the worst might be behind us, another blow landed.

The command selection list came out, and my name wasn't on it.

In the military as an officer, command is the pinnacle: the role you're groomed for, where you're entrusted with leading, mentoring, and protecting hundreds of Airmen. It's not automatic, you must rise to the top and then be board-selected. Once on the list, you must then be chosen by another commander to take a position at their installation. I believed I was ready. I had the performance, the record, the education. But my name wasn't there. It felt like a punch to the gut and honestly, after months of fertility treatments and body blows from disappointment, my gut was starting to feel like a permanent punching bag.

It felt like being told, "You're good but not good enough."

The sting wasn't just professional. It was personal. Because this wasn't just about a title or a job, it was about validation, about finally getting a win after years of nothing but setbacks.

We had poured ourselves into our careers while silently battling infertility. Now, it felt like we were failing at both. That sinking sense of "What does it take to catch a break?" settled into our bones.

With no command assignment on the horizon, we turned our attention to the next decision point: our next base.

Given our backgrounds with ICBMs, we understood that the assignments were likely to be in Montana, North Dakota, or Wyoming. Missile fields. Remote posts. Nowhere near advanced reproductive care. It hit like another blow, sharp and suffocating.

After everything we'd been through with the tests, the procedures, the surgery, we were facing the real possibility that we'd be shipped somewhere that could derail our ability to continue treatment. IVF was now on the horizon, and it was clear we couldn't afford to be hours away from a clinic.

We made our case to the assignment team. We explained the medical necessity and the importance of being close to a reputable reproductive endocrinologist. Of the three potential bases, only F.E. Warren Air Force Base in Wyoming gave us access to a top-tier clinic—CCRM in Denver was just 90 miles away. It wasn't ideal, but it was workable.

We pleaded. Explained. Asked for understanding.

But the Air Force couldn't make any promises. They "understood the situation" but refused to guarantee anything. Because I was the service member rather than a dependent, I did not qualify for the Exceptional Family Member Program, which could have kept us stationed near appropriate care. Had I been a spouse, it might have been possible, but as an active-duty officer, it simply was not an option.

The double standard was infuriating.

We were crushed, not just by the rigidity of the system, but by the coldness of it. I had given so much of myself to the mission: my time, my health, my emotional well-being. I had lived and breathed the core values, especially *Service Before Self.* And now? Now, when I needed the system to show just a little humanity, it felt like I was met with indifference.

As if the lack of access to reproductive care wasn't already enough, there was the cherry on top: the familiar, soul-punching comment I'd heard more than once from fellow officers (I assume they were joking but that didn't make it sting less).

"If the Air Force wanted you to have a family, they would have issued you one."

Every time I heard it, it felt like a slap in the face. As if my desire to become a mother was selfish. As if I was less of a leader because I dared to want something so fundamental, so deeply human.

All of it—the disappointment, the lack of support, and crushing uncertainty—only added to deepen the grief we were already feeling. It felt like every path we tried to take toward becoming parents was blocked by the very system we were trying to serve.

In the middle of all of this, a friend texted Matt with the kind of message that stops you cold: "You've got tentative orders to Minot."

Minot, North Dakota. Remote. Freezing. Isolated. And not exactly known for cutting-edge reproductive endocrinology. The news hit like a steel-toed boot to the chest. After everything we'd been through, the idea of starting over in such a remote place while trying to build a family felt like the cruelest twist yet.

But the Air Force, in its own strange way, had other plans. An unexpected cheating scandal among missileers at Malmstrom Air Force Base in Montana changed everything. The fallout was massive: firings, investigations, and a full-on culture overhaul. Daniel Coyle writes about it in *The Culture Code*[4] if you're curious to dive deeper. One of the ripple effects of that shake-up? We were rerouted from Minot AFB to Malmstrom AFB to help rebuild the culture.

So, despite the anger, the exhaustion, the pain, we held on to one thing.

Hope.

Even when it hurt.

READY OR NOT, HERE WE GO

Despite the military, medical, and emotional obstacles, we kept trying to find a way forward. After exhausting every avenue, after surgeries, tests, tracking apps, pills, herbs, timed intercourse, IUIs, diet overhauls, yoga, and prayer, we knew what came next.

IVF.

Because there were no other options left.

We'd carried the weight of our denial, our faith, and our finances for years. But there comes a point when all the reasons to wait fall away. When you stop asking, *What else can I try?* and start asking, *What if we can't have children any other way?*

There's a line you cross when your longing for a child stops being just a hope and starts to feel like a calling. A deep, soul-level knowing that you're supposed to be a parent. That something inside you was made for this.

And eventually, we knew: if there was a door left to knock on, we were going to knock.

We heard rumors that Walter Reed offered IVF for military families at reduced cost. If accepted, medications would be covered, saving us thousands, and we could start immediately after graduation from Air Command and Staff College.

It felt like a sliver of light through a crack in a very long, very dark tunnel.

We sent in our vast paperwork—every scanned medical record, every lab, every failed treatment. We waited, anxiously refreshing our inbox every day. When the email finally came through and we were *accepted*, I nearly dropped the phone.

This is happening.

There was one more twist before we could begin: my thyroid. My TSH had been fluctuating—2.7, 3.5, 5.4. To give IVF its best shot, it needed to be under 2.5. That meant starting thyroid medication, immediately.

I resisted at first. The "natural me," the clean-eating, yoga-loving version of myself didn't like the idea of more pharmaceuticals. But the me that wanted a baby? She understood. This wasn't about pride. It was about doing everything we could to make this work.

Once I started the thyroid meds, something unexpected happened.

I felt better.

For the first time in months, maybe years, I had more energy. Less brain fog. Fewer crashes in the afternoon. It was like a veil had lifted, and I wondered, *How long has this been affecting me?* What else had I been unknowingly battling?

Infertility has a way of unearthing everything: your beliefs, your body's hidden imbalances, your resilience. And in those weeks leading up to IVF, I felt like I was finally, finally, stepping into the fullness of what this fight required.

We were ready.

IVF was no longer the last resort. It was the next right step.

CHAPTER 5:

Holding It Together (Barely)

As we moved forward with our IVF plans at Walter Reed, I felt a mix of excitement and apprehension. The thyroid medication was already making me feel better, which gave me hope that we were on the right track. However, the journey ahead still seemed daunting, filled with unknowns and challenges.

One of those challenges was getting the time off from work to do IVF. In the military, not all "leave" is created equal. We have convalescent (essentially sick/medical leave), personal (our version of paid time off), and permissive (time off with commander's discretion for professional or personal development—like attending conferences or house hunting after a move). One of those distinctions hit me like a ton of bricks when I realized the leave situation. I needed at least 15 days for the IVF process at the military treatment facility, and I was told I'd have to use my personal leave, my own paid time off. My stomach churned as I processed this information. It felt like a cruel joke: I was going through this intense medical process, yet I had to burn through my hard-earned vacation days to do it. So much for sitting on a beach somewhere; my "vacation" involved ultrasounds, blood draws, and hormone shots.

I remember sitting at my desk, staring at the computer screen, trying to make sense of it all. My fingers hovered over the keyboard as I composed yet another email, this time to the base clinic. "Is there any way I could be put on convalescent leave for this?" I typed, hope mingling with frustration in my chest. The response came back quickly: "Not authorized." Two words that felt like a slap in the face.

Undeterred, I reached out to Walter Reed. Surely, they would understand the physical and emotional toll of IVF. Their response was a little more encouraging, they could put me on convalescent leave, but only for a few days after the egg retrieval. The rest? Personal leave.

As I read the email, I felt a surge of anger and disbelief. My husband, who wasn't even undergoing the treatment, could take permissive leave to "escort" me, while I, the one injecting hormones, managing mood swings, and prepping for surgery, had to drain my vacation days. How was that fair?

I paced our house, my voice rising as frustration spilled out in waves. "This makes absolutely no sense!" I said, hands flying. "I'm the one doing the shots, dealing with the hormones, having my eggs harvested—and I'm the one using my vacation time?" Matt listened, his face equal parts sympathy and helplessness. We both knew the military could be rigid, but this felt especially unjust.

In a last-ditch effort, we went to our leadership.

I still remember the nervous flutter in my stomach as we explained our situation, hoping against hope that they could pull some strings or find a loophole. But their hands were tied. The regulations were clear, no matter how unfair they seemed. I felt deflated. And I also felt resentment. Why wasn't the Air Force better equipped to support dual military couples in these situations?

I was committed to this process, determined to give us the best chance at having a family. But the stark reality of having to use up my personal leave for a medical procedure, leave I had been saving for less stressful occasions, was a bitter pill to swallow.

The impact of it all wasn't lost on me: we were wrapping up school in Alabama, headed to Virginia for IVF, and then onward to our new duty station in Montana, all within weeks. It was like the world's most stressful permanent change of station, only this one involved a medication cooler and hormone injections in hotel bathrooms. While I was busy having existential crises over both national security and my reproductive system, Matt calmly packed for what felt like the strangest deployment ever.

He'd nonchalantly ask, "Hey, where do you want me to put your collection of fertility books and Chinese herbs...do you want to take them with us?" as if he were inquiring about the weather. His ability to remain unfazed was nothing short of miraculous.

For all my fellow professional women out there, let me tell you—trying to climb the career ladder while also attempting to create life is like trying to pat your head, rub your belly, and solve a Rubik's cube...all while running a marathon. In boots. On fire.

But there I was, attempting to keep my head in the game for graduation while simultaneously preparing for the most important mission of my life. Some days, I wasn't sure if I was more worried about passing my exams or passing my next blood draw and ultrasound. And don't even get me started on trying to hide hormone-induced mood swings while listening to a bunch of pilots. Let's just say my poker face got a serious workout that year.

Through it all, Matt remained my rock, taking on most of our moving responsibilities without complaint. He became an expert at deciphering my hormone-induced code: "I need cupcakes" actually meant "Hold me, I'm scared about our future." As graduation loomed and our IVF journey was about to kick into high gear, I laughed at the chaos of it all. But with my uniform packed, my hormones (somewhat) in check, and Matt by my side, I was ready to tackle whatever came next, be it national security threats or recalcitrant ovaries.

We graduated from ACSC and, without much time to reflect on the milestone, immediately hit the road for Fort Belvoir. Our next chapter was beginning, and while the road ahead was still uncertain, we were grateful for a temporary sense of stability. Instead of spending weeks in a sterile hotel, we had the incredible blessing of staying with my sister Nicole, brother-in-law Chris, and their two kids for the majority of the time.

Being surrounded by family during such a pivotal time provided both comfort and emotional support, something we desperately needed after the stress of the past year. And yes, we camped out on their living room's pull-out sofa couch. It wasn't exactly luxury accommodations, every spring and sag reminded us we were in a season of sacrifice, but it was a roof, a soft place to land, and a reminder that we weren't doing this alone.

Beyond the financial reprieve of not having to pay for extended lodging, this arrangement gave us something far more valuable: a sense of home. After ten months of intense coursework and constant demands at school, I was ready for a mental and emotional reset. For the first time in a while, I felt like I could breathe. I looked forward to stepping away from the pressure of academics and military obligations, even if just for a little while, and focusing on what mattered most: preparing for the next phase of our fertility journey.

GOING OFF SCRIPT

We walked into the briefing room at the military teaching hospital with cautious excitement and guarded hope. The space buzzed softly with the quiet energy of other couples, all of us gathered for the same reason, to start IVF. Because this was both a teaching center and a military facility, everything ran like a mission: synchronized cohorts, precise timelines, and a clinical efficiency that felt both reassuring and impersonal.

This wasn't our first time in a fertility clinic, and none of it overwhelmed us. If anything, the structure was familiar. We had been through multiple cycles before, but this time felt different. This was what we believed to be our last real chance to conceive, the final stretch after years of trying, hoping, and recalibrating. We needed this cycle to work.

During the initial briefing, the staff walked us through what the weeks ahead were supposed to look like. They explained the protocol with a matter-of-fact clarity that came from doing this hundreds of times. We would be following an antagonist IVF protocol, meaning I would start with birth control to quiet my ovaries, then transition to daily FSH injections to stimulate multiple follicles. As the follicles developed, they would introduce Ganirelix to prevent premature ovulation and keep the timing controlled. Monitoring would be constant with blood draws at dawn, ultrasounds to track follicle growth, and tight control over medication adjustments. They described how the trigger shot would be used to finalize maturation and how egg retrieval would take place thirty-six hours later under sedation. After that came fertilization in the lab, embryo development, a possible transfer, and then the dreaded two-week wait. Then, finally, bloodwork to measure beta hCG and confirm if implantation had occurred and the cycle had been successful.

After the briefing, we walked the halls of the clinic, getting to know the exam rooms and long corridors that would hold so much of our hope in the weeks to come. The drive back to Fort Belvoir, crawling through D.C. traffic, gave us plenty of time to absorb everything we had just learned. Determined to approach this cycle with intention, I downloaded fertility meditations tailored to each day of the process. They gave me structure when everything else felt uncertain. I was cautiously optimistic. Visualization hadn't made us successful in the past, but I was willing to try anything that might keep me grounded.

By now, our lifestyle looked very different from when we started trying. We had stuck to a mostly gluten- and dairy-free diet, partly to ease my endometriosis and partly because I had read anecdotal evidence suggesting it might improve IVF outcomes. I missed pizza but reminded myself that short-term sacrifices might bring long-term joy.

We'd also backed off from our usual workouts. I even stopped doing yoga. We'd learned that once stimulation started, too much abdominal movement could raise the risk of ovarian torsion—a terrifying prospect. I joked with Matt that I finally had a valid excuse not to run. Still, I wasn't sure that the trade-off of daily injections made it worth it.

These shifts in diet, activity, and mindset became our new normal. We tackled each day with a blend of hope, commitment, and a bit of humor. If we couldn't laugh, we'd crumble.

Once I stopped the birth control, the withdrawal bleed signaled that we were ready. My baseline scan showed no cysts, a reassuring sign, and we began stimulation with 150 units of Follistim and one vial of Menopur at night. I'd forgotten how much Menopur stung.

At 6 a.m., we lined up for blood draws to track my estradiol (E2) levels. The staff affectionately called it the cattle call, and the process operated on a strict first come, first served basis. While we waited, you could feel the unspoken tension of couples quietly comparing timelines and progress, an unavoidable side effect of moving through IVF in synchronized cohorts. These blood tests were essential for avoiding OHSS, a risk when hormone levels climb too high, and the waiting room would soon become one of the most familiar spaces in our lives.

Four days in, my estradiol came back at only 25. Not great. They bumped up my meds—Follistim to 225 and Menopur to two vials—to try to coax my ovaries into action.

By day 9, things were finally moving. My estradiol was 166, and though my follicles weren't large yet, there were 23 of them. Still, I was surprised they weren't growing faster. In past IUIs, I'd triggered around day 10 with fewer meds. The doctor explained that the birth control may have over-suppressed me. I imagined my ovaries lounging on vacation, reluctant to clock back in.

With no work to distract me this time, the days dragged. I leaned hard into meditation and prayer. Anything to anchor myself.

One welcome break came when we visited our friends Angela and Brent in D.C. They had just welcomed their daughter, Liv. Holding that tiny baby filled me with a strange mix of longing and hope. We toured the Holocaust Museum together, and I was struck again by Viktor Frankl's words: "When we are no longer able to change a situation, we are challenged to change ourselves." That line stuck with me. I couldn't change our infertility, but I could change how I showed up for it.

Cycle day 11 brought better news: estradiol had climbed to 686, and my follicles were finally growing, 25 of them between 6 and 12 mm. They shifted Follistim to the morning, upped Menopur to three vials, and added Ganirelix to prevent premature ovulation. Things were moving.

On cycle day 13, I noticed the 6 a.m. cattle call line at the clinic was noticeably shorter. We always tell ourselves not to compare, but that's easier said than done, especially when you're surrounded by people on the same journey and it feels like everyone else is moving ahead.

Fewer patients were waiting for blood draws, and I couldn't help thinking, *I'm on cycle day 13. I've never gone this long without a trigger.* Granted, my past experience was with IUI using FSH injectables, but still. I realized the others must be preparing for egg retrieval, and a small pang of disappointment hit me as I wondered why my body wasn't cooperating.

My estradiol was 1265 and progesterone 0.9. They only saw 22 follicles ranging from 8–13 millimeters. I took a deep breath, reminding myself to focus on the long-term goal. *Think about our dream of having a baby. It's worth it in the long run,* I repeated to myself like a mantra. The doctor asked me to return in two days.

Cycle day 15 brought a shock: my estradiol had skyrocketed to 2597. I'd never experienced levels this high before, and I worried about the risk of ovarian hyperstimulation syndrome (OHSS). OHSS occurs when the ovaries become overstimulated, causing them to swell and leak fluid. If this escalates, it could cause dangerous complications like blood clots or fluid buildup in the lungs. I knew OHSS was a potential complication of fertility treatments, especially with the injectable gonadotropins I was taking. The rapid rise in my estradiol levels was a red flag, and I started to understand why the doctors were watching me so closely.

The ultrasound revealed 24 follicles between 8–14 mm. As the wand moved around, I felt increasingly uncomfortable. Movement was starting to hurt. They asked me to come back the next day, and I found myself in unfamiliar, nerve-wracking territory.

On cycle day 16, the waiting room was empty. Apparently, everyone else had moved on to egg retrieval. My estradiol had climbed to 3329, with follicles now ranging from 8–18mm. I learned that estradiol levels above 3000–4000 pg/mL are associated with an increased risk of OHSS. The discomfort I was feeling during ultrasounds and the high number of follicles were also typical signs of impending OHSS. My body was showing all the classic signs of overstimulation.

The doctor told me we would be triggering with Lupron instead of hCG, concerned about further elevating my estradiol and OHSS risk. I later understood that hCG can exacerbate OHSS, and by considering a Lupron trigger, they were trying to reduce my risk of developing severe OHSS while still allowing my cycle to proceed.

Panic set in as I frantically searched blogs and forums for similar experiences. Questions raced through my mind: *Was this cycle going to be a bust? Would we have to freeze? That wasn't an option... we were headed to Montana and couldn't come back...we had new jobs to start! They need us after the crisis that occurred in missiles. The missiles weren't going to manage themselves!* My mind spun in every direction at once, the classic monkey mind.

I struggled to keep my stress levels down and maintain a positive outlook. Most importantly, I tried to trust the experts. After all, they did this all the time, right? But the fear of the unknown continued to nag at me as we ventured into this unexpected turn in our fertility journey, with the looming threat of OHSS adding an extra layer of anxiety to an already emotionally charged process.

That night I got ready for my Lupron trigger shot. They wanted me to go in the next day to get my levels checked.

I took a deep breath as we stepped into the waiting room on cycle day 17. It was eerily quiet and we were the only ones there.

My heart raced as I made my way to the blood draw room, hoping for good news. The nurse smiled reassuringly as she told me my estradiol level was 3886, not too high, thankfully. The doctors believed we could proceed with the egg retrieval tomorrow. A mix of excitement and nervousness washed over me as I realized we were entering the final stretch of this intense journey.

The next day, my husband and I arrived at the treatment facility. My stomach was in knots as questions flooded my mind. *How exactly does egg retrieval work? Will I have a bad reaction to the anesthesia like I did during my endometriosis surgery? What if something goes wrong? Will it hurt afterward? Can they really get all the eggs they're expecting?* The what-ifs were endless, and I tried to push them aside as we were called back.

Egg retrieval is a crucial step in the in the IVF process. It involves removing mature eggs from the ovaries using a thin needle guided by ultrasound. The procedure is typically done under sedation or light anesthesia to minimize discomfort. The doctor uses a transvaginal ultrasound probe to locate the follicles containing the eggs and then carefully aspirates them using a needle attached to a suction device.

A lumen, in this context, refers to the hollow part of the needle used for egg retrieval. A single-lumen needle has one channel for both suction and flushing, while a double-lumen needle has separate channels for these functions, potentially improving egg collection efficiency.

When I woke up, the pain was intense. I could barely move, and the concerned looks on the medical team's faces told me something wasn't right. They explained that things hadn't gone as planned. They started with a single-lumen needle, but the eggs weren't releasing as expected. They switched to a double-lumen needle, hoping it would help, but the eggs still resisted. I was poked and prodded more than 30 times in attempts to retrieve them.

The final count was a shock: only 10 eggs retrieved out of the 20–24 they saw on the ultrasound, with just 8 mature enough for fertilization. I felt numb, struggling to process this unexpected turn of events. This scenario was never mentioned in any of the forums or blogs I'd scoured for information. I tried to remind myself that it only takes one good embryo, but the disappointment was overwhelming.

The medical team warned me again about the risk of OHSS and instructed me to go to the ER if I experienced extreme pain or increased bloating. Back at the hotel, I tried to rest and eat, sipping on dandelion tea thinking maybe it would help with the bloating. When I finally got up, the pain hit me like a freight train. I doubled over, suddenly remembering the multiple punctures the doctor made trying to retrieve the eggs. Dragging myself to the bathroom, I was shocked by my reflection. My abdomen was so distended it was almost unrecognizable. I crawled back to bed, feeling utterly drained and vulnerable.

Later, I got ready for the worst shot of the IVF process: the PIO (Progesterone in Oil). I took a deep breath, trying to steady my nerves. The needle looked like something you'd use to tranquilize a small elephant, and the oil itself was thicker than molasses in January. My already sore body protested at the thought of another injection, but this one was non-negotiable.

"You ready?" Matt asked, his voice a mix of concern and determination. I nodded, not trusting my voice, and turned away. I had read every tip out there, warm the progesterone, inject slowly, avoid blood vessels, but it did not make it any easier. I was sweating like I'd run a marathon, and we hadn't even started yet. I positioned myself by leaning over the bathroom counter to expose my upper buttock.

The things we do for a baby, I thought wryly. "Go for it," I managed to squeak out as I gripped the counter tightly. As the needle pierced my skin, I held my breath. It was not just a prick; I could feel the thick gauge pushing through layers of tissue. Then came the oil, a strange sensation of pressure and spreading warmth. It was as if someone slowly inflated a balloon under my skin. I resisted the urge to squirm, knowing movement could make it worse.

"Almost done," Matt murmured, in deep concentration. I nodded, still not daring to look. The pressure mounted and created a lump that I knew I would need to massage out. It felt like forever before he said, "Okay, that's it," and withdrew the needle. I let out a long, shaky breath and immediately started rubbing the injection site.

"Ouch," I muttered. "That's so much worse than the FSH and Menopur." Those stung, but this? This was a whole new level of discomfort.

As I massaged the lump, trying to distribute the oil, I couldn't help but laugh a little. "You know," I said to Matt, who carefully disposed of the needle, "when they said IVF would be a pain in the butt, I didn't think they meant it literally."

He chuckled and the tension eased in his voice now that the injection was over. "You're doing great," he said, giving my shoulder a gentle squeeze. "One day at a time, right?"

I nodded, feeling a mix of pride at getting through it and also felt the apprehension about the next injection. But then I reminded myself why we were doing this. Each shot, each discomfort, was a step closer to our dream. It was not easy, but nothing worth having ever is.

As I stood up, I gingerly tested how sore I was, and made a mental note to ice the area later. Tomorrow, we would do it all over again. *Sigh.*

CHAPTER 6:

The Longest Days

Now began another agonizing wait, perhaps the hardest yet. We were anxiously anticipating news on how many eggs had successfully fertilized through ICSI (Intracytoplasmic Sperm Injection). Matt had done his part, providing 12 million sperm with 80 percent motility. The embryologists would update us on fertilization results the next day, and again on day three. They didn't check the embryos daily, to minimize disturbance to their development, so it became another exercise in patience and trust.

As I lay down later, trying to find a comfortable position on the lumpy guest bed, a thought crossed my mind: *Who knew that trying to create life would involve so much poking, prodding, and waiting?* I felt like a walking science experiment, hope wrapped in hormones.

Despite the setbacks, I did my best to stay hopeful. Every step of this journey had tested our resilience, but we were still standing. I kept reminding myself that many women had faced similar odds and gone on to have healthy pregnancies. Maybe, just maybe, our story would find that ending too.

Three days after the egg retrieval, my phone rang.

My heart jumped into my throat as I saw the clinic's number flash on the screen. This was it, the update we'd been nervously waiting for. I answered, voice trembling slightly, and put the call on speaker so Matt could hear, too.

"Five embryos are still growing," the embryologist said, her voice calm, clinical, but kind.

I exhaled, not realizing I'd been holding my breath. Five. It wasn't the eight mature eggs we started with, but it was something.

I tried to focus on the positive as she explained the development stages, though I felt the sting of the three that didn't make it.

After I hung up, I caught a glimpse of myself in the mirror. My face looked tired. My abdomen was still swollen from the retrieval and the OHSS symptoms hadn't fully subsided. The physical discomfort was a constant reminder of what my body had been through. I winced as I shifted, wondering when, if, I would ever feel normal again.

"Five is good," Matt said, trying to reassure us both.

I nodded, forcing a smile. I wanted to believe him. But inside, my mind was racing. Each embryo that didn't make it felt like a lost opportunity, a tiny, imagined heartbeat that never got the chance. I tried to quiet those thoughts, tried to remember it only takes one, but the grief over even hypothetical losses was strangely real.

The next two days stretched endlessly. I swung between hope and fear, my emotions as swollen and unpredictable as my ovaries. Could I really be ready for a transfer in just two more days? The thought thrilled and terrified me in equal measure.

I meditated. I prayed. I lit candles. I bargained with God, guilt and hope tangled with doubt. I was a woman clinging to faith, whispering to whatever higher power might still be listening.

One night, in the quiet, I laid my hand on my bloated abdomen. "Come on, little ones," I whispered to the embryos I imagined growing in the lab. "Stay strong. We're waiting for you."

The pain from the retrieval was still fresh, a dull ache that flared every time I shifted wrong. *But* I told myself, *this pain is proof. It's proof of what we're willing to endure, how much we want this, how far we've already come.*

As potential transfer day loomed, the fear returned: Would any of them make it to blastocyst? Would my body cooperate? The what-ifs swirled, but beneath them was a stubborn thread of determination. We'd made it this far. We weren't quitting now.

I looked at Matt. In his eyes I saw the same fear, the same fight.

"Whatever happens," I said, surprised by the strength in my voice, "we're in this together."

He nodded, pulled me in gently, careful of my tender body. "Two more days," he murmured. "We've got this."

I let myself believe it. Just for a moment. I breathed in deep, sending one more silent prayer to our embryos.

"Grow strong, little ones," I whispered. "You can do it."

TRANSFERRING HOPE

The morning of the transfer, five days post-retrieval, I woke up with a mix of excitement and nervousness churning in my stomach. Or maybe it was just bloating from all the hormones. Either way, I was on edge, watching the clock, waiting for the clinic to call with our transfer time.

When the phone finally rang at 9 a.m., my heart leapt. "Come in at 11," they said. "We'll give you the final update then."

I turned to Matt, eyes wide, adrenaline kicking in. "This is really happening," I whispered, laughter and nerves bubbling together. We headed to the hospital, me with my swollen belly, lumpy progesterone-injected backside, and a mind full of what-ifs. But all I could think was: everything has led to this.

At the clinic, the nurse greeted us with a soft smile that didn't quite reach her eyes.

"We have good news and bad news," she said gently.

My stomach dropped.

"The good news: you still have five embryos," she continued. "The bad news: none have quite reached the full blastocyst stage yet, which is what we typically want by day five."

She went on: one embryo definitely wouldn't make it. One was still at the morula stage. Three were early blastocysts.

Given my age and the embryo quality, they recommended transferring two.

Twins? The thought hadn't seriously crossed my mind until that moment. But Matt and I barely had to exchange a glance. We both knew: this might be our only shot.

"We'll do it," I said, my voice steadier than I felt.

They handed me a cap and gown. I changed, catching my reflection in the mirror. I looked scared but there was something else there too: grit. We'd come too far to back down now.

Matt suited up too. I was so grateful he could be there with me. As I lay on the table, legs in stirrups, I felt a strange mix of vulnerability and awe. They covered me with a blanket, but modesty was long gone by that point.

"We'll use ultrasound guidance," the doctor explained. "You'll actually get to watch the embryos being transferred into your uterus."

She smiled.

I reached for Matt's hand and squeezed. My heart pounded.

On the screen, two tiny specks appeared: our potential babies.

"There they go," the doctor said softly, as she gently released them.

Tears welled up as I stared at the monitor. After all the shots, all the appointments, all the disappointments, we were here. Two microscopic bundles of hope now rested inside me.

They handed us a photo of the transfer. A black-and-white image, grainy and clinical, but to us it was magic.

"Our babies," I whispered to Matt, my throat tight.

As we left the clinic, post-transfer instructions in hand, a calmness settled over me. Whatever came next, we had given it everything we had. Those two tiny specks weren't just embryos. They were years of trying, of aching, of faith. They were love, personified.

I placed a hand over my lower abdomen. *Grow strong, little ones,* I thought. *We're ready for you.*

PUPO (PREGNANT UNTIL PROVEN OTHERWISE)

The morning after our embryo transfer, I expected to feel different, transformed somehow, but everything felt...normal. At least on the outside. I was PUPO, Pregnant Until Proven Otherwise, but implantation hadn't happened yet. Still, a tiny spark flickered inside me. Hope. Fragile, but alive.

We packed up and hit the road for Montana because, of course, duty called. The irony wasn't lost on me—here we were, potentially at the beginning of a new life, and yet we were being pulled back into our other one: the mission, the career, the military. The open highway stretched in front of us like a metaphor, both literal and emotional, for this unpredictable, winding path we were on.

Matt and I drove separately. That was part of the plan. Two cars. Too much stuff. Too many responsibilities. Too much to carry.

The doctor's orders echoed in my mind like a checklist: Take frequent breaks. Stretch your legs. Go for short walks to increase blood flow. Every few hours, I'd pull into a rest stop, sip water, and do a slow walk around the car, looking like a very cautious road tripper with an invisible cargo.

The great IVF debate about post-transfer activity levels spun in my head. *Should I be on bed rest? Should I go about my day?* I opted for a middle ground, light movement, lots of car "rest," and yoga poses with my feet up against the hotel room walls at night. I imagined little cellular fireworks inside me as I whispered, "Settle in, little ones. Stick."

And yes, I was absolutely one of those "pee on a stick" people. I decided to test out the trigger shot, watching it fade with each passing day. It became a weird little ritual: wake up, test, squint, analyze. *Is it still there? Is it lighter? Wait...is it getting darker again?!* I'd hold the test up to every light source possible. Bathroom light. Window light. Phone flashlight.

It was completely unscientific. Totally obsessive. And yet, it was the only thing I felt I had control over. The physical sensations were no help. Every cramp or flutter could've meant something... or nothing. Was that implantation? Or the fast food from that rest stop in Indiana? The guessing game was maddening.

Despite the nerves, I felt an odd mix of peace and strength. This wasn't our first time navigating uncertainty. The military had trained us to adapt, to keep moving forward even when we didn't have all the answers. IVF was just another mission—only this time, it was deeply, painfully personal.

There I was, possibly pregnant, cruising down I-90, stopping to do gentle lunges in gas station parking lots while silently cheering on two microscopic embryos. If this worked, it would make one hell of a story for the baby book. And as it turns out, a pretty good chapter in the book I didn't know I was going to write.

With every mile, I carried the weight of hope and fear in equal measure. But above all, I held tight to the belief that we were closer than ever to meeting the family we'd been dreaming of for so long.

Connecting with my husband, despite driving separately, became crucial. We'd call each other during breaks, sharing our thoughts, fears, and hopes. Sometimes we'd just laugh about the craziness of our situation, two military personnel, possibly expecting, zigzagging across the country. This shared experience, even with its challenges, strengthened our bond. Physical activity, as recommended by the doctor, became another coping mechanism. Those short walks during our frequent stops weren't just for blood flow, they became moments of freedom.

Feeling the ground beneath my feet, the air on my skin, it all helped bring me back to the present moment, away from the swirling "what-ifs" in my head. I also found comfort in writing. Each night, I'd jot down my thoughts and feelings in a journal. It became a safe space to pour out my anxieties, hopes, and dreams. Lastly, I learned to be gentle with myself. Some days were harder than others, and that was okay. I allowed myself to feel whatever emotions came up, excitement, fear, impatience, without judgment.

This self-compassion became a powerful tool in managing the rollercoaster of emotions.

While the wait was excruciating, these coping strategies and small rituals, breathing, writing, forgiving myself, helped me navigate the uncertainty with a little more grace and a lot more hope. I didn't know what the outcome would be, but I knew I was learning something vital: how to stay grounded in the middle of the unknown.

By the time we approached Montana, that lesson felt hard-earned. Excitement and nervousness bubbled up as we drove toward our next chapter. Our house on base wasn't ready yet, but my parents in Great Falls offered a temporary haven, a small blessing amidst the chaos. Reality hit fast. We signed into work almost immediately, trying to shift from IVF mode to military mode. It was jarring balancing the possibility of new life with the immediacy of our careers.

All the while, my morning ritual continued. Each day, I'd wake up early, heart pounding, to perform the pregnancy test. At 4dp5dt (four days post five-day transfer), I stared at the strip, my breath catching. Both lines were still there. Was it darker? The same? My mind raced. Surely it should be fading by now if it was just the trigger shot, right? I scrutinized my body for any signs. No cramping, no bleeding. The only discomfort I felt was from the PIO injections, a constant reminder of our journey. I tried not to read too much into the absence of symptoms, knowing it could mean everything or nothing.

Then came 5dp5dt. As I peered at the test, my heart skipped a beat. The line wasn't fading. If anything, it seemed...darker? Excitement surged through me, tempered by cautious hope. I couldn't contain myself. "Matt," I whispered, my voice trembling with a mix of fear and elation. "You have to see this!" I held my breath as he came to look, both of us hovering over this tiny strip that held so much promise. In that moment, about to start new roles at work,

I felt the first real flicker of belief. Maybe, just maybe, our dream was becoming a reality.

As we stood there, whispering and smiling in disbelief, I realized something: the practices that carried me through, the grounding, the grace, the faith, had done their job. Whatever came next, we were ready for it.

THE SECOND LINE

Work was a blur of new responsibilities and introductions, but my mind kept drifting back to those little pregnancy tests waiting at home. I wanted to test every couple of hours, the urge almost overwhelming at times. Thankfully, the demands of my new role provided some distraction, if not complete reprieve from my racing thoughts. The constant buzz of activity in the office at least slowed down the endless loop of "what ifs" in my head.

As night fell, sleep eluded me. I tossed and turned, my mind a blur of hope and anxiety. The hours crawled by as I waited for dawn, each tick of the clock seeming to echo in the quiet room. Finally, unable to bear it any longer, I slipped out of bed long before our alarm was set to go off. Heart pounding, I made my way to the bathroom, test in hand. The familiar routine of unwrapping, waiting, and watching felt different this time, charged with an electricity I couldn't quite explain. As the seconds ticked by, I held my breath, afraid to hope too much. And then I saw it. The line. There was no doubt about it—it was darker. Unmistakably, undeniably darker.

My heart swelled, a rush of emotion flooding through me that was part joy, part disbelief, and all wonder. "Oh my God!" I whispered, my hand shaking as I held the test closer to the light, making sure my eyes weren't playing tricks on me. But there it was, clear as day. A positive. A real, honest-to-goodness positive. In that moment, standing in the dim light of early morning, everything changed. All the appointments, the injections, the waiting, it all crystallized into this single, beautiful moment of possibility. I wanted to shout, to dance, to wake up Matt and share this incredible news. But I also wanted to savor this moment, just for a second, this perfect slice of time where hope became reality.

As I stood there, test in hand, I felt a wave of gratitude wash over me. For our persistence, for the support of our families, for the miracle of science that made this possible. Whatever challenges lay ahead, and I knew there would be many, we had already overcome so much. This tiny, darker line was proof of that. With a deep breath, I prepared to wake Matt and share our news. Our journey was far from over, but this moment, this beautiful, terrifying, exhilarating moment, was one I would cherish forever. In the quiet of the early morning, as Montana slept around us, our future suddenly seemed brighter than ever.

The days at the munitions squadron seemed to drag on endlessly. I found myself staring blankly at inventory lists and safety protocols, my mind constantly wandering back to those two pink lines. The urge to share our news was almost overwhelming. I'd catch myself opening my mouth to tell a coworker, only to snap it shut again, remembering our decision to keep this precious secret to ourselves for now.

Every morning brought a new surge of excitement and validation. The line on the test strip grew darker with each passing day, a visual representation of the life growing inside me. It was tangible proof of our success, a daily affirmation that yes, I was pregnant! The reality of it would hit me at the most unexpected moments, during a briefing, while inspecting equipment, or in the middle of a casual conversation with a colleague. Despite the thrill of our secret, the wait for official confirmation felt interminable. We had to wait until 14 days post-transfer for the blood draw that would definitively confirm the pregnancy.

Those two weeks stretched out like an eternity. I found myself counting down the days, hours, and even minutes until we could get that final, clinical validation. The anticipation was a mix of excitement and anxiety. Part of me reveled in this period of private joy, where only Matt and I knew about the potential new addition to our family. Another part of me was eager for the certainty that blood work would provide, a definitive answer that would allow us to fully embrace this new reality.

As I went about my duties in the squadron, I felt like I was living a double life. On the outside, I was the same dedicated officer, focused on my responsibilities. But internally, I was bursting with a secret joy, counting down to the moment when we could finally share our news with the world. Those days of waiting taught me a new kind of patience. Each morning's darker line was a small victory, a stepping stone towards the official confirmation we were eagerly awaiting. In the midst of the military precision that surrounded me at work, I was experiencing a deeply personal journey of hope and anticipation.

As the date of the blood draw approached, I found myself both eager for and apprehensive about the finality it would bring. This limbo of early pregnancy, with its mixture of certainty and uncertainty, had become a special time all its own. Whatever the official results would be, I knew I would always cherish these days of quiet excitement, shared only between Matt and me, as we stood on the threshold of a new chapter in our lives.

The day of the blood draw finally arrived, and I found myself at the lab, order in hand, my heart racing with anticipation. As the lab tech drew my blood, she casually mentioned, "You should get a call later today." I nodded, trying to appear calm while inside I was a bundle of nerves. The reassurance of that morning's positive pregnancy test helped, but this was the moment of truth.

The wait for that call felt like an eternity. When my phone finally rang, I answered with shaky hands. "Pregnant," the voice on the other end said, "and your hCG is 65!" A tear rolled down my cheek as joy overwhelmed me. It was real. It was happening. Eager to share the news, I emailed the clinic right away. Their response was both exciting and nerve-wracking: I needed to retest in 48 hours to see if the hCG doubled, indicating a viable pregnancy. *No problem,* I thought, even as a small voice in my head wondered, *When will I stop worrying about this?*

After so many negative tests, these positive results felt almost surreal. Part of me still couldn't quite believe it was happening. Matt and I tried to keep busy, attempting to distract ourselves from the wait. We did share our news with my parents since we were staying with them. Their joy was infectious, making the news feel more real.

In quiet moments, I found myself talking to the baby or was it babies? Two embryos were transferred, after all. "Hey you," I'd whisper, "Grow, baby, grow!" It felt silly and wonderful all at once. As the 48-hour mark approached, I headed back to the lab, timing it as close as possible to the exact hour. I had already researched the range my hCG should be in, the numbers etched in my mind. Now, all I could do was wait impatiently for that crucial phone call. The anticipation was almost unbearable.

Each ring of my phone sent my heart racing, wondering if this was the call that would confirm our hopes. I tried to stay positive, reminding myself of how far we'd come, but the fear of disappointment hovered like a shadow I could not shake. As I waited, I reflected on our journey: the ups and downs, the tears and laughter, the endless appointments and injections. All of it had led to this moment, this wait for a single number that could change everything.

I found myself bargaining with God and the universe, promising anything if only the numbers would be good. The rational part of me knew that worrying wouldn't change the outcome, but after everything we'd been through, it was hard not to. Finally, my phone rang. I took a deep breath, steeling myself for whatever news was coming. As I answered, I silently hoped that this call would bring us continued good news. "Your hCG is 200."

I exhaled slowly, suddenly aware that I'd been holding my breath. The reality of the situation washed over me like a wave, both exhilarating and terrifying. "This is really happening," I whispered to myself, a mix of excitement and disbelief coloring my words. With trembling fingers, I typed out an email to the fertility clinic, my heart racing as I awaited their response.

When it arrived, I devoured the instructions, committing every detail to memory. An ultrasound at six weeks. Two weeks to wait. *I can do this,* I told myself, trying to summon every ounce of strength and patience I possessed. As the days crawled by, my body began to change.

WHERE IS IT?

Morning sickness became my constant companion, although "morning" seems like a cruel misnomer. The nausea clung to me all day long, a persistent reminder of the life growing inside me. I was grateful I didn't actually vomit, but the constant queasiness was a challenge. I found myself in a bizarre cycle of eating to stave off nausea, only to feel sick from eating. It was like my body was playing a twisted game of "Would You Rather?" with itself. Through it all, I tolerated the PIO injections, each one a small victory in the marathon of hope.

When we finally got our house on base, it felt like a sign. "Perfect timing!" we exclaimed, throwing ourselves into the distraction of settling in. As the week moved on, I actually noticed my nausea decreased. *Weird*, I thought to myself.

Before I knew it, the day of our first ultrasound arrived. As we drove to the appointment, excitement bubbled up inside me, threatening to overflow. After countless vaginal ultrasounds during our fertility journey, this one felt different. Special. We were finally going to see our baby! Lying on the exam table, feet in stirrups, I tried to calm my racing heart. The wait for the technician felt endless, and I found myself counting ceiling tiles to stay sane. When she finally entered and began the ultrasound, I held my breath once again. "There's your uterus," she said, her voice steady. "Looks good. There's the yolk sac."

I watched her face intently as she focused on the screen, passing over the yolk sac again and again. A small "Hmmm" escaped her lips, and suddenly, the air in the room felt thick and heavy. "I don't see a heartbeat yet," she said, her words hitting me like a physical blow. My mind reeled, unable to process what I was hearing. *We did IVF. We should be right on track. There should be a heartbeat.*

The technician's voice seemed to come from far away as she suggested we speak with our doctor and return in a couple of days. As we left the clinic, I felt numb, lost in a fog of confusion and fear. Back home, I did what comes naturally in this age of information—I turned to the online forums. Surely someone else has been through this, I thought desperately. Maybe there's hope. As I scrolled through posts and comments, I clung to every positive story I found, determined to believe that our journey wasn't over.

As I scoured the forums, I stumbled upon stories that ignited a flicker of hope within me. Tales of rising beta levels and heartbeats discovered just days later. I clung to these narratives like a lifeline, desperately willing our story to follow the same path. With a mixture of trepidation and optimism, I did another beta test. The results showed my levels were still rising, and for a moment, I allowed myself to believe that everything might be okay. But anxiety gnawed at the edges of my hope as we waited for the next ultrasound.

Time seemed to warp in the days leading up to our appointment. Hours flew by like minutes, yet each minute felt like an eternity. Finally, we found ourselves back at the clinic, my heart pounding so hard I'm sure the technician could hear it. As I laid on the exam table once again, I tried to steel myself for whatever we might see. Part of me knew this hope might be false, but I couldn't help it. I would rather have been there, clinging to that thread of possibility, than anywhere else.

The technician's face told me everything before she even spoke. No sugarcoating the second time, there was still no heartbeat. Nothing changed. The words "blighted ovum" fell from her lips, and my world shattered. A blighted ovum, she explained, is when a fertilized egg attaches to the uterine wall, but the embryo doesn't develop. The gestational sac forms, but it's empty. It's a type of very early miscarriage.

I can't even begin to describe the tidal wave of emotions that crashed over me. Numbness and heartbreak warred within me as the reality sank in, this was not a viable pregnancy.

In that moment, all our hopes, all our dreams, all the morning sickness and injections and waiting...it was for nothing. In a daze, I called the doctor. Their words barely registered as they explained that at this point, all we could do is wait. If a miscarriage did not occur naturally, we might need to consider a D&C (dilation and curettage). As I hung up the phone, I felt hollow. Empty, like the gestational sac inside me.

Sharing the news of our non-viable pregnancy felt like reopening a wound with each conversation. Thankfully, we'd kept our circle small, avoiding the temptation to make it "Facebook official" or shout it from the rooftops. Still, telling even our closest family and friends was excruciating.

The hardest conversation, surprisingly, was with my boss. I found myself hoping he'd understand, dreading the possibility of cold professionalism in the face of my grief. To his credit, he said all the right things. He offered his condolences, told me I didn't need to explain anything, and gently reminded me that I could talk to him or take the time I needed. Still, I could tell he saw how much I was struggling. I wasn't fully present, how could I be? In fact, I was placed down on the Personnel Reliability Program. I was not to be around nuclear weapons. And honestly, I totally agreed with that decision.

Now, we faced another wait, this time for my body to expel what I'd thought was our miracle. The silver lining, if you could call it that, was no more PIO shots. But that small mercy was dwarfed by the overwhelming negative thoughts swirling in my head. Why was this so damn hard? The question echoed in my mind, a relentless drumbeat of frustration and despair. I couldn't shake the feeling that my body was failing me, failing us. We'd been so sure this time, the stars seemed aligned. IVF between PCS moves, settling into our new house...it had all felt so right.

I found myself wondering what we'd done wrong, even though logically I knew it wasn't our fault.

Nothing could have prepared me for the physical reality of the miscarriage, which hit about 10 days later. The pain was intense, far worse than any period I'd ever experienced. The cramping felt like my body was trying to turn itself inside out, and the bleeding was alarmingly heavy.

Despite the physical and emotional turmoil, I dragged myself to work the next day. At the time, there was no leave provision in the regulations for miscarriage. Just like with IVF, the system had no place for something so deeply human. I had used personal leave to try to create life and now, after losing it, I was expected to report for duty as if nothing had happened.

I felt like a ghost haunting my own life, going through the motions while feeling utterly hollow inside. The experience left me completely drained, both physically and emotionally. It was as if all the hope and excitement we had built over the past weeks had been forcibly extracted along with the failed pregnancy. I moved through each day in a fog, trying to reconcile the life I had imagined with the reality I now faced.

In the months that followed, I couldn't shake the feeling that something larger needed to change. No one should have to choose between duty and healing. The experience opened my eyes to how little space the system made for grief and how many women, silently and professionally, carried heartbreak beneath their uniforms.

CHAPTER 7:

Optimism, With a Side of Tears

As I reframed our experience, a new perspective emerged. For the first time in our journey, I had seen a true positive pregnancy test. That had never happened before, and it felt like a significant milestone. We were making progress, the most progress we'd made so far in our years of trying. That realization fueled my determination. If we could just find the right doctor, someone who would truly take care of us with the right protocol, I believed we could be successful.

The memory of that positive test, fleeting and bittersweet as it was, gave me hope. It was proof that my body could do this, that we were on the right track. We just needed to fine-tune our approach.

What was that mysterious force that kept propelling me forward through all the ups and downs of this fertility journey? Maybe it was that primal, instinctive urge to reproduce, the whisper of biology telling me, "This is what you were made for."

This drive was a curious thing. It was the same force that somehow managed to keep the crushing disappointment at bay when each new cycle began. I'd wake up, see that telltale sign, and the next day think, *Alright, let's go again.* And let's not forget about the financial aspect. As the costs kept piling up, that same determination kept us in the game. I'd look at our bank account, wince a little, and then remind myself that you can't put a price tag on dreams.

There were days when I felt like a warrior, battling through hormone surges and mood swings with the grace of a bull in a china shop. Other days, I felt more like a mad scientist, mixing potions and following arcane rituals in pursuit of the ultimate creation. But through it all, that drive kept me going. It was there in the injections, in the countless doctor's appointments, in the hopeful two-week waits, and even in the tears of disappointment. It was the voice that whispered, "just one more try" when everything else in me wanted to give up.

After the miscarriage, my doctor had me undergo regular hCG blood draws until my levels returned to zero, ensuring I had completely discharged the pregnancy and returned to normal. Thankfully, it only took a few tests and a few weeks to confirm this, allowing us to set our sights on finding our next reproductive endocrinologist.

As we contemplated our next steps, the financial reality of another IVF cycle weighed heavily on our minds. We had benefited from a reduced rate at Walter Reed, but returning to that facility was out of the question after our experience. The prospect of funding another cycle when we had already invested tens of thousands of dollars seemed daunting. I threw myself into researching options, scouring the internet for anyone even remotely close to Montana who could help us. This search, along with my job, kept me busy, providing a welcome distraction from worrying about my body's recovery.

Our research narrowed down our options to two promising candidates.

The first was CCRM in Denver, Colorado, one of the most renowned clinics in the nation with impressive success rates. The second was Dr. Sher at SIRM in Las Vegas, Nevada. What drew me to Dr. Sher were his extensive blog posts on the effects of endometriosis on fertility. He detailed the best IVF protocols for these situations, focusing on optimizing egg quality and success rates.

As I pored over Dr. Sher's writings, I felt a glimmer of hope. Here was someone who seemed to truly understand the complexities of endometriosis and its impact on fertility—that my uterus wasn't just being dramatic, it was under siege. His approach resonated with me, and I began to imagine a future where our unique challenges were met with an equally unique plan. The decision ahead of us was significant, but I felt more empowered than ever before. We had experienced setbacks, yes, but we had also gained valuable knowledge and insight. Each step of the journey, even the painful ones, had brought us closer to our goal. As we prepared to make our choice between these two promising options, I felt a renewed sense of optimism. We were no longer fumbling in the dark—we were making informed decisions, armed with experience and determination.

I reached out to both clinics, eager to gather more information about their pricing and wait times. The response from CCRM left me a bit disheartened. Their price sheet revealed a hefty cost of at least $15,000 for a fresh IVF cycle, and that didn't even include medications. To add to the challenge, their waitlist stretched out for at least a couple of months. I just turned 37. Waiting even longer felt like another hurdle in our already lengthy journey.

SIRM, on the other hand, offered more promise. They had a military cycle price of $10,000, which, while still significant, felt more manageable than CCRM's offering. What really caught my attention was their considerably shorter wait time—just 45 days. After all we'd been through, the prospect of moving forward sooner rather than later was incredibly appealing. As we weighed our options, Dr. Sher at SIRM stood out. His expertise in endometriosis and its impact on fertility resonated with our situation.

We decided to take the next step and meet with him virtually to get his advice. With a mix of nervousness and anticipation, we sent over our medical records. As we waited for our virtual appointment, I felt a renewed sense of hope. Here was a doctor who seemed to understand the complexities of our case, and we were potentially just days away from charting a new course in our fertility journey.

We sat at our dining room table on our phone, waiting for the video call to begin and Dr. Sher to jump on. The familiar jitters of anticipation coursed through me. As the video call connected and Dr. Sher's face appeared on the screen, I felt an immediate sense of ease. His warm smile and calm demeanor radiated through the pixels, making our high-stakes fertility consultation feel almost like a casual chat with a knowledgeable friend.

When Dr. Sher began to speak, I was momentarily taken aback by his South African accent. At first, it was a bit challenging to decipher, and I found myself leaning in closer to catch every word. But as he continued, my ear adjusted, and the initial struggle gave way to a rhythmic cadence that was almost soothing. I launched into my thoughts, explaining my theory about the previous protocol—how it felt like a slow response followed by overcorrection. I gestured with my hands, animated and passionate.

Dr. Sher nodded thoughtfully and began to explain his approach. His mention of the "toxic" environment created by endometriosis sent a shiver down my spine. He believed that endometriosis, my ovarian stimulation cycle, and the Lupron trigger all contributed to the failed cycle. As he laid out his recommendations, I felt a growing sense of clarity.

He proposed a long pituitary down-regulation protocol: one to two months on birth control to lower LH and reduce stromal activation, followed by low-dose FSH and a touch of LH/hCG from day three of stimulation. If fewer than 25 follicles were present, he would continue stimulation until half reached 14mm. Once E2 exceeded 2500 pg/ml, all stimulation would stop. We'd track E2 daily until it dropped below 2500, then administer a 10,000U hCG trigger. Retrieval would occur 36 hours later. ICSI would be necessary because coasted eggs lack cumulus cells and won't fertilize easily.

We'd also complete reproductive immune testing through Reprosource. Dr. Sher explained that natural killer cell activity, antiphospholipid antibodies, and immune factors could play a significant role in implantation or miscarriage. If something showed up, we'd address it directly.

Near the end of the call, he gave us his personal phone number. I was floored. This was so different from the sterile, procedural feel of Walter Reed. As soon as we ended the call, I let the tears fall and collapsed into Matt's arms. "This is it," I whispered. "I think we've finally found our path forward. He is the doctor."

But after the euphoria faded, anxiety crept back in. "I don't know if I have three more cycles in me," I admitted, my voice barely above a whisper. "The physical toll, the emotional strain—it's like running a marathon with no finish line."

Matt wrapped me in a hug. "One step at a time," he said gently. "We'll figure out the logistics, the cost. We'll make it happen."

And I believed him. Even in the midst of fear, exhaustion, and uncertainty, I believed. Because this time, we weren't starting over—we were stepping forward, stronger and wiser than we'd ever been.

TRY AGAIN BECAUSE THAT'S WHAT WE DO

Just when I thought I could focus solely on our fertility journey, another challenge reared its head: squadron command hires. The memory of last year's disappointment still stung, and I was determined not to let anything stand in my way this time. "It's my time," I muttered to myself, clenching my fists with determination.

But then came that conversation with my group commander. As I sat across from him, his words hit me like a punch to the gut. "I know you want to have a baby, but do you think you can do that and command?" For a moment, I was stunned into silence. My mind raced, indignation rising like bile in my throat. *Would he say this to a male in the same position? I don't think so.* It was bullshit. The unfairness of it all made my blood boil.

I could feel the stress piling on, layer by layer. *What do I have to do to get selected? To prove myself? Are fertility treatments going to get in the way of my dream of being a commander?* These thoughts swirled in my head like a tornado, threatening to sweep away all the hope and optimism I'd been feeling. Taking a deep breath, I pushed down the hurt and anger bubbling inside me. Instead, I looked him straight in the eye and said, "No offense, but IVF is not a sure thing. We've been trying for years with negative results." I could hear the edge in my voice, but I pressed on. "What I do know is that at 37, if I don't do IVF now, I WILL regret it later. There are no guarantees it will be successful, but data has shown it would get even harder the older I get, and I cannot wait any longer."

As I walked out of his office, the emotions I'd been holding back crashed over me like a tidal wave. Hurt, anger, and frustration battled for dominance. Perhaps I was just low on generous assumptions that day, but I couldn't shake the feeling that this conversation shouldn't have happened at all. In this moment, it felt deeply personal. Between hormones, exhaustion, and the emotional whiplash of fertility treatments, everything felt sharper, heavier, harder to let roll off my shoulders. I know he meant well but to me doing IVF should not have even been in the equation. The thought kept repeating in my mind, each iteration fueling my indignation. *Isn't that discrimination?* I wanted to scream it from the rooftops, to challenge the unfairness of it all.

Instead, I found myself in the bathroom, gripping the edges of the sink as I stared at my reflection. The woman looking back at me seemed simultaneously fierce and fragile, determined yet vulnerable. I took a shaky breath, trying to center myself. This was supposed to be my time—for command, for starting a family, for everything I'd worked so hard to achieve. And now, it felt like I was being forced to choose, to prove myself worthy of both my career ambitions and my personal dreams.

As I splashed cold water on my face, I made a silent vow to myself. I would not let this setback define me. I would fight—for my career, for my family, for the right to pursue both without judgment or discrimination. The path ahead might be harder than I'd anticipated, but I was ready for the challenge.

With one last look in the mirror, I straightened my uniform and walked out, head held high. The battle wasn't over—in fact, it was just beginning. But I was ready to face it head-on, armed with determination, perhaps a little righteous anger, and the unwavering belief that I deserved both my dreams of command and motherhood. And I was going to prove it to everyone, including myself.

In the days that followed, I found out something that only deepened my unease: during the wing commander hiring meeting, my IVF treatment had come up. A trusted friend who was in the room told me that the Operations Group Commander had spoken up, reminding the room that this was not an appropriate or legal factor in hiring decisions. I was stunned. Even though someone spoke up, the fact that it had come up at all left me feeling exposed and scrutinized.

I hadn't asked for special treatment. I had simply wanted to be seen for my qualifications, not reduced to a medical decision that should have remained private. The fact that it had entered the room, even briefly, made me feel vulnerable. It reminded me how precarious this balancing act was, pursuing both command and motherhood. Sometimes I wondered if this was just the cost of being a woman in a male-dominated career field, always managing expectations, always having to prove that your personal life wouldn't interfere with your professional one. I know my boss cared, the team cared. I do. But care doesn't always prevent damage and that's what made this so hard to sit with.

BOX OF HOPE

We pressed forward with IVF by paying for it with what little savings we had and putting the rest on our credit card. Financially, this weighed heavy on us. We still had to add in the trip and hotel costs, which meant staying in Las Vegas for at least ten days. And, of course, we had to take our personal leave.

Once we submitted payment, the next round of testing began. I completed the uncomfortable sonohysterogram, a saline ultrasound that evaluates the uterus for fibroids, cysts, or scar tissue. Thankfully, it only detected endometriomas. This was confirmed by my baseline ultrasound, which also checked my antral follicle count and endometrial lining.

Because one endometrioma measured over 14mm, Dr. Sher would need to drain it before starting stims. My immune testing also came back with "abnormal" antiphospholipid antibodies, which are immune system proteins that can mistakenly attack normal cells and increase the risk of blood clots or implantation issues. And just like that, Lovenox was added to the cocktail. For those unfamiliar, Lovenox is a blood-thinning injection used to reduce clotting risks and improve implantation. Another needle to add to the lineup.

When the fertility pharmacy's "Box of Hope" arrived, I eagerly printed out my cycle calendar, feeling like a kid counting down to Christmas. Except this calendar wasn't filled with chocolates or gifts—it was filled with birth control pills and hormone injections. This time, Lupron joined the lineup, not as a trigger shot but for down-regulation. I dove into research mode and learned that Lupron was so potent it was banned in the Olympics. The medication warnings would have filled a full "side-effect bingo" card: hot flashes, mood swings, headaches, and delightful injection site reactions. Lupron was also supposed to help with endometriosis, but once I started it, my endo pain basically laughed at the idea.

Morning and night, I stood in front of the fridge with a marker, crossing off another day on my cycle calendar. Some days those lines felt like small triumphs; other days, they were just a reminder that I was still in the game. I placed my hand on my belly, murmuring, "One day closer to you, little one."

Leading up to Vegas and the start of stimulation medication, I was on birth control, then Lupron and dexamethasone. Because of the large endometrioma, we headed to Vegas early so Dr. Sher could drain it. We planned for two weeks there—at least 14 days of leave—starting in early December. The trip down was uneventful. We stopped in Utah, taking in old memories from our previous assignment, before completing the drive to Vegas. We stayed in a hotel room with a kitchen so I could stick to my mostly gluten- and dairy-free diet and eat as cleanly as possible heading into IVF.

At the clinic, Dr. Sher performed the ultrasound and was ready to drain the endometrioma. It hurt a little, but my excitement about starting stims overshadowed the discomfort. Though I was spotting, he reassured me it would resolve, and I could start Follistim (225 IU), Menopur (75 IU), and Lovenox (30 mg) that night.

I had no problem doing the injections, though I dreaded the sting of Menopur. Little did I know Lovenox would be just as bad and over time, I dreaded that one even more. I'd brace myself before each shot, repeating, "This is worth it." After a few days, my Follistim dropped to 150 units until retrieval.

Each morning, I'd wake up and compare this cycle to the last. How was I feeling? The bruises from Lovenox were multiplying. I rotated injection sites, searching for tender-free territory. Between appointments and blood draws, Matt and I did our best to stay distracted. But this wasn't a Vegas vacation. This was the highest-stakes gamble we'd ever take.

Thankfully, our friends Sam and Diana visited with their son Boston. Their presence was a wonderful distraction from our IVF. At the Bellagio, we marveled at the Christmas decorations—giant wreaths, sparkling lights, the scent of pine—and for a brief moment, I let myself feel joy.

One day Matt and I hiked the Vegas hills, letting the wide sky clear our minds. Another day, we helped assemble bikes for a Christmas charity. We even visited the National Atomic Testing Museum, a fascinating diversion. We were living in the in-between, doing whatever we could to hold onto hope.

When egg retrieval day arrived, I was nervous, flashing back to the trauma of my previous procedure. As I lay on the cold table, I whispered, "You've got this." The anesthesiologist smiled. I joked, "I hope your magic potion works." She laughed and I drifted off.

Waking up, I noticed a key difference versus the last egg retrieval: I wasn't in agony. The doctor entered and said, "Seven." My heart sank a little. Not terrible, not great. "Lucky number seven," I said weakly. I tried to remember: quality over quantity.

Recovery was much better than before. The next day, I was walking, albeit slowly. Then came the call: six eggs had fertilized. My heart soared. I alternated between prayer, visualization, and meditation. *Just grow, little ones.*

As I lay in bed, my eyes fixed on the ceiling, I replayed the events of the past few days in my mind. Five days had passed since the egg retrieval, and it was supposed to be the day we'd been anxiously awaiting. The day that could change our lives forever. My stomach was a knot of nerves as we waited for the clinic to call. The last update we'd received two days ago mentioned five growing embryos, but so much could change in 48 hours. When the phone finally rang, I swear my heart did a somersault in my chest. "Hello?" I answered, my voice barely above a whisper. "We have some good news and bad news," the voice on the other end said. I held my breath. "The good news is the embryos are still growing, but the bad news is that they're not blastocysts yet. We want to wait another day before doing the transfer."

My heart plummeted, and I felt a lump form in my throat. Tears welled up in my eyes as a torrent of thoughts flooded my mind. Would they continue to grow? Our last IVF cycle never made it to blastocysts. How could I possibly handle another day of this excruciating wait? Matt, bless his heart, tried his best to distract me. But I couldn't stop myself—I dove headfirst into a Google rabbit hole, searching for success rates at six days post-retrieval. The numbers seemed to be the same, but that did little to quell my anxiety. I've never experienced a day drag on so slowly. It felt like time had decided to take a leisurely stroll while I was stuck in high-speed mode. I alternated between fervent prayers, quiet tears, and attempts at meditation, all while sending every ounce of positive energy I could muster to our embryos. That night, I went to bed early, hoping sleep would make the time pass faster.

Instead, I tossed and turned, my dreams a jumbled mess of petri dishes and microscopes.

Finally, morning arrived. We took our dogs out, their wagging tails and happy faces a welcome distraction from the weight of anticipation. As we waited for the phone to ring, I found myself bargaining with the universe. "Please," I whispered, "just let them grow." When the call came, I nearly dropped the phone in my haste to answer. "Come in," they said, "we have two blastocysts ready to transfer." My heart soared! This was really happening! We'd finally made it to this crucial step. I wanted to dance, to shout, to let joy spill into the world but instead I smiled, whispered a thank you, and got ready to head to the clinic. At the appointed time, we arrived, a mix of excitement and nervousness coursing through our veins. The nurse offered me some Valium to calm my nerves, which I reluctantly accepted. Here I was, about to have embryos transferred into my uterus, and they thought a little Valium was going to do the trick?

Twenty minutes later, the doctor arrived with a photo of our embryos. Two little bundles of cells, full of potential and hope. As I settled into the stirrups, I tried to focus on staying relaxed. The ultrasound-guided transfer began, and I heard them read out our ID number to ensure we had the right embryos. It was a surreal moment—in mere seconds, I would be PUPO (Pregnant Until Proven Otherwise) once more. Of course, logically, I knew this wasn't actually the case. But in that moment, I refused to think otherwise. These were our embryos, our potential future children, and I was going to give them every ounce of positivity and possibility I could muster.

As we left the clinic, I felt a strange mix of emotions—hope, fear, excitement, and exhaustion. We decided to rest for the night and leave early the next morning. Vegas had been our home for longer than we'd anticipated, and we were both ready to sleep in our own beds once more. As I drifted off to sleep that night, my hand resting gently on my stomach, I allowed myself to dream.

To hope. To believe that maybe, just maybe, this time would be different. This time, our little embryos would stick around for the long haul. And as I closed my eyes, I whispered a quiet "goodnight" to the potential life growing inside me.

We set out early the next morning, our sights set on Utah. The journey ahead of us was daunting—a 14-hour drive that stretched out like an endless ribbon of asphalt. As Matt took the wheel, I settled into the passenger seat, trying my best to relax despite the surge of emotions swirling inside me. The monotony of the highway became a backdrop for my thoughts. I found myself visualizing the microscopic drama unfolding within my body. In my mind's eye, I could see our tiny embryos, those precious bundles of cells, nestling into the warm, welcoming lining of my uterus. "Please," I whispered, a mantra that matched the rhythm of the car's tires on the road, "please let this work." I tried to push away the darker thoughts, the what-ifs and maybes that lurked at the edges of my consciousness. The alternative was too painful to contemplate, so I focused on sending waves of positive energy to my potential passengers.

CHAPTER 8:

Miracles on Gumwood Street

Crossing state lines, I found myself chuckling at the craziness of it all. Here we were, racing across the country while, inside me, life might be taking root at its own leisurely pace. *Hey, little ones,* I thought, patting my belly gently, *I hope you're enjoying the ride as much as we are.* The hours ticked by, marked by gas station stops and drive-throughs. We swapped stories, shared hopes, and even managed to laugh about some of the more ridiculous moments of our fertility journey. It felt good to find humor in the situation, a welcome respite from the anxiety that had been our constant companion. As the sun began to set, painting the sky in hues of pink and orange, we finally crossed into familiar territory. Home was within reach and with it the promise of our own bed and the comfort of our surroundings.

We pulled into our driveway, exhausted but relieved. As I stepped out of the car, stretching my stiff limbs, I realized with a start that it was just a week until Christmas. The holiday season was in full swing, lights twinkling on neighboring houses and a chill in the air that spoke of winter's arrival. The timing seemed almost poetic—a season of hope and new beginnings coinciding with our own tentative steps towards parenthood. The blood draw that would determine our fate was scheduled for after Christmas. It felt like an eternity to wait, yet also far too soon. How would we make it through the holiday season with this monumental question hanging over our heads?

I made a silent pact with myself: I would embrace the joy of the season, allow myself to hope and dream, but also prepare for whatever outcome lay ahead. After all, we had already come so far, overcome so much. Whatever the future held, we would face it together.

As we settled back into our routine at home, I found myself grappling with an overwhelming urge to know. The waiting game had always been the hardest part of this journey, and this time was no different. I had made up my mind—I was going to test out the trigger shot again, just like last time. I remembered how it had worked before: the second line on the pregnancy test would gradually fade as the trigger hormone left my system, and then, if I was pregnant, it would start to darken again. It wasn't foolproof, but it was something to cling to, a way to feel like I had some control in this wildly unpredictable process.

We had returned to work, which provided a welcome distraction. With Christmas approaching, things had slowed down a bit at the office, and the festive buzz around us helped keep our minds off the constant wondering.

As the days after the transfer ticked by, I settled into a familiar routine of early morning testing and anxious waiting. I saw two lines, faint but unmistakably there on 4dp6dt (four days post six-day transfer). Sleep became an elusive luxury as my mind spun with a constant loop of hope and worry.

By then, my upper butt had become a lumpy landscape of progesterone injection sites, each bruise a merit badge in endurance. If Girl Scouts gave out a gold award for perseverance, I would have qualified twice over.

Every twinge or ache sent my mind spiraling. Had it really worked? Was my body welcoming these precious embryos? I found myself silently willing my uterus to be the perfect, receptive environment for our potential little ones.

When day 5 post-transfer arrived, my heart was pounding like a drum in my chest. This was the turning point last time, when the second line had started to darken. The significance of this day weighed heavily on me. At 4 a.m., sleep having completely abandoned me, I decided I might as well test. There was no way I was going back to sleep anyway. With trembling hands, I unwrapped the test and went through the motions that had become second nature by now. The wait felt interminable. I watched the test intently, hardly daring to blink. As the seconds ticked by, I held my breath, my eyes fixed on the window where the lines would appear.

And then I saw it. The second line looked slightly darker, didn't it? Yes, it did! I turned the test this way and that in the dim bathroom light, scrutinizing it from every angle. My heart and mind raced in tandem, a riptide of emotions threatening to overwhelm me.

I need to tell Matt! I thought, the excitement bubbling up inside me. I rushed back to our bedroom, test in hand. Matt stirred as I approached, his eyes blinking open in the semi-darkness. "Matt," I whispered, my voice quivering with emotion, "look!" He sat up, suddenly alert, and took the test from my outstretched hand. As realization dawned on his face, a smile spread across his features. We embraced, a tangle of arms and hope and cautious joy. In that moment of celebration, we both knew this was just the start. A multitude of questions raced through my mind: Would the line continue to darken? Would we make it through the dreaded Two Week Wait to the beta test? And if we did, would we reach that coveted first ultrasound? As we held each other, I allowed myself to bask in this small victory. We had cleared one hurdle, but the road ahead was still long and uncertain. Yet in that pre-dawn moment, wrapped in Matt's arms with the positive test clutched in my hand, I felt a surge of optimism.

I'll admit it: my impatience got the better of me. The idea of waiting until morning to test again felt like an eternity. My mind, ever the scientist, reasoned that if I took a test at night, it was bound to be darker, right? After all, if beta hCG levels double every 48 hours, surely there'd be a noticeable difference.

With my heart pounding, I snuck back into the bathroom that evening. As I unwrapped the test, I couldn't help but think what a strange ritual this had become. I probably should've checked if Costco sold First Response pregnancy tests in bulk.

The wait for the results felt even longer this time, my anticipation building with each passing second. When I finally looked at the test, I had to blink a few times to make sure I wasn't seeing things. It was still positive, and yes, perhaps slightly darker! I held the test up to the light, turning it this way and that, a grin spreading across my face.

As 6dp6dt rolled around, coinciding with Christmas Eve, I decided to go all out. I reached for the other pregnancy test we had, the digital one that actually spells out "Pregnant" or "Not Pregnant." My hands shook as I took the test, and the wait for the result felt like an eternity. When the word "Pregnant" appeared on the little screen, I let out a gasp that was half laugh, half sob. There it was, in black and white (well, digital pixels, but you get the idea). We were pregnant! I burst out of the bathroom, nearly colliding with Matt in the hallway. "Look!" I exclaimed, thrusting the test towards him. His eyes widened as he read the screen, and then he swept me up in a bear hug, both of us laughing and crying at the same time.

We could hardly contain ourselves, the joy bubbling up and spilling over. It seemed the IVF had worked! Of course, we knew we were still in the early stages, and there were many more hurdles to overcome. But in that moment, on Christmas Eve, it felt like we'd received the most precious gift of all. As we stood there in our hallway, arms around each other, we marveled at the timing. It was as if the universe had decided to give us our own little Christmas miracle. "Merry Christmas, little one," I whispered, my hand resting gently on my stomach. Matt placed his hand over mine, and we shared a look of pure wonder and love.

As Christmas Day dawned, the world seemed a little brighter, tinged with the glow of our secret joy. Yet, a cautious undercurrent ran beneath our excitement. We had been here before, just four months ago, and the memory of that heartbreak tempered our enthusiasm. Still, I felt a surge of hope each time I saw those test lines getting darker. It was like watching a tiny miracle unfold, one faint line at a time.

Finally, the day arrived for the beta hCG test. As I headed to the lab, I couldn't shake the feeling of déjà vu. *Here we go again,* I thought, a mix of anticipation and anxiety swirling in my stomach. The wait for the phone call felt interminable. When it finally came, I answered with bated breath. "Yes, you are pregnant," the nurse said, her voice matter-of-fact. "Your hCG is 60." I let out a breath I didn't realize I'd been holding. *Phew,* I thought, *one step closer.* It was good news, but I knew we weren't out of the woods yet. The next hurdle was already looming, the follow-up test in 48 hours.

Those two days crawled by, each hour stretching out like taffy. When the results finally came in, my jaw dropped. The hCG had more than doubled! As the initial shock wore off, a new question popped into my mind: *Does this mean twins?* The possibility hadn't even occurred to me until that moment, but suddenly it seemed like a very real option. Unable to resist, I dove headfirst into the online forums, searching for answers. Was there a correlation between high hCG levels and multiples? I scrolled through countless threads, absorbing stories and statistics, but in the end, the results were inconclusive.

I shut my laptop and chuckled at myself. Here I was, already trying to peek ahead at the next chapter when we were still in the early stages of this pregnancy journey. I placed a hand on my stomach, imagining the tiny life, or lives, growing inside. "Whatever you are, little one(s)," I whispered, "we're just happy you're here."

As the days ticked by, the next major milestone loomed ahead of us, the first ultrasound. My stomach churned with a mix of anticipation and dread, remembering all too vividly how things had gone wrong at this stage last time. Ironically, the intense morning sickness and overwhelming fatigue that had set in provided a strange sort of comfort. Unlike our previous experience, where my symptoms had begun to ease, this time I felt consistently terrible.

I never thought I'd be grateful for nausea, but here I was, clinging to every wave of queasiness as a sign that things might be different this time.

When the day of the ultrasound finally arrived, my nerves were at an all-time high. As we sat in the waiting room, I squeezed Matt's hand, drawing strength from his steady presence. "It'll be okay," he whispered, but I could hear the tension in his voice too.

Once in the exam room, I found myself face-to-face with my old friend, the vaginal ultrasound wand. As I positioned myself on the table, I thought about how many times I had been in this exact position, hoping and praying for a miracle.

I took a deep breath and turned to the technician. "I should probably tell you about our last experience," I said, my voice wavering slightly. I briefly recounted our previous loss, watching as empathy flickered across her face. As she began the ultrasound, moving the wand with practiced precision, I held my breath. The question that had been haunting me for weeks bubbled to the surface: Would we see a heartbeat (or maybe two)?

The technician's voice broke through my anxious thoughts. "Okay, let me explain what we're seeing here," she said, her tone reassuringly calm. "This is the gestational sac." I stared at the screen, trying to make sense of the grainy black and white image. My heart was pounding so loudly I was sure everyone in the room could hear it. I keyed in on the fact she said one gestational sac. "And here," she continued, pointing to a tiny thing on the screen, "is the baby." I felt Matt's hand tighten around mine. We both leaned forward, eyes glued to the monitor.

"Now, let's see if we can detect a heartbeat," the technician said, adjusting the wand slightly. The room fell silent as we all focused on the screen. And then, suddenly, there it was—a rapid, rhythmic pulsing. The most beautiful sight I'd ever seen. "There's the heartbeat," the technician confirmed, a smile in her voice. "Strong and steady, measuring right on track for your gestational age."

I felt tears welling up in my eyes, a mix of relief, joy, and lingering disbelief. We'd made it past the hurdle that had tripped us up before. There, on the screen, was undeniable proof of the little life growing inside me. Matt leaned down and kissed my forehead, his own eyes glistening. "We did it," he whispered.

As the technician continued her measurements, pointing out various features and explaining what we were seeing, I allowed myself to start believing. This was real. This was happening. Of course, I knew we still had a long way to go. The road ahead was filled with more tests, more milestones, more potential hurdles. But for now, in this moment, listening to the steady whoosh-whoosh of our baby's heartbeat, I felt a surge of hope stronger than any I'd experienced before. This time it didn't feel fragile, it felt alive!

We were in the business, as we jokingly called it, further than we'd ever been on this infertility journey. The memory of that first ultrasound flooded back, the tiny flicker on the screen that had filled us with such hope. We saw the heartbeat, and things felt good. Well, except for my so-called 'morning sickness' that actually lasted all day. I could almost taste the bland crackers that had become my lifeline. My diet was steady with carbs and more carbs, but I was in survival mode. I'd have eaten cardboard if it meant keeping the nausea at bay.

CHAPTER 9:

Unexpected Challenges

About a week after the ultrasound, everything changed. I began to bleed. So much blood. *This cannot be happening*, I'd thought to myself. To come this far and then have a miscarriage? I couldn't even fathom it. The drive to the ER was a blur, punctuated by the agonizing wait once we arrived. We impatiently waited to be seen, my hands twisting in my lap. In my mind, I knew if I was having a miscarriage, there was nothing they could do. The helplessness of that realization hit me all over again. I found myself shedding tears that I tried to hold back, but it was impossible. I sighed, remembering the frustration that had mingled with my fear. *Why was this so dang hard?*

When they finally called my name, it took every ounce of strength I had to stand up. I mustered the strength to get up and walk back to the room with Matt. The cold exam table, the dim lights of the ultrasound room. They had me lie down for an ultrasound yet again. We explained we had done IVF and had just seen the heartbeat a week ago. The anticipation was almost unbearable as the technician began the exam. The ultrasound wand came out and they searched for the heartbeat. I held my breath and waited. Then, those magical words: the baby was still alive and still had a heartbeat.

Relief and terror flooded over me. So why was I bleeding so much? The doctor's explanation came next, introducing a term I'd never heard before: subchorionic hematoma. It was a pocket of blood between the placenta and the uterine wall, which could potentially threaten the pregnancy. The odds of maintaining a pregnancy with a subchorionic hematoma varied, but studies suggested that about 70 percent of pregnancies with this condition resulted in live births as long as it got smaller.

Right now, it was bigger than the baby. They couldn't tell us if the baby would survive. The uncertainty was almost as terrifying as the bleeding itself. I took another deep breath and listened to the doctor. I needed to contact my reproductive endocrinologist to see if I should stay on Lovenox since I was bleeding so much. The blood thinner had been part of our treatment plan, but now it seemed like it might be doing more harm than good. *Ok, what do we do now? Just take it one day at a time.*

From what I'd read, our chances of the baby surviving would improve if the bleeding stopped. But it didn't. The constant sight of blood was a terrifying reminder of how precarious our situation was. We added more ultrasounds to our calendar, scheduling one every other week until we were out of the first trimester. After that, we'd have the 20-week ultrasound. If we made it that far, the baby's chances of survival would increase significantly. Most subchorionic hematomas resolve by then—or if they don't, sadly, the baby is often miscarried.

We took it day by day, ultrasound by ultrasound, our hearts in our throats each time. The bleeding persisted, a constant source of worry. By 15 weeks, it had lessened considerably, and for the first time, I felt a glimmer of hope.

I was being held together by Matt's unwavering support, countless prayers, and a steady diet of carbs. The only real reassurance I had was that I still felt sick, a strange but familiar comfort in the world of pregnancy after infertility.

My anxiety was through the roof. In a moment of desperation, I ordered a home heartbeat detector, hoping it would help ease my mind. I remember taking it with me on a work trip, clinging to the gentle whoosh-whoosh of the heartbeat like a lifeline.

But the downside was just as powerful. On the nights I couldn't find the heartbeat right away, panic would surge through me. My mind would spiral through every worst-case scenario until the sound finally returned and I could breathe again.

As the 20-week mark approached, I could barely contain my nervous excitement. The day of the ultrasound finally arrived, and I held my breath as the technician began the exam. With our hearts full of awe and joy, we learned the baby was still alive and growing right on track. We could still see the subchorionic hematoma but it was extremely small. And then came the words that made my heart soar—we were having a precious baby girl! The news was like music to our ears.

I stared at the gentle curve of my growing belly, a mix of awe and trepidation washing over me. The journey to this point had been anything but easy. As I eased myself onto the spin bike for another low-impact session later that day, I couldn't help but think about the irony. Here I was, a former fitness enthusiast, now celebrating the small victory of a 20-minute gentle ride.

"Well, little one," I whispered, patting my bump, "looks like we're both learning to take it slow."

The past few months had been a series of doctor's appointments, cautious optimism, and an ever-growing list of dos and don'ts. My body, once a reliable instrument of strength and endurance, now felt like a delicate ecosystem I was doing my best to maintain.

Every twinge and flutter sent my mind racing, a constant internal dialogue of worry and hope. As I moved through a series of gentle yoga poses, I found myself reflecting on the strange duality of my current reality. On one hand, I was nurturing a precious new life, my long-awaited miracle. On the other, I was preparing to take on one of the biggest professional challenges of my career.

Pregnancy had made me hyper-aware of balance—how to breathe through discomfort, surrender control, and trust the process. Those same lessons were about to be tested in a very different arena.

When the news of my selection for command came, it felt like a tidal wave of emotion. Pride, excitement, and a hint of panic all surged at once.

A commander and a new mom, I mused, stretching into a cat-cow pose.

It was the dream. It should have felt like a full-circle moment, but the high was tempered by the memory of how closely my personal life had been scrutinized just to get here. The questions. The conversations that shouldn't have happened. The lingering awareness that IVF had made its way into rooms I wasn't even invited into.

Now that I had been chosen, another voice in my head whispered: Would they regret it now that I am pregnant?

Beneath the excitement, a quiet doubt persisted. Would I be judged for being a new mother in command? Would people silently question whether I could handle both, even if no one ever said it aloud?

I pushed the thought aside, reminding myself how hard I had fought for this. But the tension never fully left me. This was what I wanted. Still, I believed I would have to prove, again, that I belonged.

There were more pressing matters at hand, like figuring out how to survive the end of the pregnancy.

As the weeks flew by, my due date of September 6 loomed ever closer, as did my change of command ceremony on July 5. The timing seemed perfect, just enough of a buffer to settle into my new role before our little one made their grand entrance.

"Two months to settle into command, and then figure out how to keep a tiny human alive," I joked to my husband one evening,

"No pressure, right?" He squeezed my hand, his eyes reflecting the same mix of excitement and terror I felt. We were in this together, navigating uncharted waters with a map made of hope and determination.

Around the 24-week mark, my body decided to throw me yet another curveball. Braxton Hicks contractions arrived on the scene, uninvited and decidedly unwelcome. At first, I thought I was imagining things, surely it was too early for this? But as the days wore on, there was no denying the uncomfortable tightening sensations that seemed to come and go at random. "Seriously?" I muttered one afternoon, pausing in the middle of a briefing to take a deep breath. "I thought we had a deal, little one. You stay put, and I'll handle the rest." No matter how much water I guzzled or how often I changed positions, these "practice contractions" persisted. It was as if my uterus had decided to start its own training regimen, completely disregarding my carefully planned schedule.

"Maybe the baby's just trying to prepare you for command," my husband suggested with a grin. "You know, keeping you on your toes, expecting the unexpected." I rolled my eyes but didn't stop smiling. Despite the annoyance, I tried to view these Braxton Hicks as just another part of the journey, a reminder that my body was doing exactly what it needed to do, even if the timing wasn't always convenient. It was a lesson in flexibility and patience, two qualities I knew I'd need in abundance in the months to come.

Amidst the frenzy of preparations and unexpected bodily surprises, my best friend forever Angela stepped in like a fairy godmother, determined to throw us the baby shower of our dreams right before my change of command. As I watched her fuss over every detail (she really is the best party planner), I felt a lump form in my throat. "You know," I said, "there was a time I thought this day would never come." Angela paused, her eyes meeting mine. "I know," she said softly. "That's why we're going to make it perfect." And perfect it was.

As I sat surrounded by friends and family, opening gifts, a surge of gratitude rose in me so strong it nearly brought tears to my eyes. This journey had been long and difficult, marked by setbacks and heartbreak, but it had also revealed the incredible strength of the human spirit and the steady support of those who loved me.

As the party wound down, I found a quiet moment to myself. Resting a hand on my belly, I felt a strong kick from within.

"Alright, little one," I whispered, a smile tugging at my lips. "We've got quite the adventure ahead of us. But don't worry. Mommy's got this—most of the time, anyway."

In that quiet moment, I realized just how alike these two journeys were: leading others and nurturing new life. Both required patience, presence, and faith in something unseen. Whether in uniform or in motherhood, command wasn't just about authority. It was about service—the kind rooted in showing up for something bigger than yourself.

And I was ready to lead, in every sense of the word.

WHO IS IN COMMAND?

The morning of my change of command ceremony dawned bright and clear, as if the universe itself were celebrating with me. As I donned my maternity uniform, carefully adjusting it, a wave of emotions washed over me. Excitement, pride, and a touch of nervousness all swirled together in a heady mix. "This is it," I whispered to my reflection, smoothing down my airmen battle uniform one last time. "The moment you've been dreaming of since you were a fresh-faced LT." The irony wasn't lost on me—here I was, about to take command of the very unit I had served in as a wide-eyed 2nd Lieutenant. It felt like coming full circle, a testament to how far I'd come and the journey that lay ahead. I sat down to struggle with my boots. My feet were a little more swollen, but I finally got them on. I let out a huge sigh. "Eight more weeks of this to go," I said to myself.

As I made my way to the ceremony, the gentle flutter in my belly reminded me that I wasn't embarking on this new adventure alone. My hand instinctively rested on my bump, a silent promise to both my unborn child and my future command. "We've got this, little one," I murmured. The ceremony itself was a blur of crisp salutes, heartfelt speeches, and the weight of responsibility settling on my shoulders. But what stood out most was the sea of familiar faces—family, friends, mentors, and colleagues who had supported me every step of the way. Their proud smiles and encouraging nods buoyed me, filling me with a sense of gratitude so profound it nearly brought tears to my eyes. As I took the podium to deliver my first address as commander, I felt a surge of determination. This wasn't just my moment—it was a triumph for everyone who had believed in me, pushed me, and helped me reach this pinnacle.

Taking the flag was amongst the best moments in my career. In that moment, I knew that whatever challenges lay ahead—be it the complexities of command or the adventures of impending motherhood—I was ready to face them head-on. As the ceremony concluded and well-wishers surrounded me, I took a moment to soak it all in. This was more than a professional milestone—it was the beginning of a new chapter, one filled with promise, responsibility, and the unwavering commitment to honor those who had helped me reach this point. The journey ahead would be challenging, no doubt, but with the support of my unit, my family, and the little one growing inside me, I knew we were ready for anything. This was our time to shine, and I was determined to make every moment count.

I settled into my new role as commander with gusto, eager to make the most of the eight weeks I had left before my due date. There was so much I wanted to accomplish before the baby arrived, and I was determined to stay the course. I attended meetings, checked on the troops, and did my best to understand the unit. Beneath the surface though, my body was already reminding me who was really in charge.

The Braxton Hicks contractions were becoming more frequent, but I brushed them off as just another quirk of late pregnancy. I thought I could out-schedule biology, manage pregnancy like a project plan.

I didn't realize then how little control I actually had.

It was a Sunday, just over two weeks after my change of command, when everything shifted. I woke up feeling off, a vague unease settling in my stomach. Trying to shake it off, I sipped some water and nibbled on a paleo muffin, hoping rest would help. But the contractions persisted, and they felt different—stronger, more insistent.

"Something's not right," I murmured to my husband, worry creeping into my voice. With a mix of reluctance and growing concern, I called my doctor. By some stroke of luck, he was on duty at the hospital and told me to come in for a check-up.

At exactly 34 weeks pregnant, I had no idea what to expect. The drive to the hospital was thankfully short, leaving little time for emotions to catch up fully. I wasn't sure what I was feeling or what I was walking into.

TINY BUT MIGHTY

We arrived at the hospital around noon. As the nurse strapped me to the fetal heart rate monitor, explaining it in a calm voice, I felt a sudden contraction. And then, with a gush that seemed to echo in the small room, my water broke. The nurse's matter-of-fact statement hit me like a thunderbolt: "I guess you're having your baby today." In that moment, all my carefully laid plans, all my expectations of how this was supposed to go, came crashing down. Tears welled up in my eyes, a mix of fear, shock, and utter disbelief. "But...but we haven't even finished our birth classes," I stammered, as if that would somehow pause the unstoppable process my body had initiated.

The reality that I had mistaken active labor for Braxton Hicks contractions suddenly seemed absurd. Here I was, the woman who prided herself on being prepared for every contingency, completely blindsided by the most natural process in the world. We did not have our birth plan nor any of our hospital items because we hadn't packed our bags. As the medical team sprang into action around me, I caught my husband's eye. He looked as shell-shocked as I felt. "It will be ok" he said, squeezing my hand. This wasn't how we planned it, but then again, when had anything in this journey gone according to plan? We were about to meet our baby, ready or not (*not—assuredly not!*).

The moment they wheeled me into the delivery room, the sterile smell of disinfectant hit me like a wave, a stark reminder that this was really happening. The fluorescent lights seemed to pulse in time with my racing heart, casting harsh shadows across the medical equipment that suddenly looked more menacing than reassuring. As another contraction crashed over me, I gripped the bed rails, my knuckles turning white. The pain was unlike anything I'd experienced before—a tidal wave of sensation that threatened to pull me under. I gasped for air, feeling as though I were drowning on dry land.

Breathe, just breathe, I coached myself silently, trying to recall the techniques from the birth classes we hadn't finished. *You've faced tough situations before. You can do this.* But as the next contraction hit, even harder than the last, I felt my confidence waver. This was a battle I hadn't trained for, an experience with no clear roadmap.

"Do you want an epidural?" the nurse's voice cut through the haze of pain, her words a lifeline I desperately wanted to grasp. "Yes," I managed to choke out between ragged breaths, "how soon can the doctor get here?" The words tumbled out, tinged with a desperation I barely recognized in my own voice.

My doctor arrived, his calm demeanor a stark contrast to the chaos I felt inside. As he explained that our baby was coming early, I tried to focus on his words, to process the information like I would an important briefing. More staff in the room. No signs of distress. But the details blurred as another contraction gripped me, turning my world into a tunnel of pain and fear.

The wait for the epidural felt relentless. Each second stretched into an eternity, marked by the relentless rhythm of contractions. The nurses moved around me in a choreographed dance, their gentle touches and soothing words a balm to my frayed nerves.

But with each wave of pain, nausea rose in my throat, threatening to overwhelm me.

"You've got this," I heard Matt's voice, steady and sure. I clung to his words, trying to channel the strength and composure I'd always prided myself on. When the anesthesiologist finally arrived around 4 PM, the shift was immediate and profound. As the medication took effect, I felt as though I could breathe again, the pain receding like a tide going out.

Everything was happening at breakneck speed, a sprint of activity that left me struggling to process each new development. I clung to a single goal, repeating it like a mantra: *Give birth safely. Just get her here safely.*

But when it came time to push, I found myself woefully unprepared. The mechanics of breathing and pushing eluded me, my body refusing to cooperate with my mind's commands. Frustration welled up inside me, hot and bitter. "I don't know how to do this," I admitted, tears of frustration stinging my eyes. "I should have been more prepared. I should have..."

"If we can't get her out soon, we might need to consider a C-section," my doctor's words cut through my self-recrimination, concern etching his features. "She might be in distress."

Fear gripped me, cold and sharp. This wasn't how it was supposed to go. We were supposed to have more time, more preparation. I was supposed to be in control. In a stroke of inspiration, they brought in a mirror so I could see my progress. The sight was shocking at first, but then something clicked. It was as if seeing was believing, and my body finally understood what it needed to do. *You can do this,* I told myself, staring at my reflection. *You're bringing your daughter into the world. Now push!*

When she finally emerged, the room erupted into a flurry of activity. The NICU team swooped in, their urgent movements a blur of blue scrubs and focused expressions. The silence was deafening—where was her cry? My heart seemed to stop, waiting for that precious sound.

"She's breathing," someone called out, the words a lifeline in a sea of uncertainty. "But we need to get her to the NICU."

I held her for the briefest moment, her tiny form warm against my chest. She was so small, so fragile, yet in that instant I felt a love so fierce it took my breath away.

We hadn't even packed our hospital bags, let alone settled on a name. We had a short list of favorites, but we had figured we'd decide over the next six weeks. Except she clearly had other plans. As we stared down at her tiny face, though, the choice was obvious. She wasn't a maybe or a shortlist contender. She was Avery. She had always been Avery.

The nurse swooped in, placed her in the incubator, and whisked her away to the NICU.

"Go with her," I urged Matt, my voice cracking with emotion. "Don't let her be alone." As they prepared me for the final stage of delivery, I braced myself, drawing on every ounce of strength I had left. The process of delivering the placenta was indeed uncomfortable, at times terrible, but my mind was elsewhere. Every fiber of my being was focused on Avery, willing her to be strong, to fight. In that moment, as I lay there feeling more vulnerable than I ever had before, I realized that this was perhaps the greatest challenge I would ever undertake.

CHAPTER 10:

What Happens Next?

I never imagined my journey into motherhood would begin in such a way. The contractions had started suddenly, weeks before my due date, and everything after that was a blur of panic and pain. As I lay in my hospital bed, still groggy from the intense labor and delivery, my phone buzzed with a new message. It was Matt, sending photos from the NICU. My heart raced as I swiped through the images, each one revealing our tiny Avery, all 4 pounds 14 ounces of her. Pride swelled in my chest—I had brought this little fighter into the world—but it was quickly overshadowed by a tidal wave of fear.

"What happens next?" I whispered to myself, my fingers tracing the outline of Avery's incubator on the screen. The nurses had told me I could visit her later, but for now, I was stuck in my room for observation. I felt like a caged animal, desperate to break free and rush to my baby's side. The clock on the wall seemed to mock me, its hands moving at an agonizingly slow pace.

As soon as they gave me the all-clear, I was out of bed faster than I thought possible for someone who'd just given birth. My legs were wobbly, so they wanted me to be in a wheelchair, but I didn't care. I had a mission. The hallway stretched before me like a marathon track, but I was determined to reach the finish line—my daughter.

Stepping into the NICU was like entering another planet. The constant beeping of monitors created a symphony of anxiety, each alarm making my heart skip a beat. The air smelled of disinfectant and something else I couldn't quite place—fear, perhaps? And there she was—our little Avery, looking even tinier in person, surrounded by a tangle of wires and tubes. Her skin was almost translucent, and I could see the faint blue lines of her veins beneath the surface.

"Our baby," I breathed, pressing my hand against the incubator. Tears welled up in my eyes, a mixture of love and heartache. She was alive, she was fighting, but seeing her like this...it was almost too much to bear. I wanted nothing more than to scoop her up and hold her close, to shield her from the harsh realities of this sterile environment.

A nurse approached, her scrubs adorned with cheerful cartoon characters that seemed out of place in this serious setting. Her voice was gentle but firm. "Have you started pumping yet? If you want your milk to come in and stay, you need to start as soon as possible."

I blinked at her, momentarily confused. Pumping? Oh right, breast milk. In all the chaos, I'd completely forgotten about that part of motherhood. "I...no, not yet," I admitted, feeling a pang of guilt. Was I already failing as a mother?

She nodded understandingly, her eyes kind. "Try to pump every three hours. It'll help build your supply. Don't worry if you don't get much at first—it's normal."

And so began my adventures in pumping. I felt like a dairy cow hooked up to some bizarre milking machine, the rhythmic whirring of the pump becoming the soundtrack to my days and nights. That first session? One. Single. Drop. I stared at the tiny bead of liquid in disbelief, wondering if this was some sort of cosmic joke.

"Is that normal?" I asked the nurse, trying not to feel discouraged. My breasts felt heavy and sore, but apparently, they hadn't gotten the memo about milk production.

She smiled reassuringly, patting my arm. "For now, yes. Keep at it, your body's still figuring things out. Think of it as training for a marathon—you've got to build up your endurance."

Here I was, a new mom, and I couldn't even produce enough milk to fill a thimble. But Avery needed it, needed me, so I persevered. I set alarms on my phone, turning my life into a never-ending cycle of pump, eat, sleep (barely), repeat.

Days blurred together in a haze of NICU visits, pumping sessions, and stolen moments of sleep. My body surprised me with its resilience, healing faster than I'd expected. The soreness gradually faded, replaced by a new strength I didn't know I possessed. But emotionally? I was a wreck.

One moment, I'd be overjoyed at finally being able to hold Avery against my skin, marveling at her tiny fingers and toes. I'd count each perfect digit, memorizing every detail of her face. The next, I'd be sobbing into Matt's shoulder, overwhelmed by the uncertainty of it all. The constant beeping of monitors became a cruel reminder of how fragile our situation was.

"She's so small," I whispered during one of our kangaroo care sessions, feeling the rapid flutter of her heartbeat against my chest.

"But so mighty," Matt added, his voice filled with pride and hope. He was my rock through all of this, always ready with a hug, a joke, or food.

We clung to every milestone like a lifeline. The first time she took a full feed, we cheered as if she'd won an Olympic medal. The day she hit 5 pounds, nearly two weeks after birth, was cause for major celebration. We must have looked ridiculous—two adults giddy over a number on a scale—but at that moment, it felt like the most important achievement in the world.

Nothing had prepared us for this entire premature birth and the NICU experience. It was like being dropped into a foreign country without a map or translator. We had to learn a whole new language of medical terms, navigate the complex world of insurance and hospital bureaucracy, all while trying to be there for our tiny daughter.

I found myself obsessively Googling preemie statistics late at night, each search sending me spiraling further into anxiety. The glow of my phone screen illuminated my worried face as I read story after story, some hopeful, others heartbreaking.

As the days turned into weeks, I settled into a new normal. Pumping every three hours became second nature, my body responding more readily as time went on (although we still needed to supplement with formula). I read stories to Avery through the incubator window, my voice barely above a whisper as I shared tales of rabbits and love and blue trucks that beeped. I played classical music for babies through my phone (because apparently, that's good for brain development), imagining Avery as a future musical prodigy. And always, always, watching those monitors, willing them to show improvement.

The NICU became our second home. We spent more time there than our actual one. The nurses became like family, celebrating each small victory with us and offering comfort during the tough moments. It wasn't the start to motherhood I had imagined or expected. There were no joyful homecomings, no proudly showing off our newborn to friends and family. Instead, there were long days in the hospital, nights interrupted by the mechanical whir of the breast pump, and a constant undercurrent of worry. It was harder, scarier, and more emotionally draining than I ever could have anticipated.

But as I watched Avery grow stronger each day, I realized it was also more rewarding than I could have dreamed. Every ounce she gained felt like a personal victory. The first time she latched on to breastfeed, I cried tears of joy. When she finally opened her eyes and seemed to really look at me, I felt a connection so profound it took my breath away.

We were on this unexpected journey together, our tiny warrior and us, and we were determined to see it through to the other side. As I sat by her incubator, my hand resting gently on her tiny body, I made her a promise. "We've got this, little one," I whispered. "You keep fighting, and we will be right here beside you, every step of the way."

As I gently placed our tiny miracle into the car seat, my heart raced with a mixture of excitement and trepidation. After 21 long, grueling days in the NICU, we were finally heading home. The moment felt surreal, like stepping out of a time warp into a new reality we'd been desperately longing for.

THIS IS WHAT WE WAITED FOR

The drive home was a blur of conflicting emotions. Every traffic light seemed to last an eternity as I obsessively checked the rearview mirror, half-expecting to see the familiar flashing monitors that had become our constant companions over the past three weeks. The absence of beeping machines was both a relief and a source of anxiety.

How would we manage without the reassuring presence of nurses and doctors at our beck and call? As we crossed the threshold of our home, the weight of responsibility settled heavily on our shoulders. Our little fighter was now solely in our care. The nurses' parting words echoed in my mind: "Keep her warm, track her feeding, and a nurse will visit weekly to monitor her progress." Those first few days were a vortex of sleepless nights and constant worry.

Every tiny sneeze or hiccup sent us into a panic. We took turns holding her, relishing the freedom from the tangle of wires and tubes that had been her constant companions in the NICU. Her warmth against my chest was the most precious feeling in the world, a reminder of the fragile life we were now responsible for nurturing. The reality of our new normal quickly set in. Sleep became a distant memory as we navigated the challenges of caring for our preemie.

We invested in the Owlet baby monitor to ease my anxiety about her well-being. It is a sock that tracked her heart rate, oxygen levels, and sleep patterns, and that provided much needed reassurance in the months following our NICU time. We did get a few false alarms but we learned to be calm and assess the situation. Most of the time the sock had just gotten out of place.

I found myself in a constant cycle of feeding, pumping, and worrying. My body ached from the relentless demands of milk production, but I persevered, knowing that every drop was liquid gold for our little warrior. Humor became our lifeline, a way to cope with the overwhelming emotions and exhaustion. As the days turned into weeks, we slowly found our rhythm. Each ounce gained was still a victory celebrated, each milestone reached a cause for jubilation. The weekly visits from the nurse became less daunting and more reassuring as our confidence grew.

A few weeks after bringing our little fighter home, we found ourselves facing a new challenge. Our once-peaceful baby transformed into a bundle of distress, crying inconsolably day and night. The clockwork nature of her screams left us bewildered and exhausted. "Is this the infamous purple crying we've heard about?" we wondered, desperately seeking answers in our sleep-deprived state.

As she approached her 40-week gestational age, we recalled reading about premature babies "waking up" around this time. But nothing could have prepared us for the reality of it. Our perplexity turned to panic when we discovered blood in her diaper. My heart raced as I frantically searched online for answers, my mind conjuring worst-case scenarios. Gradually, the pieces of the puzzle began to fall into place.

The constant spit-up, the constant screaming, and now this—it all pointed to reflux and a potential allergy. The culprit? Likely the milk proteins in my breast milk. The realization that my diet could be causing her such distress was gut-wrenching. We found ourselves on a new mission: eliminate dairy from my diet and wait an agonizing 21 days for it to clear from her system. Discussions with her doctor led us down the path of specialized formula options to supplement my breast milk—at a staggering $50 per can. It felt like a financial gut punch until we discovered Tricare might cover it as a medical necessity. The process of securing this coverage became yet another item on our ever-growing to-do list. Amidst this whirlwind of dietary changes and formula investigations, the looming specter of my return to work added another layer of stress.

The thought of leaving our struggling little one, even for a few hours, filled me with anxiety. Yet, a small part of me craved the distraction that work might bring, a sense of normalcy amid the chaos and challenges. In hindsight, I'm still amazed at how we navigated that time. The stress was palpable, seeping into every aspect of our lives. We were new parents, still finding our footing, suddenly fluent in medical terminology and specialized diets we'd never imagined needing. But through it all, we learned what it truly meant to advocate for our child.

We became researchers, detectives, and medical coordinators overnight. We discovered she was allergic to multiple things—soy protein and more—which made our foray into solids a whole other adventure. The journey was far from easy, but it forged us into more resilient, knowledgeable parents. As we watched our little one slowly begin to heal, we realized that this challenging phase, like so many in parenting, was just that—a phase. We emerged on the other side stronger, more confident, and even more in love with our tiny warrior.

But just as we were beginning to find our rhythm, life reminded me that command—like parenthood—doesn't pause.

Towards the end of my maternity leave, my unit experienced a suicide.

The call came from my boss. His voice was calm but serious: he was letting me know what had happened, and then he asked the question that stopped me, "Are you coming back early to deal with this?"

There was no easy answer. My body and mind, still healing. My baby, still needing me. My team, grieving. I paused for just a moment, then responded with what I knew to be true: "My team has the Chief, the Operations Officer, and the First Sergeant. My baby has me."

I wasn't flippant. I was heartbroken. Torn. I trusted my team—they had been there longer than me. I also knew what it meant to live my values. Command was my dream. But so was this little girl. And the entire point of fighting to become a mother was to be one.

When I returned from maternity leave, my boss pulled me aside. "Everyone's been talking," he said, "about how you didn't come back early when it happened. I just don't want you to regret your decision."

I nodded, feeling that old ache return—the sense of being watched, measured, maybe even quietly judged. Again, I believe he cared. Truly. But care doesn't erase the discomfort. Once more, I felt exposed—like my motherhood was being weighed against my leadership.

That moment taught me something I'll never forget: as a leader, you will face decisions for which no answer feels clean. Someone will be disappointed no matter what you choose. The only compass you have is your values. And if you don't know what they are—if you haven't done the work of defining them for yourself—the storm will decide for you.

This wasn't just challenging. It was excruciating. I grieved for the Airman we lost. I grieved the quiet judgment I sensed. And I grieved the fantasy that I could somehow do all of it perfectly.

But I also came away with clarity: my command was never meant to come at the cost of my motherhood. And I would not lead from a place of regret. I would lead from truth.

CHAPTER 11:

Try Again, Seriously?

When Avery was about 10 months old, I found myself staring at the calendar, acutely aware of the relentless march of time. At nearly 39, I felt like a ticking biological clock personified. The thought made me laugh—here I was, a grown woman, imagining myself as some sort of human egg timer. But the humor was tinged with anxiety. "We're not getting any younger," I said to my husband. "What do you say we give Avery a sibling?" He agreed, and we decided to give nature a chance.

In the back of my mind, I was already formulating a backup plan. I reached out to our fertility clinic, the same one that had helped us conceive Avery through IVF. Just hearing the receptionist's voice brought back a series of memories—the hope, the fear, the endless waiting. "What's the schedule looking like?" I asked, trying to sound casual while my heart raced. "And, um, the pricing?" I winced at my own question, knowing full well that we hadn't even paid off our last IVF cycle.

As I jotted down notes, I could almost hear Dave Ramsey in my head, preaching about saving cash first. "Sorry, Dave," I muttered under my breath, "but you've clearly never felt your fertility clock ticking louder than your savings account."

The statistics weren't exactly on our side. At 39, with no prior issues, the chance of conceiving naturally in any given month was around 10 percent, and it declined with each passing year. IVF offered better odds, with a success rate of about 23 percent per cycle for women aged 38 to 40. Still, even those improved chances felt like a roll of the dice. And with my endometriosis, my odds fell faster than a Hunger Games tribute in the first five minutes in the arena.

I never thought I'd feel a rush of excitement at the thought of a phone call with a fertility clinic, but here we were, Matt and I, sitting on our couch, ready to dive back into this emotional roller-coaster. The familiar voice of Dr. Sher echoed through the receiver, and I could almost picture him in his white coat, his warm smile radiating through the phone line.

"What's awesome," I said to Matt, "is that they picked right up where we left off. It felt like we were continuing a conversation that had merely been paused."

As we spoke, I could hear the genuine curiosity in Dr. Sher's voice. "How's little Avery doing?" he asked. My heart swelled with pride as I shared stories about our miracle baby. "She's growing like a weed and keeping us on our toes!" I gushed.

The conversation quickly turned to the tests we needed to repeat: the labs, immune testing, fluid ultrasound, and semen analysis. *Here we go again,* I thought, feeling a familiar tingle of anxiety mixed with determination. At least I was now a pro at this whole fertility thing.

When Dr. Sher mentioned that he wasn't surprised we hadn't conceived naturally yet but felt optimistic based on our last IVF results, it was like a spark ignited in my chest. "You have a good chance of success within a couple of IVF cycles," he assured us. His cautious optimism was enough to fan the flames of hope in my heart.

Of course, I knew better than to romanticize it. Multiple cycles meant money, leave, and emotional whiplash. But this time, we had something we didn't before: optimism and proof it could work. If another child joined our family, wonderful. If not, we were deeply grateful for our little miracle.

I told Matt, "If someone had told me years ago that I'd be excited about hormone injections and blood draws, I would have thought they were crazy." Matt grinned back at me. "Well, they do say love makes you do crazy things." "And apparently," I teased, "so does the desire for another baby."

I found myself reflecting on our journey so far. The path to parenthood had been far from easy, but it had also been incredibly rewarding.

I never thought I'd be there again, staring at a calendar, plotting my life around ovulation cycles and hormone injections. But there I was, preparing to embark on another rollercoaster of emotions, needles, and cautious optimism. I remember thinking, *Okay, body, time to get back in baby-making shape*, as I popped a prenatal vitamin. The irony wasn't lost on me. I was managing the chaos of motherhood and work during the day, while trying to decode my reproductive system at night.

I dove headfirst into the world of fertility supplements, embracing what felt like a chemistry experiment inside my own body. The CCRM cocktail became my new best friend—or maybe my frenemy. I couldn't quite decide as I gagged down another fish oil capsule. I read and reread everything I could about improving egg quality. I still avoided BPA like the plague (receipts, plastic, etc.), still used natural and chemical-free personal products (room air fresheners long gone), and added pycnogenol, NAC, and PQQ to the growing supplement stack. My nightstand looked like a mini pharmacy. *I will improve my egg quality*, I told myself. I was already taking melatonin and still sleeping terribly. *This will be my best IVF.*

"You've got this," I'd mutter to myself in the mirror each morning, trying to channel the same confidence I projected at work into this personal mission. Stress management became my secret weapon, though some days it felt more like stress juggling.

Telling my new boss about our IVF plans was nerve-wracking. I rehearsed the conversation a hundred times in my head, imagining scenarios ranging from understanding nods to career-ending disappointment. When I finally mustered the courage, the wave of release that washed over me at his supportive response was almost dizzying. It felt like the universe was finally cutting me some slack.

"Thank you," I said, my voice steadier than I felt. "I promise this won't affect my performance." He smiled and replied, "I know it won't." I left his office feeling like with his support I could conquer the world—or at least my own fertility.

As summer faded into fall, each passing month felt like sand slipping through an hourglass. After meeting with Dr. Sher, we had a tentative IVF cycle scheduled for October, but part of me still hoped we'd get lucky on our own before then. My cycle was as punctual, but apparently my eggs and my husband's swimmers couldn't seem to sync their schedules. By September, the familiar twinge of disappointment had become an unwelcome monthly visitor. "October it is," I sighed.

As we packed our bags for Las Vegas, I felt a mix of excitement and trepidation. This wasn't just any trip—it was the final, most challenging leg of our fertility journey. But this time, we had a little miracle in tow, our 15-month-old daughter, Avery—living proof that faith, science, and sheer determination could rewrite the odds.

The drive stretched out before us like a ribbon of possibility. With Avery on board, our usual quick pit stops turned into mini-adventures.

"You know, kiddo," I said, catching Avery's eye in the rearview mirror, "you're kind of a good luck charm on this trip." She responded with a toothy grin that melted my heart.

As we settled into our familiar room at the Staybridge Suites, a wave of déjà vu washed over me. The same walls that had witnessed our anxious waiting now echoed with Avery's giggles. That night, as I lay in bed, my mind raced with a familiar cocktail of hope and fear. I placed a hand on my abdomen, wondering if it would soon be home to another little miracle. "We've done this before," I whispered to myself, "we can do it again."

The next morning, we headed to our first appointment. Dr. Sher's face lit up at the sight of Avery. "Well, hello there, little one!" he cooed. "You're the best advertisement for our work, you know that?" As Dr. Sher performed the ultrasound, found an endometrioma (yes, again), and drained it, I focused on Avery's curious eyes taking in the unfamiliar surroundings. The discomfort of the procedure seemed to fade into the background.

We filled our days with sightseeing: Hoover Dam, long walks, and even fancy dinners we missed the last time around. In quiet moments, I worked on my next round of professional military education, Air War College. Between the toddler-wrangling and hormone injections, switching between military strategy coursework and embryo protocols felt oddly grounding, like commanding chaos on two fronts.

One night, Avery took several unassisted steps for the first time right there in our hotel room. I burst into tears, scooping her up. "You are the proof that this is all worth it," I whispered.

We used the same protocol as before and egg retrieval came quickly. Matt took charge of Avery while I went through the familiar ritual. They retrieved 16 follicles. Eight were mature. Seven fertilized. The number sat with me—not high, but hopeful. On day three, we got the call: six still growing strong. "Come on, little ones," I whispered into the night. "Keep going."

By day five, we got the news: two beautiful blastocysts, ready for transfer. I was stunned—thrilled—and more than a little in awe as this had never happened before. Avery squealed and clapped as I danced around the room with her in my arms. It felt poetic: one miracle cheering on the next.

The transfer was calm. Valium in my system, Avery reading animal books beside us, Matt holding my hand. The embryologist showed us our embryos on the screen. Not genetically tested, but they looked strong and full of potential. *We did everything right,* I told myself as they completed the transfer.

The day of the beta test finally arrived, bringing a blend of anticipation and cautious hope. The at-home pregnancy tests had shown progressively darker lines, boosting my confidence that we'd hear good news. Still, a flutter of nerves followed me into the lab for the blood draw. The wait for results felt like its own kind of limbo, with time stretching thin, slow, and sticky like wet paint.

When the phone finally rang a few hours later, I answered with bated breath. The nurse's voice was calm and steady: "Yes, you are pregnant. Your beta is 62." Those long-hoped-for words washed over me, bringing a wave of quiet relief and joy. From that moment, things began to fall into place. My next beta rose to 149, right on track for a healthy pregnancy. With each milestone, we allowed ourselves to hope a little more. A sense of peace settled in, not loudly, but gently. Hope was still there, softened now, tempered by the road we had traveled.

Then came the day of the ultrasound. As we waited for the technician to begin the search for a heartbeat, the anxiety that had become so familiar during our fertility journey resurfaced. The room was quiet except for the soft hum of the equipment, the atmosphere thick with anticipation. And then we saw it—that tiny, flickering light on the screen. A heartbeat. Our baby's heartbeat. My own heart swelled with an emotion so profound it defied description. Tears welled up, threatening to spill over as we gazed at that beautiful, rhythmic pulse of life.

In that moment, all the struggles, the disappointments, the endless waiting—it all faded into the background. Here was tangible proof of our perseverance, our hope made visible in the most miraculous way. As Matt and I exchanged glances, our eyes shining with unshed tears, I felt a sense of gratitude and wonder that words could scarcely express.

Around the same time, an email landed in my inbox. It was quiet and unassuming but carried its own kind of hope. Two more of our embryos had made it to blastocyst and were safely frozen. Despite my "very advanced maternal age," this had been our best IVF cycle yet. All the supplements, all the research, all the relentless effort had worked. Knowing we had those two tiny sparks of potential waiting brought a strange, quiet comfort. A backup plan. A cushion of possibility. Just in case.

We had never had embryos to freeze before, so we hadn't even thought about it. I wasn't sure why the update took so long to come through, but the surprise made it feel like an extra win. One we hadn't dared to expect.

This pregnancy seemed to fly by at warp speed, a mad dash of activity as I juggled my role as a commander with caring for our energetic toddler. Despite my initial fears of experiencing bleeding like in my previous pregnancy, those worries thankfully never materialized.

A significant milestone came with the noninvasive prenatal testing. The results brought a wave of calm and confidence—low risk across the board, and the exciting news that we were expecting another girl! Another beautiful miracle to join our family. The 20-week ultrasound further confirmed that everything was on track and normal, a reassuring checkpoint in our journey.

Yet, even with these positive developments, I found it challenging to fully relax. Worry became my constant companion—would she continue to grow properly? Would she stay put until at least 37 weeks, sparing us another NICU experience? These thoughts swirled in my mind, a testament to the lasting impact of our previous experiences.

As our daughter grew, so did the complexity of our lives. My time in command was drawing to a close, and a new assignment loomed on the horizon—this time, to the Pentagon. The timing felt almost laughably tight: change of command, have the baby, and then execute a full-blown Permanent Change of Station (PCS). Oh, and somewhere in that mix? I had to finish Air War College distance learning. For those unfamiliar, it's a required professional military education program for field grade officers—you don't get promoted without it. Mentors strongly encourage knocking it out early, especially in case you don't get selected for the in-residence version (like we experienced as Majors with Air Command and Staff College).

Whether it was the constant worry or the pregnancy itself, sleep became elusive. I often found myself wide awake at 3 or 4 in the morning, my mind racing with all that lay ahead. Rather than toss and turn, I decided to put these early hours to use, chipping away at my Air War College assignments in the quiet of the pre-dawn. I juggled diapers, duty, and doctrine at 3 a.m., tapping out essays on military strategy between kicks from the tiny life inside me; trying to keep all the pieces moving forward.

At around 24 weeks, the contractions began, triggering immediate concern due to my history. The doctor's words echoed in my mind: "If they get worse, 5–6 in an hour, you need to get checked." As the weeks progressed, the contractions intensified despite my best efforts to hydrate, rest, and prevent preterm labor.

A significant shift occurred around 30 weeks when I felt a powerful movement, followed by the unsettling realization that her head was now in my ribs. The doctor confirmed our fears—she was breech. This new development added another layer of complexity to an already precarious situation.

At 31 weeks, while at work, I counted six contractions within an hour. My heart raced as I called my husband, knowing we needed to head to the hospital. Once there, the monitors confirmed what we feared—I was in preterm labor, with contractions persisting and dilation beginning. The news hit me like a punch to the gut. The medical team decided to administer steroids to help the baby's lungs develop, just in case.

The next couple of days in the hospital were miserable. Sleep eluded me due to the constant monitoring and worsening contractions. I heard the term "irritable uterus" being tossed around, and I wondered if I'd make it to term. They slowed the contractions enough for me to go home.

After discharge, I was put on bed rest until 35 weeks—if I could make it that far. I adapted by turning the couch into a command post, with my work laptop and water bottle always within reach, while also trying to rest as much as possible. I did everything I could to encourage her to turn head down: frozen peas on my belly, Spinning Babies techniques, acupuncture. But she stubbornly refused to budge. Maybe it was an early sign of the personality she'd bring into the world.

Amidst all this, I was also planning my change of command ceremony. I desperately hoped to make it to that date, just shy of 37 weeks. I found myself constantly talking to her, pleading for her to stay put until then. Reaching 35 weeks felt like a small victory—we'd surpassed Avery's gestation. I started working half days, determined to make it to my change of command. We also scheduled an attempt to turn the baby the day after the ceremony, when she'd be exactly 37 weeks—a safer point if anything were to go wrong.

The day of my change of command finally arrived. Standing was a challenge, with contractions coming relentlessly. "You can do it, little one," I whispered. "Just hold out until after this." I barely made it through the ceremony, each moment a test of endurance as contractions came and went.

But we did it. She stayed put. Immediately after the ceremony, I went home and broke down in tears—a mix of relief and sheer exhaustion. I had successfully completed my first command and was almost at 37 weeks. It felt like crossing a finish line I wasn't sure I'd reach, a testament to both my determination and our little girl's resilience.

CHAPTER 12:

We Made It

My appointment to try and turn her was scheduled at 8 in the morning. I woke up around 4 AM yet again, restless and uncomfortable. Eventually, I decided to ease my discomfort with an Epsom salt bath. The warm water helped soothe the contractions and general uneasiness I was feeling.

As I was getting dressed downstairs, I suddenly felt what I can only describe as a rubber band snapping. In that instant, my water broke, gushing everywhere. The realization hit me immediately—*Well, I guess I'm having a C-section!* I thought to myself.

I called out to Matt. When he responded with a groggy, "What?" I exclaimed, "It's time! Grab Avery!" We quickly tried to set our plans in motion, calling my parents to take Avery, but they didn't answer. We then tried our friends, but they didn't pick up either. Left with no other option, we took Avery with us to the hospital.

The car ride was intense. I tried my best to breathe through the contractions, which were coming faster and growing more painful by the minute. As soon as we arrived at the hospital, they checked my dilation. I was already at 6 cm. The staff's urgency was palpable as they said, "Oh man, we need the C-section right now."

Everything moved quickly from that point. They wheeled me into the operating room almost immediately to prepare for the procedure. Thankfully, my parents made it in time to take Avery, allowing Matt to join me in the room.

The routine of a C-section began. They put the sheet up, administered the spinal block, and started the procedure. I could feel them moving around (a strange sensation) and working to deliver our baby. Matt was right there by my side, a comforting presence in the midst of the controlled chaos.

And then, in no time, there she was. They brought her to my face, and I saw her for the first time. She was beautiful! She was safe! She was breathing! In that moment, I felt overwhelmed with gratitude. After all those weeks of wondering if I could make it to term, we had done it, and she was perfect. The awe and joy I felt were indescribable. All the worry, the discomfort, the challenges—it all faded away as I gazed at our precious daughter. We had made it, and she was finally here, safe and sound.

Just like with Avery, we waited until we saw her to choose her name. We had a few favorites, but when we looked at her, really looked at her, we both knew in our hearts: she was Aliana. Aliana Faith. That was her name. That was who she had always been.

Unlike with Avery, I was able to hold her in recovery after the C-section—a moment that felt nothing short of awe-inspiring. Skin to skin, heart to heart, I took her in. The softness of her cheeks, the warmth of her body, the miracle of her presence. It was quiet. Sacred.

A couple of days later, we went home. I was careful not to lift anything due to my C-section. Having Matt around to help was amazing, and people brought us meals to get us through those early days. We knew we had a few months of maternity leave before our move, so I did my best to soak in every moment with my last baby. I took all the photos and pumped all the time.

After 3–4 weeks, I decided to exclusively pump and bottle-feed so I wouldn't stress about how much milk she was getting. I was producing more than I did with Avery, but I knew once she hit her max of 28–30 oz a day, I'd have to supplement a little.

And just like Avery, she turned out to be allergic to milk proteins. But unlike last time, we identified it quickly with no weeks of guessing, no drawn-out discomfort. This time, we knew what to look for.

It still wasn't easy, but it wasn't unknown. And that made all the difference.

As we found our rhythm in those early weeks, time moved faster than I expected. Before I knew it, maternity leave was over, and we were packing up for our next big chapter: our assignment at the Pentagon. Despite the rush of changes, we felt happy, excited about our future, and confident that our family was finally complete.

LONGEVITY RULES

Our time at the Pentagon was a blur of staff work and temporary duty assignments (TDYs). Amidst the constant churn of military life, we marveled at how quickly Avery and Aliana were growing. The days seemed to blur together, filled with new milestones and precious moments. Often, it felt like we were tag-teaming, trading off responsibilities between trips. During those long trips and quiet flights, I found myself diving into something new: longevity. Somewhere between motherhood and mission briefs, I became even more fascinated with wellness, biohacking, human optimization, and what it truly means to thrive—not just survive.

Upon reflection, I suppose all that research paid off. I never imagined I'd become one of *those* people obsessed with tracking every aspect of their health, but there I was, staring at my Oura ring like it held the secrets to the universe. (In case you're wondering, the Oura ring is a sleek little ring that tracks sleep, body temperature, heart rate variability, and more—basically a wellness-obsessed crystal ball for your finger.)

Looking back, it started innocently enough with yoga, acupuncture, a few supplements. What began as an attempt to "boost fertility" slowly turned into a mission to build the perfect environment for life itself. Fertility desperation will do that to you. I tried it all: supplements with names I couldn't pronounce, castor oil packs (messy, not worth the laundry), morning sun exposure, grounding—both the barefoot kind and the "maybe this will keep me sane" kind. If someone on a fertility forum mentioned it, odds are I gave it a shot.

At the time, I told myself I was just being healthy for pregnancy. I had no idea I was inching toward full-blown wellness-nerd territory. Then one day, I looked down at my Oura ring and realized, oh no, I'd become that person. You know, the one tracking sleep, heart-rate variability, and temperature like their life depended on it. But to my surprise, the data didn't make me obsessive—it made me empowered. For the first time, I could actually measure progress instead of just guessing.

I used to laugh at people obsessed with "optimization." Then life humbled me. Infertility, command, motherhood—they all demanded endurance, not perfection. Biohacking became less about control and more about survival. It was my way to invest in longevity—to be the kind of mom who could chase toddlers and purpose with the same energy.

Somewhere along the way, it stopped being a phase. Biohacking—yes, that overused buzzword—became something deeply personal. Not needles-in-your-eyeballs extreme, but strategic self-care with a scientific twist. To me, it meant fine-tuning the basics: sleep, sunlight, hormones, nutrition, and mood. Not for abs or algorithms but because I wanted to be a vibrant, active "old mom," the one doing handstands at 50 while her kids roll their eyes.

The more podcasts I listened to, the more supplements and small, weird wellness tweaks I tried. Sure, coworkers teased me for being a "biohacker," but I didn't mind. Everything I was doing aligned with my values and the future I envisioned. I wasn't chasing youth. I was practicing stewardship—fine-tuning the only vessel I get in this life.

In the end, it wasn't necessarily about adding years to my life.

It was about adding life to my years.

CHAPTER 13:

What Do You Do With Embryos?

When Aliana reached about 15 months old, I found myself reflecting on our family's future. One evening, I turned to Matt and said, "Maybe we should use our embryos." The words hung in the air, laden with possibility and emotion.

Each month, the embryo storage bill arrived in the mail. At first, it felt like just another piece of paperwork, but over time, it became something else. A quiet nudge that whispered, Remember us?

Those embryos weren't just biological material. They were pieces of our story, suspended in liquid nitrogen over 2,000 miles away in Las Vegas. Symbols of hope, resilience, and the dreams we once held so tightly. Every time that bill arrived, I was transported back to the lab where science, faith, and love had come together in one final effort to grow our family.

As we discussed our options, we both felt a deep sense of responsibility toward these embryos. As Catholics, the idea of simply discarding them or donating them to science didn't sit right with either of us. These weren't just cells in a lab. They were potential siblings for Avery and Aliana, created from the same love, faith, and determination that had brought our daughters into the world.

The decision ahead of us was weighty. Using the embryos would mean embarking on another pregnancy journey with all its joys and challenges. It would mean expanding our family further, changing our dynamics once again. But it also felt like the most fitting way to honor the struggle and hope that had gone into creating those embryos in the first place.

As we contemplated this next step, we knew it would require careful planning, considering both our military careers and the needs of our growing family. Yet, the possibility of giving life to those frozen embryos filled us with a mix of excitement and nervous anticipation.

Towards the end of our time at the Pentagon, I received exciting news—I had been selected for command again at Hill Air Force Base. The prospect of returning to Utah filled me with delight, as we had loved our previous time there. During this period, I confided in my amazing team at the Pentagon about the possibility of using our frozen embryos for another sibling. While I wasn't entirely certain, I felt a strong pull towards this option. At 41, I was acutely aware of the "now or never" nature of this decision.

Matt and I decided to see how our Permanent Change of Station would unfold before making a final decision. However, our plans were thrown into disarray when COVID-19 hit in February/March 2020, just as we were in the process of buying a house. The pandemic forced us to purchase our new home sight unseen, adding an extra layer of uncertainty to our move.

Matt and I agreed we'd revisit the decision once we were settled at Hill. But deep down, I already knew: those frozen embryos weren't just waiting in storage. They were waiting for us.

TRY, TRY AGAIN

June arrived, bringing with it the nerve-wracking experience of moving across the country with two little kids during the pandemic drama. Despite the challenges, we were excited about the new adventure ahead. When we finally saw our house for the first time at the end of June, we were relieved to find it even better than expected.

As we settled into our new jobs, I found myself quickly consumed by the demands of command. The AMMO troops had a knack for getting into trouble, and I was working nearly every weekend. Combined with daycare closures due to COVID, it created a challenging situation at home, especially for Matt, who carried the bulk of the childcare responsibilities. It began to take a toll on his work, just as the constant pressure wore on me. I was exhausted, caught between the weight of command and the demands of motherhood. Any sense of balance or harmony felt completely out of reach. It wasn't just elusive. It felt like a myth.

Amidst this chaos of change and challenges, we made a significant decision, we would use our frozen embryos. I reached out to the local fertility clinic and was pleasantly surprised to learn they had purchased SIRM, our previous fertility clinic. Even better, they offered to transfer our embryos to Utah free of charge. At least one thing was free. A frozen embryo cycle would cost us around $4,000, and they wanted to do a mock cycle for $500 to see how things would go.

By now, I was fluent in acronyms and hormone panels. My life had become a string of lab results and cycle charts, and my foray into biohacking kept me current on the lingo. When the fertility team mentioned doing an Endometrial Receptivity Analysis (ERA), I had mixed feelings. Part of me wanted to skip straight to the embryo transfer and just *go*. But the other part, the methodical, spreadsheet-loving, leave-no-variable-unchecked part, was intrigued. The ERA, they said, could tell us exactly when my body would be most receptive for implantation.

So, we added another test to the queue. At that point, what was one more? Waiting for results had practically become a full-time job. First up: AMH. The number popped up—2.72. I stared at it like it held the key to everything. Was that good? Bad? Google said it was great for 41. That result opened the door to even more possibility, and with it came a surprising surge of optimism. For a fleeting moment, I even considered another fresh cycle. Who was I?

Next, TSH: 2.2. Under the magic 2.5 line. I swear I could hear my thyroid give me a high five.

Finally, the ERA results arrived. Sitting in the doctor's office, heart hammering, I waited for what felt like the final clue in a fertility escape room. "You're just a bit late," the doctor said with a smile, "Your transfer window comes a little later than average." I laughed. "Fashionably late, of course. Even my uterus has a flair for the dramatic." He nodded. "But everything looks normal."

Those three words, *everything looks normal*, were the closest thing to poetry I'd heard in years.

As we geared up to start our frozen embryo transfer, I felt a mix of excitement and nervousness. The process seemed simpler this time around, back on estrogen to build up my uterine lining, followed by progesterone to mimic a natural cycle. No more injections to stimulate egg production or the stress of egg retrieval. It was a welcome change after the intensity of our previous IVF cycles.

We were thrilled when we got word that our embryos had safely made the journey to Utah Fertility Center. As the transfer date approached, I found myself marveling at how much easier the FET protocol felt compared to a fresh cycle. No trigger shots, no anxious waiting to see how many eggs were retrieved. Just medications to prepare my body and a scheduled transfer date.

Before we knew it, transfer day had arrived. One worry that had been nagging at us was whether our embryos would survive the thawing process. I held my breath as we waited for news, exhaling with relief when we learned they had made it through successfully. As we prepared for the transfer, the embryologist gave us an update on their quality. These weren't top-grade "A" embryos, but rather "B" grade with some fragmentation. A flicker of doubt crossed my mind—were they good enough? Without preimplantation genetic testing, we had no way of knowing if these embryos were chromosomally normal and viable. But in reality, we were willing to give it a try.

As we prepared for the transfer, Matt and I shared a quiet moment of prayer, hoping for the best outcome for our family. This time around, I noticed a surprising sense of calm washing over us. Perhaps it was the familiarity of the process, or maybe it was the feeling of closure that came with using our remaining embryos. It felt like we were turning the final pages of this chapter in our lives.

Despite our relative composure after the easy transfer, the infamous two-week wait proved to be just as challenging as before. The days crawled by, even with work and the ongoing Covid situation keeping us occupied. I found myself constantly aware of every little twinge and sensation in my body, wondering if it could be a sign. Just like in our previous attempts, my impatience got the better of me. I couldn't resist the urge to test early, armed with a stash of First Response tests I'd tucked away. Three days after the transfer, I carefully unwrapped the first test with trembling hands. As I waited for the results, I stared intently at the stick, willing a second line to appear. My heart sank as I registered the single, solitary line. Negative. I tried to reassure myself, *It's still early. No need to worry yet.*

I managed to hold out for two more days, remembering how my previous positive results had shown up around five days post-transfer. With a mixture of hope and trepidation, I tested again early on the morning of day five. Those three minutes of waiting felt like an eternity. I paced the bathroom, alternating between staring at the test and avoiding looking at it altogether.

When the timer on my phone chimed, I took a deep breath and looked down at the test. My heart dropped. Negative. Again. With a heavy heart, I went to find Matt. "It looks like it didn't work," I said, my voice barely above a whisper. I let out a long, deep breath, feeling a complex mix of disappointment, resignation, and a strange sense of finality. "Okay," I said, more to myself than to Matt, "so it is what it is. Let's wait and I will test closer to the 14-day mark."

As the days ticked by, I found myself in a constant battle with my own impatience. Despite my best intentions to wait the full 14 days post-transfer, the urge to know was overwhelming. It was like an itch I couldn't stop scratching, each negative test a painful reminder of our struggle.

The night before the scheduled blood draw, I decided to take one final home test. As I waited for the results, I felt a strange mix of hope and dread. When the single line appeared, confirming yet another negative, I felt a heavy weight settle in my chest. It was as if the last flicker of hope had been extinguished, leaving me in darkness.

"Okay," I whispered to myself, my voice barely audible in the quiet bathroom. "I need to prepare for the actual negative blood draw confirmation." The words felt hollow, but I clung to them like a lifeline, trying to brace myself for the official results. The morning of the blood draw arrived, and I felt oddly numb. As the nurse drew my blood, I couldn't muster even a glimmer of hope. I knew in my heart what the results would be, but I wasn't sure how I would react when faced with the final, irrefutable confirmation.

When my phone rang later that day, I answered with trembling hands. As the nurse gently confirmed what I already knew, the test was negative, a tidal wave of emotions crashed over me. Sadness came first, a deep, aching sorrow that seemed to emanate from every cell in my body. Tears welled up in my eyes as I thought of the future we had imagined, now slipping away like sand through my fingers.

But intertwined with the grief was a surprising thread of acceptance. We had given it our all, left no stone unturned. There was a certain peace in knowing we had done everything we could. Pride swelled in my chest as I reflected on our journey. We had faced each challenge with courage and determination, supporting each other every step of the way. Regardless of the outcome, that was something to be proud of. As the initial shock of the news began to subside, anxiety crept in. What now? Did we have it in us to go through IVF again? The thought of more injections, more appointments, more emotional rollercoasters was daunting. But so was the thought of giving up on our dream of expanding our family.

Confusion clouded my mind as I tried to sort through these conflicting emotions. Part of me wanted to close this chapter of our lives, to find contentment in what we had. Another part wasn't ready to let go of the vision of a larger family.

I felt a strange mix of exhaustion and restlessness. The journey had been long and arduous, but was it truly over? Or was this just another bend in the road? I took a deep breath, allowing myself to fully experience each emotion as it washed over me. Sadness, relief, pride, anxiety, confusion—they were all valid, all part of this complex journey we had embarked upon. As I exhaled, I looked to Matt for a hug. I knew we would be okay, we had each other, and we had our amazing miracle kids. We had so much to be grateful for and I had so much love for the journey we had been on and what we learned in the process.

After our final IVF attempt, Matt and I decided to take a step back and just let things be. The prospect of going through another round of IVF felt overwhelming: emotionally, mentally, physically, and financially. We were profoundly grateful for our beautiful girls, and that gratitude helped soothe the ache of unfulfilled dreams.

That's not to say the thought of trying again didn't cross my mind. It did, flitting through my consciousness like a persistent butterfly. But ultimately, we settled on a "if it happens, it happens" approach. We wouldn't actively try, but we wouldn't prevent either. It felt like releasing a long-held breath, allowing ourselves to relax into whatever the future might bring.

ALIGNMENT

As we exhaled from the final round of IVF, another quiet but seismic shift was taking shape: my relationship with the military. I had spent years pouring myself into service, through sleepless nights, missed milestones, and choices made with one eye on the mission and the other on my family. But as our girls grew, so did the tension between the life I was living and the life I wanted.

When I came up as an alternate for Air War College, I declined. I didn't want to leave my family to go back to Alabama for a year. I was burned out, stretched thin, and increasingly disillusioned by policies that had not evolved as much as I had. Then one day, I felt it—that unmistakable truth retirees always talk about: you'll just know when it's time.

And I did.

I stepped away and retired from the Air Force not out of resentment, but out of alignment. I was ready to be fully present with the family I had fought so hard for. It was not a dramatic farewell. It was a quiet exhale. A closing of one chapter, and the start of something not yet fully defined, but deeply needed.

In the months that followed, I leaned into that space. I slowed down. I spent real, unrushed time with my kids. I completed my International Coaching Federation coach training through the Human Potential Institute, a program grounded in personal development, health optimization, and high-performance coaching, with deep roots in biohacking and holistic transformation. I also began facilitating leadership courses for Air Force Global Strike Command and guiding others through Arbinger's Outward Mindset concepts while continuing to explore the science and art of human performance on a deeper level. It all felt aligned with a deeper calling rooted in growth, service, and connection. I said yes to work that sparked joy instead of obligation and gave my nervous system the reset I hadn't realized it had needed for so long.

And just when I thought the season of surprises had passed, life had other plans.

CHAPTER 14:

Expect the Unexpected

Fast forward about three years from our last FET. I had been retired from the Air Force for about eight months when I had the strangest dream on a Saturday night. In it, I felt an urgent need to take a pregnancy test, specifically the leftover test from our last fertility treatments. The dream was vivid, oddly specific, and stuck with me when I woke up. It didn't make any sense. Why would I need to take a test now?

Out of habit, I checked my Oura ring data. My temperature had spiked a couple of weeks earlier, but that wasn't unusual for the luteal phase. By all accounts, my period was due any moment. I tried to dismiss the dream, chalking it up to a random blip in my subconscious. But the feeling lingered, a quiet tug I couldn't ignore.

Around 1 p.m., I finally gave in to the urge. *I'm just going to take it,* I told myself firmly. *I'll take it, and then I'll know for sure the dream meant nothing*. With a mix of exasperation and amusement at my own actions, I dug out the last test from the box that had been sitting untouched for years.

After taking the test, I set it down on the bathroom counter and busied myself with other tasks. I brushed my hair, wiped away some smeared makeup, anything to distract myself from watching the test develop. When I finally allowed myself to look down, my heart nearly stopped.

There, faint but unmistakable, was a second line forming. I gasped, unable to believe my eyes. My hand shook as I picked up the test, watching in disbelief as the line continued to darken. "This can't be right," I muttered to myself. "I don't understand." In a daze, I set the test down and stumbled out of the bathroom in search of Matt. I found him on the couch, dozing while our kids watched a show. The normalcy of the scene felt surreal against the thundering of my heart and the whirlwind of thoughts in my head.

"Matt," I said, my voice trembling slightly. "You need to come here." He stirred, blinking sleepily at me. "What?" he mumbled, clearly not sensing the magnitude of the moment. I stood there, frozen, trying to find the words to explain what had just happened. How do you tell your husband that after years of struggle, treatments, and finally acceptance, you might be pregnant? How do you convey the shock, the disbelief, the sudden explosion of hope and fear?

I led him into the bathroom, my heart racing as I held out the test for him to see. The moment his eyes landed on it, I could tell he was just as shocked as I was. "I need you to go to the store and buy more tests," I said, my voice a mix of urgency and disbelief. "We need to make sure this is real."

Without hesitation, he nodded and dashed out the door, heading to the nearest store. As he left, I paced the bathroom, my mind racing with thoughts and emotions. I felt a flutter of excitement mixed with anxiety. What if this was truly happening?

My anticipation built as I waited. When he finally walked through the door, I practically leaped at him to grab the tests. Without wasting a moment, I took another one. As I watched the results develop, my heart and mind raced. Pregnant. OMG, I can't believe this is happening! I am 44! I will be 45 when this baby comes! The reality of it hit me like a tidal wave, and I felt a mix of exhilaration and sheer panic wash over me.

As I stared at the faint second line on the pregnancy test, my heart began to race, and a familiar cocktail of emotions washed over me. Excitement, fear, and disbelief battled for dominance in my mind. This was a moment I must have visualized thousands of times but the reality of it, the proof in my hands, felt almost impossible.

My thoughts immediately catapulted back to our infertility days, a time filled with endless doctor's appointments, hormone injections, and enough disappointment to last a lifetime. The memories came flooding back, each one as vivid as if it had happened yesterday.

"I need a beta test," I whispered, my fingers drumming nervously on the bathroom counter. "And then another beta test to see if this is viable!" The urgency in my voice surprised even me. Suddenly, reality hit me like a bucket of cold water. I didn't have a doctor anymore. I'd retired from the Air Force and hadn't seen one since. The realization made my stomach churn with anxiety.

Okay, think, I coached myself, taking deep breaths to calm my racing heart. *You've got this.* As if on cue, a lightbulb went off in my head. *Utah Fertility Center! I already have a relationship with them. I can call them tomorrow and see if I can get a beta test.* My mind, ever the strategist, was already formulating a battle plan. *I can take another test and see if it gets darker.*

But then doubt crept in, its icy tendrils wrapping around my newfound hope. *What are the odds of someone like me even getting pregnant?* I wondered to myself. *With my history of infertility and endometriosis? At my age, it's less than 1 percent per cycle without preexisting conditions. The doctors said we'd never be able to get pregnant on our own and now look at us!*

My mind raced at a supersonic speed. *Another baby?* The idea was simultaneously thrilling and terrifying. I closed my eyes, feeling the cool bathroom floor beneath my bare feet, grounding me in the present moment. My hand instinctively moved to my belly, and I allowed myself to imagine—just for a second—the possibility of new life growing there. A mix of emotions swirled within me—hope, fear, excitement, and determination. It was a familiar cocktail, one I'd tasted many times before during our fertility journey. But this time, there was something different. A spark of possibility that hadn't been there before. "Well, little one," I whispered, a tentative smile spreading across my face. "If you're really in there, you've certainly got your parent's stubborn streak. Against all odds, huh?"

IS THIS REAL?

I barely slept that night, my mind racing with a mixture of hope and anxiety. As soon as the first rays of sunlight peeked through my curtains, I was on the phone with Utah Fertility Center, my fingers trembling as I dialed the number.

"You can come in for a beta test this morning," the receptionist said, her voice tinged with surprise when I explained my situation. I could almost hear her eyebrows raising through the phone.

As I approached the doctor's office later that morning, a wave of déjà vu washed over me. The lobby hadn't changed a bit since our last failed cycle—same magazines, same slightly uncomfortable chairs, same artificial plant in the corner that had seen better days. I half-expected to see my past self sitting there, full of nervous anticipation. The tech called me back immediately for the blood draw. As she prepared the needle, I recounted my story, watching her eyes widen with each detail.

"I have never heard such a thing," she said, shaking her head in disbelief. "We'll test your beta hCG and progesterone. I can't wait to see the results!" Her enthusiasm was infectious, and I felt a spark of optimism ignite in my chest. As she inserted the needle, I barely felt the pinch, too preoccupied with the possibilities spinning in my mind.

"We'll call you as soon as we know," she promised as I left, giving me a conspiratorial wink. The next few hours dragged by like molasses. I tried to distract myself by preparing for an upcoming facilitation, but my thoughts kept drifting back to the test. My stomach did that anxious somersault thing with a mix of excitement and dread. I found myself absentmindedly rubbing my abdomen, wondering if there really was new life growing inside.

When my phone finally rang, I practically lunged for it, answering before the first ring had finished. My heart pounded so loudly I was sure the caller could hear it. "Your beta hCG is 378 and progesterone is 14.3," the voice on the other end announced.

I felt my knees go weak, and I sank into the nearest chair. "You need to set up care with the OBGYN because we can't help you anymore," she continued, but her words seemed to come from far away as some reality of the situation sank in. I was pregnant. Against all odds, it had happened.

As the reality of our unexpected pregnancy sank in, Matt and I found ourselves navigating a flurry of emotions and medical decisions. Given my history, I was concerned about my progesterone levels and took matters into my own hands, using topical progesterone as a precaution until I could speak with a doctor. At my age, I knew low progesterone was a possibility and I had never done a cycle without it. It felt strange not to rely on something that had always been part of the process.

More than anything, I wanted to know I had done everything I could to support this pregnancy. If I were to miscarry, I didn't want to be haunted by what-ifs or wonder if I should've acted sooner.

The next crucial step was confirming the pregnancy's progression through another beta test. Fortunately, I secured an appointment within 48 hours to check if my beta levels had doubled. Surprisingly, I felt energized rather than ill—perhaps it was the adrenaline from the shock of our situation coursing through my veins.

After the blood draw, the waiting game began anew. True to my Type A tendencies, I obsessively checked the app for results, knowing they sometimes appeared there before the official call. When I saw the numbers, my heart leaped—my beta had skyrocketed to 956, and my progesterone had risen to 18. This pregnancy was undeniably progressing.

The nurse's call confirmed what I'd seen in the app and brought news of the next step: an ultrasound scheduled for the following week to search for a heartbeat. Remembering my history, I requested a progesterone prescription, which they readily agreed to provide.

Matt and I kept this development to ourselves, all too aware of the uncertainties that lay ahead, especially given my age. We'd been down this road before and knew better than to take anything for granted. As we waited impatiently for the ultrasound appointment, my mind raced with a torrent of "what ifs" and possibilities, each thought a mix of hope and trepidation for what the future might hold.

Keeping this monumental secret felt surreal, but we were determined to protect our children from potential heartbreak. As we arrived for our appointment, I went through the familiar routine of disrobing from the waist down, a procedure that had lost none of its awkwardness over the years. The ultrasound wand emerged, and we found ourselves transfixed by the screen, hearts pounding in anticipation. The sac and pole appeared, but the crucial heartbeat was absent. "Are you sure of your dates?" the technician asked, her brow furrowed.

I hesitated, suddenly uncertain. "Well, according to my last cycle and my Oura ring data, I thought I ovulated before Valentine's Day. But I had been traveling, so I could be off," I admitted, doubt creeping into my voice.

"Hmm," she mused. "Let's do another beta test and have you come back in a couple of days for another ultrasound." We agreed, and I underwent yet another blood draw, the familiar process now tinged with anxiety. When the results appeared on my app, my beta had surged to 11,260. *Perhaps my ovulation was later than I thought,* I reasoned, clinging to hope.

Trying to push our concerns aside proved nearly impossible. Our minds raced with a barrage of questions: How would we manage another baby? Should Matt retire? Would I continue working? How would our children react? The sheer number of life-altering decisions looming before us was overwhelming.

On the day of our follow-up ultrasound, we arrived early, our nerves frayed. The singular question burned in our minds: Was this pregnancy viable? Having experienced the heartache of miscarriage before, we approached this moment with guarded emotions, our hopes tempered by the lessons of the past. As we waited to be called in, I squeezed Matt's hand, drawing strength from his presence.

I took a deep breath as I settled onto the examination table for yet another transvaginal ultrasound. The familiar setting felt both comforting and nerve-wracking. I could hear the soft hum of the machines and the rustle of papers as the technician prepared. This time, however, there was a spark of hope igniting within me. I had a feeling, deep in my soul, that today we would see a heartbeat.

As I positioned myself, knees bent and feet resting in stirrups, I found myself cracking a joke to lighten the mood. "You know, if I had a dollar for every time I've been on this table, I could probably fund my own ultrasound clinic!" The technician laughed, and for a moment, the tension eased.

The probe was gently inserted, and while there was a slight pressure that accompanied it—similar to the feeling of a Pap smear—it was nothing I couldn't handle. As the technician maneuvered the wand inside me, I focused on the screen, my heart racing with anticipation.

Then it happened—the flicker appeared. There it was! A tiny heartbeat pulsing on the monitor. Relief washed over me like a warm wave. But alongside that joy was a cautious reserve; we were still in the early days of this pregnancy, and anything could happen.

I glanced at my husband across the room; his eyes mirrored my mix of excitement and apprehension. We had been through so much together already. This journey had its share of ups and downs, and we both knew better than to let our hopes soar too high just yet. After the scan, I met with my OBGYN, who radiated warmth and confidence. She reviewed my lab results with an approving nod. "I think you're healthier than some of my 20-year-old patients," she said with genuine admiration. I agreed. I had been on this health journey long enough to have very good insights on my health—although I never thought I would be in this position again!

We decided we would get another ultrasound at 11 weeks with the kids and tell them the news. My heart raced at the thought. How do you explain something so life-changing to a 5-year-old and a 7-year-old? We had barely come to terms with this being real, and I could not imagine what they would think. Would they be excited? Confused? Upset? The anticipation was like a roller-coaster ride of emotions.

As we drove to the ultrasound place, I felt like I was about to burst with nervous energy. The kids, oblivious to the significance of this outing, were more concerned with their growling stomachs and the playground we had passed. "Can we go there after?" they asked, their eyes wide with hope. I mused at the contrast between their carefree attitude and my internal turmoil. When we finally were brought into the room, the technician came in and scanned for the baby. The cool gel on my skin made me shiver, both from the temperature and the anticipation. And then, there it was. The grainy image appeared on the screen, and my breath caught in my throat. The heartbeat was perfect, a rapid flutter that seemed to echo my own racing pulse.

The girls had a hard time comprehending at first. Their little faces scrunched up in confusion as they stared at the screen. "You have a baby in there?" my eldest asked, her voice a mix of disbelief and awe. I nodded, unable to speak past the lump in my throat.

As the reality began to sink in, I could see the excitement building in their eyes. They seemed thrilled at the possibility, their earlier hunger and desire to play forgotten in the face of this new adventure. I felt a soft exhale of reassurance followed quickly by a surge of love for these amazing little humans who were about to become big sisters.

As we left the ultrasound, my mind was reeling. The girls chattered excitedly in the backseat, their imaginations running wild with thoughts of a new sibling. I caught my husband's eye, and we shared a silent moment of understanding. This was real. This was happening. The mixture of emotions was overwhelming. Joy, fear, excitement, and a touch of panic all swirled together in a dizzying cocktail. Here we were, about to embark on this incredible journey once again, and all I could think about was how we were going to fit another car seat in our vehicle.

Another thought that would not leave my mind was, is this baby chromosomally normal? The question nagged at me constantly, a persistent worry that I couldn't shake off. We had done NIPT (Non-Invasive Prenatal Testing) for both girls due to my advanced maternal age, and now I was what? Very advanced maternal age? The term made me chuckle nervously, but the underlying concern was real. I needed to know our risks, so we did the test. The waiting period that followed was excruciating. I found myself checking my phone obsessively, jumping every time it buzzed, hoping it was the clinic with our results.

My impatience was reaching new heights, a trait that was becoming a recurring theme in this pregnancy. When the notification finally came that the results were in, a swirl of apprehension and cautious hope wash over me. I decided to FaceTime Matt so we could see the results together. After all, this test would not only give us crucial information about the baby's chromosomal health but also reveal the gender. The anticipation was almost unbearable.

As I sat down to my laptop with my phone in my hand, I was ready to open the results. I could feel my heart pounding in my chest, and I'm pretty sure Matt could hear it too. We exchanged a look, a silent communication of support and shared nervousness. With a deep breath, I tapped the screen, and zoomed the phone in to read the information that could potentially change everything. The moments that followed felt like an eternity, our eyes scanning the report, searching for the crucial information. I held my breath, my mind racing with possibilities.

We saw the gender—boy! My heart skipped a beat as the realization sank in. After two girls, we were going to have a son. I glanced at Matt, seeing my own mix of surprise and joy mirrored in his eyes. But the real relief came as we read further. We were low risk for chromosomal abnormalities! The tension that had been building in my shoulders for weeks suddenly released, and I felt like I could breathe properly for the first time in ages. Thank goodness! It was such a profound relief that I found myself wiping away a tear.

They were happy tears and my mind was already racing ahead. A boy, that was something we hadn't done before! I placed a hand on my belly, feeling a new connection to the little life growing inside. "Hello, little man," I whispered, a smile spreading across my face. The journey ahead still felt daunting, but now it was tinged with a renewed sense of joy and anticipation. We were having a boy, and he was healthy.

CHAPTER 15:

Welcome Home, Anxiety, My Old Friend

The excitement was palpable, but so was the anxiety. The question remained, when would we tell our employers and our families? We wanted to wait until 13 weeks, after the first trimester. It felt like we were carrying this enormous secret, one that was simultaneously thrilling and terrifying.

The exhaustion and nausea hit me like a freight train. I felt terrible, and my new bedtime was 7… if I made it that far. Some days, I'd find myself nodding off at my desk, desperately trying to keep my eyes open during Teams meetings. I'd catch myself thinking, *If only they knew why I look like I've been hit by a truck.* The struggle to keep our secret was real, especially when all I wanted to do was curl up in a ball and sleep for days. I was truly in survival mode.

I felt guilty that Matt had to take on the girls by himself a lot of the time because I just felt too sick or too tired to do anything. He took on the challenge easily—or at least he made it look easy. I'd watch him from the couch, my fortress of blankets, as he juggled dinner prep, homework help, and bedtime routines. *He is superdad,* I thought to myself as I struggled to eat anything that wouldn't cause me to feel sick. *I am so lucky to have such an amazing husband.*

The days crawled by as we waited to reach that 13-week milestone. Each morning, I'd wake up (usually because of another wave of nausea) and think, *One day closer.* It became my mantra, a reminder that this challenging phase was temporary and that something beautiful awaited us on the other side.

As we approached the end of the first trimester, the anticipation of sharing our news grew. We decided to break the news over the phone and FaceTime, given the distance between us and our families. It was a mix of excitement and nervousness as we dialed each number, wondering how they'd react to our surprise announcement.

Matt's identical twin brother guessed it right off the start. Must be that twin connection! Matt and I exchanged shocked glances, laughing at how quickly he'd figured it out. So much for our carefully planned reveal!

I think our parents were as surprised as we were. Over FaceTime, we could see the shock on their face, followed by excited exclamations. Even in telling them, it felt surreal, like it wasn't really happening. Saying the words "We're having a baby" out loud to our family members made it feel both more real and somehow more dreamlike at the same time. The physical distance added to the strange feeling, as if we were actors in a play rather than actually sharing life-changing news.

I am not kidding when I say it took probably until the third trimester to accept that our new addition was actually real. Despite the growing excitement of our families and the constant stream of congratulatory messages, there was still a part of me that couldn't quite believe it. It was as if the reality of the situation was taking its time to fully sink in, even as my body was changing and we were making plans for the future.

The next step was telling my employers that I was pregnant. I had already been traveling to facilitate the Air Force Global Strike Command Commander's Course while pregnant (and let me tell you that was really difficult when I felt so sick all the time). I still don't know how I made it through that last trip! The constant nausea, the exhaustion, and trying to maintain a professional demeanor while feeling like I'd been hit by a truck—it was a challenge I wouldn't wish on anyone.

Both of my bosses were amazing when I shared the news. Even though I had a good feeling about how they might respond, I found myself hesitating—past experiences with pregnancy in the

Air Force had taught me to be cautious when sharing personal news. I hadn't realized just how much anticipation I'd been carrying about those conversations until the words were out. I think part of me had been bracing, not for judgment exactly, but for the disruption. I'd finally found my rhythm again, felt confident in both jobs, and now this unexpected curveball had entered the scene.

The anticipation and anxiety had my stomach in knots and not just from the morning sickness.

Now I see it wasn't deep struggle I was feeling, but complexity. I felt physically drained and emotionally stretched, and I also knew that this baby would shift everything: my time, my energy, my focus. I had just begun to feel like myself again after leaving the Air Force. I was exploring different parts of who I was by chasing creative goals, accepting opportunities, and living with a sense of freedom and direction.

And now everything would change again.

It wasn't that I didn't want this baby. I absolutely did. But I also felt a tug of grief for the momentum I'd been building. That's what made it so confusing—the excitement and the apprehension living side by side. I questioned myself constantly: *Am I ungrateful? Am I failing to honor the blessing in front of me?* But the truth is, both things can be true. I was thrilled to welcome this new life, and I was also adjusting, again, to the impact it would have on the rhythm I'd worked hard to create.

The mental chatter was real, but what helped was the unwavering support I received from both of my bosses and employers. Their kindness made room for grace. It reminded me that I didn't have to figure everything out at once, and that this didn't have to feel like a setback—it could be a shift.

When I told my Arbinger boss, Mike, he said something that stayed with me: "Naomi, this is a season." That simple truth helped me breathe. This wasn't the end of my momentum—it was a new chapter. And like every season, it would come with its own growth and lessons.

My other boss, Rob, was equally supportive. We talked openly about how this pregnancy—especially at 45—was a surprise, and how it would shift things for our family. I appreciated the honesty in those conversations and the space they created for me to process without judgment.

The support I received reminded me that much of my earlier tension was self-imposed. I had built up a version of how this would go, all restriction and loss, but the reality was more generous than that.

Of course, my body had its own ideas. I had taken breaks from yoga during my previous pregnancies, and this time was no different. I always found my way back to the mat and to teaching but the heat was too much, and I had to pull back again. The hot yoga studio had been a sanctuary for me, and stepping away from it was just another reminder that things were shifting.

As summer set in, I started to feel a bit better, but the limitations were still there. I couldn't run with the kids or ride the rollercoasters at the theme park. I watched from the sidelines as Matt and the girls darted around, laughing and carefree. I loved seeing their joy—but part of me longed to join in.

Then, at 21 weeks, the familiar contractions began, just like with my other pregnancies. It was my body's way of reminding me: *we've been here before.* That tightening of the abdomen—physical and symbolic—was a signal that I'd need to surrender again, to adjust again, to trust again.

And in doing so, I realized: this wasn't just about navigating pregnancy. It was about embracing a new kind of growth. A quieter one. A slower one. But no less meaningful.

WILL I MAKE IT?

At 45, I was now considered a "geriatric" mother, a term that made me smile and cringe in equal measure. It was a reminder that this journey would require a different approach than my previous pregnancies, even if I felt the best going into it.

I remember staring at my computer screen, bleary-eyed from hours of searching online for answers. PubMed became my late-night companion as I desperately looked for ways to slow the contractions or prevent another case of preterm premature rupture of membranes, which had happened with Avery. It occurs when the amniotic sac ruptures before 37 weeks of pregnancy and before labor begins, increasing the risk of complications for both mother and baby. The irony wasn't lost on me. Despite everything I'd been through, I was once again deep in research, hoping to find something, anything, that could help.

"Be hydrated," the articles said. Check. "Take vitamin C." Done. "Supplement with progesterone." Already on it. "Healthy nutrition." I almost laughed out loud. If anything, I'd been eating healthier than ever before. It felt like the universe was playing a cruel joke, giving me advice I was already following to a T.

With a heavy heart, I made the decision to scale back on my beloved exercising. My routines of intense workouts were replaced with gentle walks and what felt like an endless amount of rest. The contractions, however, seemed to have missed the memo about taking it easy and kept coming with unwavering persistence.

This time around, I was taking it easier than I ever had in my previous pregnancies, especially since I was retired and not working 10–12 hours a day. Gone were the days of trying to prove I could do it all. My focus was solely on nurturing this unexpected little life growing inside me.

The limitations upset me more than I cared to admit. Before this surprise pregnancy, I was in one of the best shapes of my life: strong, flexible, and ready to take on the world. Now, I felt like I was watching all those hard-earned gains slip away, replaced by an ever-growing bump and a constant worry about the baby's well-being.

I tried my best to stay positive, repeating my new mantra: *This is an opportunity to start from scratch and rebuild to an even better place after birth.* But let's be real, some days it felt more like a consolation prize than a genuine silver lining.

There were moments when the frustration of my physical limitations would creep in like an unwelcome guest. I missed the rush of endorphins from a good yoga or Pilates session, or the joy of a family jog with the kids. My body, once a source of strength, now felt foreign and unpredictable.

But then, just as I'd be wallowing in self-pity, I'd feel a little kick or movement from the baby. It was as if this tiny being was reminding me, "Hey mom, I'm still here, and I'm worth it." Those moments would instantly melt away my frustration, replacing it with a mix of awe and determination.

Work continued to be a welcome distraction, even as I had to adjust my schedules. I was grateful for the mental stimulation that took my mind off the pregnancy challenges. However, even this aspect of my life required adjustments. My once-packed schedule had to be carefully pruned, with my doctor drawing a firm line at the start of the third trimester for travel given my history.

As I entered the later stages of pregnancy, I began to think of this as my redemption pregnancy. I was deeply committed to having a VBAC, driven by a renewed determination to prepare for a natural birth. I downloaded Hypnobabies and threw myself into the program, practicing daily. I also hired a doula, someone who could support me through natural labor and advocate on my behalf if needed.

In addition to Hypnobabies and the support of my doula, I had another quiet force in my corner: my acupuncturist. I'd been seeing her regularly before and throughout this pregnancy, and she became a vital part of helping me stay grounded. Each session gave me more than relief, it gave me reassurance. She supported my body through the relentless contractions, helping calm things down when we needed to keep him in, and gently activating points to encourage labor once I hit 37 weeks.

My fellow biohacking acupuncturist and friend was also a lifeline during this time. While I couldn't take all the same peptides or try every new thing, her companionship kept me sane. Sometimes, support doesn't come in a protocol. Sometimes it looks like someone who just gets what you're trying to do with your body and your life and offers zero judgement.

As we packed our bags for our summer vacations, I was overcome by a mix of excitement and apprehension. Our trips to Yellowstone and Disney World were supposed to be our last hurrah before the baby arrived, but here I was, waddling into my third trimester with a belly that seemed to have its own zip code.

Yellowstone was breathtaking, but Disney World pushed me to my edge. As we approached the gates of Magic Kingdom with my husband's twin brother's family, I scanned the sea of people and felt my uterus tighten in protest. I placed a hand on my belly and whispered, "Not today. We're here to have fun, remember?"

Thankfully, I'd had the foresight to rent a scooter. I zipped through crowds on my trusty chariot like a pregnant Evel Knievel, the kids hitching rides and giggling at my expense. Here I was, a grown woman, scooting through the happiest place on earth with a belly the size of Space Mountain. But hey, getting ahead in lines wasn't a bad perk.

But beneath the laughter, there was a twinge of frustration. As I watched my kids dash from ride to ride, their faces lit up with joy, I felt a pang of longing. I wanted to be right there with them, screaming on rollercoasters and getting on all the rides. Instead, I was often relegated to the sidelines, my uterus throwing a contraction party.

It's okay, I'd tell myself, forcing a smile as I waved to my family from the waiting area. *You're growing a human. That's a pretty mag-*

ical ride in itself. But even as I repeated this mantra, I couldn't shake the feeling of missing out.

Despite the limitations, we managed to have a blast. We had photos and meals with the characters, gorged ourselves on Dole Whip (okay, maybe just me), and the kids stayed up way too late watching fireworks. And through it all, my little passenger kept reminding me of his presence with kicks and rolls that rivaled any Disney ride.

As we boarded the plane home, exhausted but happy, I felt a shift in my perspective. This trip, with all its challenges, had been a turning point. We were finally entering the acceptance phase. This baby was really happening, ready or not.

Back home, I threw myself into birth preparations. The nursery was completed, a testament to our growing excitement. But even as we nested, my body kept reminding me that it was on its own schedule.

The term "irritable uterus" became my new normal. It felt like an understatement—my uterus wasn't just irritable, it was downright furious. The contractions came so frequently that I started to wonder if my body was trying to set some sort of record.

At 31 weeks, a particularly intense bout of contractions sent me to the hospital. I found myself in triage, hooked up to monitors, my heart racing as I wondered if this was it. When they told me it wasn't real labor, the tension drained from my body. I hadn't realized how tightly I'd been holding myself until that moment.

From then on, my calendar became a sea of doctor's appointments. Weekly stress tests became my new hobby, and I swear the nurses started taking bets on how many contractions they'd see each time. As I lay there, watching the monitor spike with each tightening, I'd have silent conversations with my belly.

Listen, kiddo, I'd think, *I know you're eager to join the party, but let's not rush things. You've got a bit more cooking to do.* As the weeks ticked by, the reality of our impending arrival began to sink in.

This surprise pregnancy, which had once seemed like such an upheaval, was now the center of our world.

As my due date loomed closer, I found myself in a constant battle between determination and exhaustion. I had always prided myself on my ability to push through challenges, but at 36 weeks, my body was staging a full-scale rebellion. The contractions had become an unwelcome constant companion, making it impossible to find comfort in any position for more than a few minutes.

My last facilitation scheduled at 36 weeks proved to be my breaking point. I desperately wanted to complete it but my uterus had other plans. Sitting became an exercise in squirming, standing felt like a balancing act, and lying down? Well, that was out of the question entirely. With a mix of frustration and resignation, I had to admit defeat and bow out early.

Nights became a cruel joke. Our bed, once a haven of rest, now felt like a torture device designed by a sadistic chiropractor. I'd surround myself with a fortress of pillows, arranging and rearranging them like some sort of sleep-deprived architect. But no matter how I positioned myself, comfort remained elusive.

I know Matt didn't get any sleep as I constantly rolled, rearranged, and sighed the whole night. I knew my irritability was affecting everyone. The kids would tiptoe around me, exchanging glances that seemed to say, "Careful, Mom's having one of her moments." And poor Matt, bless him, was trying his best to be supportive while probably secretly wondering if he could invent a time machine to fast forward through this last stretch.

As we hit the 37-week mark, I found myself having daily pep talks with my belly. "Alright, little man," I'd say, poking at a particularly vigorous kick in the wee hours of the morning, "the eviction notice has been served. You're free to vacate the premises any time now."

But of course, this stubborn little boy had plans of his own. While his sisters had been eager to make their debuts, he seemed determined to overstay his welcome. I started to wonder if he was holding out for a penthouse suite instead of a regular nursery.

Desperate times called for desperate measures. I took to walking up and down our street, waddling like a penguin on a mission. Our neighbors must have thought I'd lost my mind, pacing the curb with the intensity of a general inspecting troops. "Come on, water, break already!" I'd mutter under my breath, earning concerned looks from passing neighbors and dog walkers.

CHAPTER 16:

The Redemption

Finally, at 37 weeks and 5 days, my body decided to cooperate. I woke up at 6 am to that unmistakable sensation of a rubber band snapping inside me. For a moment, I lay there in disbelief. Could it be? And then, as I stood up, the flood began.

"Matt!" I called out, a mix of excitement and panic in my voice. "It's showtime!"

As water pooled at my feet, a strange calm washed over me. This was it. The moment we'd been waiting for, dreading, and eagerly anticipating all at once.

We sprang into action, quickly loading our bags into the car and calling our friend Dayton to come over and watch the kids and get them ready for school. I fired off a text to our doula, asking her to meet us at the hospital. Meanwhile, the contractions were picking up speed, each one more insistent than the last. Our friend couldn't arrive fast enough, and when he finally did, Matt started to chat with him. But there was no time for pleasantries. "No way," I interrupted, urgency in my voice. "We need to get moving right now."

As we prepared to leave, I paused for a moment, placing one hand on my belly. Despite the discomfort, sleepless nights, and emotional rollercoaster of this pregnancy, a wave of love and anticipation washed over me. This journey, as challenging as it had been, was about to bring us our little boy. Just then, another jolt from a contraction reminded me of the task at hand. Thankfully, the ride to the hospital was short.

In the truck, I struggled to find comfort, shifting in my seat as I played my Hypnobabies tracks to focus on my breathing. Each contraction felt like a powerful wave crashing over me, but

I reminded myself that each one brought us closer to meeting our baby. *I can do this without an epidural,* I thought determinedly. I'm not going to lie; it was painful. But instead of timing the contractions, I concentrated on breathing through them.

When we arrived at the hospital, we headed straight to maternity. Thanks to pre-registration, check-in was swift and seamless. We had requested a room with a tub, and luckily it was available. They had me settled in no time.

In preparation for the day, I had printed the "Believe" sign from Ted Lasso. One of the first things Matt did was hang it up as my reminder that I could do this; I just needed to believe in myself. That simple word became my mantra as I prepared for what was to come.

The contractions intensified rapidly, and I felt a wave of calm when our amazing doula arrived. She understood exactly the kind of birth experience we wanted and proved to be a fantastic advocate. With each contraction, she applied counterpressure to my hips, providing much-needed relief. In a stroke of genius, she handed me a comb to squeeze, a simple yet effective distraction from the pain.

During the first cervix check, I was already effaced to a 6. The tub was calling my name, and although my doctor had vetoed a water birth, she agreed I could labor in there before pushing. I waited anxiously as the nurse struggled to place the fetal monitor and get a reading. It was intermittent but she let me go in. Finally settling into the warm water, I felt a moment of blissful respite. However, the intermittent monitoring meant I couldn't stay submerged for long. I clung to every second in that tub, relishing how it eased the increasingly intense contractions.

Reluctantly, I climbed out and onto the bed. The pain was escalating, and I found myself asking, "If I wanted an epidural, how long would it take?" The response—at least 20 minutes for the anesthesiologist to arrive—made me question if I could keep going. Just then, I felt a massive release of bodily fluids, and I knew instinctively that it was beyond epidural time. This baby was coming, ready or not.

It was about 8:15 a.m. The doula and nurse tried positioning me different ways, but I settled on all fours, finding it the most bearable. About 20 minutes later, it was time to push. We switched the Hypnobabies soundtrack to "push," and I braced myself.

The phrase "ring of fire" suddenly took on a whole new, visceral meaning. As I pushed with all my might, I remember pleading with my doctor, "Can't you just grab him?" I knew the answer, of course, but the intensity of the moment overtook my rational mind. The doula kept me focused, applying ice to cool me down, while the Hypnobabies track guided my pushing efforts.

After what felt like an eternity but was likely just a few more pushes, at 9:02 a.m., one final, herculean effort freed him. Matt was there to catch our son, a moment of pure magic. The baby boy's cry pierced the air, immediately followed by my own tears of joy and relief. We had done it, this was the redemption birth I had dreamed of but never thought possible with my previous deliveries.

I was in awe: of this tiny human we'd created, of my body's incredible strength, of my amazing husband, and of the skilled team of doctor and doula who had made this happen. As I held our son for the first time, the challenges of the past nine months melted away. This surprise pregnancy, which had started with such uncertainty, had culminated in a moment of pure, indescribable joy. We had our little boy, and I had experienced the natural birth I had always hoped for. It was more than just a birth; it was a powerful reminder of what we're capable of when we believe in ourselves and have the right support around us.

As he lay on my chest, I was still shaking from the adrenaline and exertion. We studied him quietly, soaking in every detail, his soft cries, his perfect features, the weight of him in my arms. Just like with our other children, we had gone into the birth with a short list of names, knowing we'd want to meet him before deciding.

"Declan," we said. It was one of our top contenders, but as soon as we saw him, it just felt right. He was Declan. There was no question. Naming him felt like naming something we had always known but hadn't yet spoken aloud.

So many people have asked me what I did differently to have this baby. It's a question that always makes me pause, partly because it's hard to pinpoint the exact thing that made the difference, and partly because I'm still in awe that it happened at all.

But as I reflect on my journey to motherhood again at 45, there are certainly some things that I believe contributed to this healthy pregnancy and birth.

PART II

I didn't realize it at the time, but IVF wasn't a standalone solution. It was just one piece of a much larger puzzle. The changes I made to my health, mindset, nervous system regulation, and overall well-being didn't just support our IVF success. They also created the internal environment that made natural conception possible.

In this section, I lay out exactly what I did over the past fourteen years, how a pursuit that began with fertility became a deeper commitment to longevity, healing, and alignment.

If Part I was the story, Part II is the strategy. This is the roadmap, the science-backed tools and holistic practices that made the impossible possible.

But before we begin, I want to say this clearly: This is *my* roadmap. It's not a guarantee, a formula, or a promise. You could do everything I did and still have a different outcome. Or you might find your path looks nothing like mine and still leads to healing, clarity, or a miracle of your own.

The truth is, my journey wasn't marked by a single, definitive factor. I wish I could point to my $n = 1$—that one crucial change that made all the difference—but the reality is more complex. It wasn't just sunlight in my eyes that perfectly restored circadian rhythm. It was the accumulation of small, consistent efforts to optimize my health, manage stress, and align with who I truly am.

And even if this journey hadn't ended with a baby, it still would've been worth it. I felt stronger, more whole, more aligned. I came back to myself.

Before we get into the specifics,
I invite you to hold this awareness:

Each body is its own ecosystem shaped by time, choice, and spirit. While my experience offers one pathway, it's not a blueprint, it's a resonance. And resonance, by nature, is both shared and unique.

Healing doesn't follow a script. It follows presence.

This next part isn't just about what I did—it's about how I learned to listen. To my body. To my breath. To the quiet signals that said, "Yes." "Not yet." "Let go."

So, take what resonates. Leave what doesn't. Trust that your own knowing will guide you better than any protocol.

And now, a friendly warning: If you came here just for the memoir, the emotional highs, the military love story, the fertility rollercoaster, you're welcome to close the book now. No hard feelings.

But if you're curious about what I actually *did*: the science, the mindset work, the crunchy stuff like nervous system regulation, this is where it all unfolds. Like any woman on a mission, I went deep. Part II is where I share how I basically became a one-woman research project on fertility, longevity, and living in alignment.

This section is divided into five thematic chapters, each reflecting a pillar of how I rebuilt my health, aligned with my values, and supported fertility and healing.

CHAPTER 1: Alignment and the Nervous System.
How I got honest about my stress, purpose, and values and why nervous system regulation was the foundation of everything.

CHAPTER 2: The Inner Work of Healing.
From trauma processing to mindfulness, belief work, and visualization, this chapter dives into the inner rewiring that mattered most.

CHAPTER 3: Functional Foundations.
Labs I explored, what I learned from them, and how I used that data to guide personalized healing.

CHAPTER 4: Food, Movement, and Breath.
What I ate, how I moved, how I breathed and how all of it supported blood sugar, inflammation, and energy.

CHAPTER 5: What I Let Go, What I Added.
From red light therapy to targeted supplements, and from endocrine disruptors to energetic clutter, this is where I fine-tuned my environment.

Each chapter shares what I did, why I did it, and how it evolved over time. This isn't about perfection; it's about progress, curiosity, and experimenting with what works for *you*.

At the end of each chapter, you'll find a simple "Starting Point," a small action or reflection inspired by the practices in that section. Whether you're facing infertility, you're optimizing your health, or you're simply curious, these are accessible steps that *anyone* can try. They're not meant to be overwhelming or prescriptive—just gentle invitations to move forward, wherever you are on your journey.

Let's begin.

CHAPTER 1:

Alignment and the Nervous System

By the time I started paying attention to alignment and my nervous system, I had already experimented a lot: labs, diets, protocols, all of it. But something still felt off. Deep down, I was beginning to realize that healing isn't just about what you do, it's about who you are while you're doing it. Was I living in a way that was true to me? Or was I chasing someone else's idea of what "healthy" or "successful" looked like?

This chapter is about how I began to uncover the hidden cost of inauthenticity and how disconnecting from my true self had silently worn down my body over decades. For so long, I had been living from the neck up, pushing, striving, performing. But when I started to truly listen—to my body, my nervous system, my emotions—I realized how far I had drifted from my own internal compass. Returning to authenticity, to what felt aligned and real, became the foundation of my healing. It's where I learned that transformation begins when you slow down, regulate your stress, and get radically honest about what your body has been trying to tell you all along.

THE IMPACT OF CHRONIC STRESS

A significant factor in my journey was the impact of chronic stress, which I now recognize as a silent culprit that affected me for years. During my 26-year career in the Air Force, particularly within missile maintenance and nuclear weapons, perfection wasn't just encouraged, it was expected. The mantra "Perfection Is the Standard" became the expectation I placed on myself. However, this constant pursuit of flawlessness had unintended consequences. I believe it led to a heightened activation of my sympathetic nervous system, keeping me in a persistent state of fight, flight, or freeze. And beneath that state lived a quiet truth: I was often operating from a version of myself that felt externally curated rather than internally aligned.

Emerging research shows that military women face three known causes for infertility: exposure to toxins, prescriptions for psychiatric medications, and a higher-than-average rate of reported sexual trauma.[5] In fact, a 2018 survey revealed that 37 percent of active-duty women self-reported experiencing infertility, a rate three times higher than the national average.[6] Recent research emphasizes that chronic stress itself, independent of external exposures, can play a significant role in infertility. Prolonged activation of the body's stress response system disrupts hormone regulation, impairs ovulation, and can lead to increased systemic inflammation, which has been linked to conditions like endometriosis and polycystic ovary syndrome (PCOS). For many military women, including myself, this constant pressure may be a key, yet under-recognized, factor in infertility.[7]

It wasn't until I retired that I fully grasped the toll chronic stress had taken on me. The unwinding was immediate and undeniable. What I had long accepted as "normal" was actually a state of chronic dysregulation. Interestingly, many veterans I've spoken with describe the same feeling, an immense sense of release post-retirement, even if they hadn't realized how tightly they'd been wound while still in service.

This newfound awareness marked a turning point. I began to see not just the stress itself, but the identity I had constructed around perfectionism, hypervigilance, and control. Working in an environment where one mistake, especially around nuclear weapons, could have devastating consequences only heightened these patterns. I started to unpack the deeper impact of chronic stress and the constant hijacking of my nervous system. Over time, I began to understand that my disconnection from authenticity, my true self, had created the very conditions in which many of my physical symptoms had taken root.

Emerging research supports what I intuitively experienced: authenticity is not just a personal value; it plays a biological role in resilience, stress regulation, and overall well-being. A 2023 study published in *Frontiers in Neurology*[8] explores the intersection of authenticity, brain function, and health, suggesting that when we live in alignment with our true selves, we foster neurological and psychological resilience.

The study defines authenticity as "being true to oneself," a dynamic process that is deeply connected to self-awareness and emotional regulation. People with higher authenticity scores tend to have increased activity in brain regions responsible for self-awareness, emotional stability, and resilience to stress, such as the prefrontal cortex and precuneus, areas also implicated in mindfulness and cognitive control. On the flip side, a lack of authenticity can heighten stress responses, leading to dysregulation of the nervous system and, over time, increased vulnerability to anxiety, burnout, and even neurodegenerative diseases.[9]

This science validated what I had lived. I was operating under an identity shaped by military culture, external and internal expectations, and long-standing habits of self-suppression. I had unknowingly muted parts of myself to meet standards that, while admirable in context, were ultimately unsustainable. Only when I began realigning my daily life with my actual values, through coaching, teaching yoga, and being fully present with my family, did things really shift. My nervous system calmed. My health improved. And, incredibly, my body became capable of something I never thought possible: having Declan.

We may not yet have large-scale reproductive health trials proving that authenticity improves fertility, but the growing body of evidence offered me another piece of the puzzle. Living in alignment with who I truly was didn't just feel good—it seemed to matter on a biological level.

Authenticity, it turns out, is protective. Research shows that people who live in alignment with their values experience lower systemic inflammation, better brain function, and greater psychological resilience. This is why tools like mindfulness, nervous system regulation, and emotional healing are so vital. They don't just support well-being—they help the body function more optimally and age more gracefully.

In hindsight, I now see that my fertility journey was never just about medical interventions or supplements. It was about returning home to myself. I began to actively examine what I valued and if my life reflected those values. Human Potential Institute coach training during my last military command helped me ask deeper questions. If I truly valued family, why was I spending most of my time at work? If I valued creativity and connection, why did my calendar tell a different story?

This process of self-discovery and stress reduction created a more favorable environment both mentally and physically. It allowed me to approach my journey from a place of greater balance and self-compassion, which I believe played a significant role in making our bonus baby possible.

As I started getting honest about stress and alignment, something deeper began to shift—not just in my nervous system, but in my sense of self. I wasn't just managing symptoms. I was remembering who I was underneath the performance, the pressure, and the external validation.

There's a tool called the Scale of Positive and Negative Experience (SPANE). It measures the frequency and intensity of positive and negative emotions—what we feel most often and how deeply. While authenticity isn't listed as an emotion, the researchers behind SPANE noted something interesting: the more often we experience positive emotions, the more aligned, and yes authentic, we tend to be.[10] Authentic individuals also show a reduction in internal conflict, which helps lower stress and feelings of anxiety.

Authenticity raises your frequency. Not in a woo-woo way, but in a physiological, real-feeling-in-your-body kind of way. When I stopped bracing, stopped forcing, stopped trying to be the version of myself I thought was acceptable or impressive, something softened. And in that softening, healing happened.

Some say authenticity vibrates higher than love. I can't confirm that scientifically, but I understand the sentiment. Because when I began showing up more as myself, something shifted in every layer of my being, my biology, my energy, my purpose. Everything began to move differently. Gently. Powerfully. In sync.

Being authentic isn't about being dramatic, loud, or telling people, "I am what I am." It's about not abandoning yourself. It's about telling the truth, gently, steadily, first to yourself and eventually to the world.

That became the real work. Not just the labs or the protocols. But coming home.

As I reflect on that transformative period, I realize how closely my journey aligns with the concept of *eudaimonia*, the ancient Greek idea of living in a deeply meaningful, satisfying way. My post-retirement work of facilitating leadership courses, coaching, and teaching yoga brought me fully into that space. I had been teaching yoga for over a decade already, but now I could feel it: I was where I needed to be. No longer chasing achievement, but contributing from a place of truth.

My nervous system knew it too. And most importantly, my kids felt the difference.

As soon as I retired, they saw me each morning. I wasn't stuck in my inbox, or mentally rehearsing a meeting, or physically at work. I was present. Truly present. And in that presence, our relationship flourished.

It was this return to self, this shedding of inauthenticity and embracing of aligned living, that changed everything.

RECOGNIZING CHRONIC STRESS

One of the trickiest things about stress is that it can become so ingrained in our daily lives that we don't even realize it's there. I know I didn't. I just thought I was "pushing through," staying focused, being productive. But in reality, my body was constantly in overdrive. It wasn't until I stepped away from that high-stress environment that I realized how much it had been affecting me.

So, how do you know if stress is running the show? Here are some key signs:

Physical Symptoms

Our bodies are great at giving us warning signs, but we're not always great at listening. Chronic stress can show up as:[11]

- Constant headaches or tension in the neck and shoulders.
- Digestive issues (bloating, nausea, IBS-like symptoms).
- Feeling exhausted but still struggling to sleep.
- A racing heart or feeling on edge for no obvious reason.
- Unexplained aches or pains, or frequent colds.

Emotional and Mental Symptoms

Stress doesn't just live in the body; it takes up space in the mind too. It can look like:

- Feeling overwhelmed or irritable over small things.
- Struggling to focus or feeling like your brain is in a fog.
- Increased anxiety or a constant sense of worry.
- Mood swings or feeling emotionally drained.
- That nagging sense of burnout or dread that just won't go away.

Behavioral Symptoms

When we're stressed, our habits tend to shift...sometimes without us even noticing. Some common signs include:

- Withdrawing from people or avoiding social situations.
- Relying more on caffeine, alcohol, or other coping mechanisms.
- Emotional eating (or losing your appetite completely).
- Procrastinating, feeling unmotivated, or struggling to finish tasks.
- Feeling constantly "busy" but never actually getting anywhere.

WHEN STRESS BECOMES CHRONIC

The thing about stress is that we're often really good at ignoring it, until we can't. Short-term stress is one thing, but when it and these symptoms stick around for weeks, months, or even years, it can take a serious toll on our health. Hormonal imbalances, inflammation, and even fertility challenges can all be linked to prolonged stress.

For me, I didn't fully understand the weight of it until I stepped out of that environment and felt the immediate unburdening. What I had accepted as normal was actually chronic dysregulation. If you're constantly running on empty, your body is telling you something. The key is to listen before it turns into something bigger.

STRESS AND TRAUMA

During my military service, I experienced chronic stress, but it wasn't until I delved deeper into research on trauma and stress[12] that I discovered the profound impact of PINE (Psycho-Immune-Neuroendocrine) system dysregulation. This research revealed that both "little t" traumas, such as chronic stress, and "big T" traumas, involving sexual violence or life-threatening experiences, can significantly affect our overall health.

Dr. Sara Gottfried's work in "The Autoimmune Cure"[13] sheds light on how trauma can rewire our bodies, potentially triggering autoimmune diseases. She notes that up to 80 percent of patients with autoimmune conditions experienced significant emotional distress before the onset of their illness. This aligns with my own experience and the patterns I observed in fellow veterans.

When exposed to prolonged stress or trauma, our stress response can become stuck in the "on" position, throwing our immune, nervous, and endocrine systems off balance. If left unaddressed, this dysregulation can manifest as illness or disease, a concept explored in books like "The Body Keeps the Score" by Bessel van der Kolk and "When the Body Says No" by Gabor Maté.

I've come to understand that this emotional and mental environment is the foundation upon which all other aspects of health are built. You could have the best diet and take all the right supplements, but if you don't address the underlying emotional and mental challenges, it's like putting a Band-Aid on a bullet wound, ineffective at best.

As I began to connect the dots after my retirement, I realized this imbalance and chronic activation of my Psycho-Immune-Neuroendocrine (PINE) system was a missing link in my journey. My endometriosis, which has growing recognition as an autoimmune-related condition, may well have been influenced by this prolonged stress response. This understanding has been both enlightening and validating, shedding light on why addressing stress and supporting overall immune function has been so critical in my journey towards health and fertility.

Only later did I understand and recognize that I experienced not only the "little t" trauma of chronic stress from my military service but also a significant "Big T" trauma from my childhood.

When I was in second grade, a horrific accident occurred that left both physical and emotional scars. My grandmother, who was deaf, was dropping my sister and I off at school. As I closed the car door, my jacket got caught, and my grandmother unknowingly dragged me for five blocks. The terror and helplessness I felt during those moments are still vivid in my memory. By some miracle, another parent at the school noticed and stopped my grandmother before she entered a one-way street, saving my life.

This traumatic event left me with physical scars around my hips and road rash in my sacral region, but the emotional scars ran much deeper. For years, I grappled with intense shame that I couldn't fully explain. I felt "less than," ashamed of my scars, and I avoided talking about the incident at all costs since it was like reliving it each time. After reading all of the information on the impact of physical and emotional stress, I believe this trauma contributed in some way to our infertility.

I also had less stressful events like my parents' divorce and ongoing custody battles but that seemed minimal compared to my accident. Like the chronic stress from my military service, I pushed these feelings deep down, not realizing how they were impacting my overall well-being and contributing to the overload of my PINE system.

It wasn't until I retired and had more time for self-reflection that I began to process some of this trauma. While our IVFs were successful previous to retirement, I cannot help but wonder: if I had taken care of this earlier, would we have been successful on our own? If I had taken a step back from all the "doing" or if I had separated from the military or done some therapy, would it have worked? I can't prove causation, but I've come to believe that unresolved stress and unprocessed experiences shape the body in profound ways.

Emerging research supports the idea that early-life trauma can have lasting effects on female reproductive health.[14] Studies show that childhood trauma, whether physical, emotional, or environmental, can lead to persistent dysregulation of the body's stress response systems. This includes long-term activation of the sympathetic nervous system and disruptions in the hypothalamic-pituitary-gonadal (HPG) axis, both of which are critical for reproductive function. Women with trauma histories are at greater risk for infertility, endometriosis, and pregnancy complications due to these stress-related changes.

My journey has taught me that healing from trauma and chronic stress is not just about treating symptoms, but about addressing the whole person, body, mind, and spirit. It's about creating an environment where the body can heal itself, by aligning with our authentic selves and living our values. This holistic approach has not only supported my fertility journey but has also led to a deeper, more enduring sense of well-being and flourishment, a true embodiment of *eudaimonia*.

This doesn't mean trauma work guarantees pregnancy or perfect health, far from it. But it can restore the inner conditions so healing becomes possible. I believe that chronic stress and trauma had quietly shaped my biology, but authenticity and self-compassion began to reshape it back. This shift, from striving to safety, from suppression to self-connection, created space for my body to do what it was designed to do.

Through this process, I thought resilience was "toughing it out" or ignoring pain. Instead, it's about developing the ability to adapt to stress and adversity, to learn from difficulties, and to grow from these experiences. This journey of healing and self-discovery has been challenging, but it has also been incredibly rewarding, leading me to a place of greater self-understanding, compassion, and overall well-being. This is why I felt so compelled to share this journey.

RESONANCE RESET: A QUICK ALIGNMENT STARTING POINT

Before you add anything new, another supplement, protocol, or planner, pause. Ask yourself: *Is the life I'm living aligned with the life I say I want?*

Start here:

Core Values Check: What are your top three values right now? Be honest, not aspirational. What actually drives your choices?

Time + Money Scan: Where do your hours and dollars go? Does that reflect what matters to you or just what's loudest?

Environment Review: What's around you? On your desk, in your pantry, in your phone? What's nourishing, and what's noise?

People Inventory: Who are you spending time with? Do they expand you and support you or keep you small?

Media Diet Check: What are you feeding your mind? Is it making you smarter, softer, and stronger or just more anxious?

Start with awareness. Don't overhaul, just observe. One small shift toward alignment can unlock momentum in ways you won't expect.

As I started living in closer alignment with what truly mattered, something else became clear: the stress wasn't just external. It was internal, too, woven into my thoughts, my inner dialogue, and how I related to my body and this journey. The next phase wasn't about doing more; it was about changing how I *thought* and *felt*. That's where the inner game began.

CHAPTER 2:

The Inner Work of Healing

That brings us to what I call the inner work of healing. This is where I started untangling the mental and emotional knots that had quietly shaped my fertility journey and my sense of self. It wasn't always pretty (or Pinterest-worthy), but learning to work with my mind, not against it, was one of the most powerful shifts I made. Let's talk about mindfulness, forgiveness, and all the ways I (mostly) retrained my brain to stop catastrophizing at 2 a.m.

BRIDGING STRESS THROUGH MINDFULNESS

Infertility is more than just a medical condition...it's an emotional, psychological, and even spiritual challenge. The endless cycle of appointments, hormone injections, and waiting can create a crushing weight of stress, anxiety, and self-doubt. I know firsthand how consuming it can be. At times, it felt like my life was on hold, every decision revolving around something I couldn't control. Pile work stress on top if it and it can feel suffocating.

For so long, I believed that if I just worked hard enough, if I followed every protocol to the letter, I could force a successful outcome. But infertility doesn't work like that. It demands patience in the face of uncertainty, resilience in the face of repeated disappointment. I had to learn that controlling my thoughts and emotions was just as important as controlling my treatment plan.

Science supports this shift in mindset. A 2022 meta-analysis found that Cognitive-Behavioral Therapy significantly reduces anxiety and depression in women with infertility, improving emotional well-being and quality of life.[15] Another study on Mindfulness-Based Stress Reduction confirmed that mindfulness techniques can lower infertility-related stress, helping women manage the emotional ups and downs of treatment.[16] Most compelling, a randomized controlled trial on the Body Mind Spirit approach found that women who engaged in mind-body practices had lower anxiety, improved resilience, and even higher pregnancy rates compared to those who didn't.[17]

But this shift isn't just about doing yoga or meditating. It's about something deeper that I mentioned earlier with the alignment of being my authentic self and feeling good about it on the inside. True well-being doesn't come from checking off self-care boxes; it comes from living in a way that is congruent with who you are at your core. And when I finally did that, I didn't just feel better, I thrived.

This also isn't about simply staying positive or ignoring the pain that infertility brings. It's about training the mind to respond differently to stress. I became a reframing master, shifting my internal dialogue from self-blame to self-compassion, from fear to focus. One of the biggest shifts was learning to take things one step at a time, instead of fixating on the final outcome, I focused on what I could control in the moment.

This is the same strategy I used to write this book in between working full time and raising three kids. I didn't have long stretches of uninterrupted time; I had to break it down into small, manageable pieces (usually in the wee hours of the morning, before the house was awake!). When I felt overwhelmed, I asked myself, *What can I do in the next 15 minutes?* and then focused on that moment. In both infertility and life, I realized that trying to control everything at once was impossible, but taking small, intentional steps was within my power.

But some things required more than just breaking them into smaller steps. Some things needed to be released entirely.

FORGIVENESS: HARDER THAN ANY INJECTION

I also had to learn something even harder: how to forgive, both myself and my body.

I had to forgive myself for the self-criticism I carried, especially around my time in the Air Force. For the relentless questioning: Did I wait too long? Miss something important? Make the wrong choices? I held so much guilt and shame, wondering if I had somehow caused this infertility struggle. My inner voice played every decision on repeat: every failed cycle, every moment I felt like I wasn't enough.

And then there was my body. For years, I felt betrayed by it. I was angry it didn't do what it was "supposed" to. I compared myself to friends who got pregnant effortlessly, to strangers online announcing their surprise babies with casual joy. I doubted and analyzed everything, my diet, my stress, my workouts, searching for a reason, something to blame.

Military life had taught me accountability, but not gentleness. So, I had to learn that too. I had to forgive myself for the perfectionism, the overthinking, the belief that I should have done it all better.

Science shows that forgiveness isn't just an emotional act, it's a neurological shift that can rewire how we process stress and pain. A study published in *Frontiers in Human Neuroscience* found that the act of forgiveness activates brain regions associated with empathy, emotional regulation, and cognitive control, including the precuneus, right inferior parietal areas, and the dorsolateral prefrontal cortex.[18] These areas help us reframe our experiences, regulate emotions, and engage in self-compassion.

Another study found that people who practice forgiveness show increased gray matter volume in the superior temporal sulcus, a part of the brain responsible for social cognition and emotional perception.[19]

Beyond brain function, forgiveness has profound effects on physical health. According to Johns Hopkins Medicine, practicing forgiveness can lower blood pressure, reduce anxiety and depression, improve sleep, and even decrease the risk of heart disease.[20] Letting go of resentment and self-blame isn't just good for the mind, it's essential for overall well-being and it is anti-inflammatory.

I had to make peace with my body. Instead of seeing it as broken, I started thanking it for what it was enduring: for waking up every day, for carrying me through each injection, for being strong even when I felt weak. Instead of punishing it, I needed to nurture it. I realized that forgiveness wasn't about excusing my body for what it hadn't done; rather, it was about freeing myself from the weight of shame and blame.

In the following sections, I'll share the cognitive techniques and mindfulness exercises that helped me regain a sense of peace and control. These aren't just tools for getting through infertility but lifelong strategies for handling uncertainty, stress, and emotional setbacks with greater resilience.

VISUALIZATION FOR EMOTIONAL RELEASE

Imagine yourself in a tranquil garden at dawn. The air is crisp and clean, filled with the promise of a new day. As you walk along a winding path, you feel the cool grass beneath your bare feet, grounding you to the earth.

You come to a quiet pond, its surface like a mirror reflecting the soft light of the rising sun. Find a comfortable spot on the bank and settle in, allowing your body to relax and your mind to quiet.

Take a deep breath, filling your lungs completely. As you exhale, visualize releasing any tension you've been holding. With each breath, sink deeper into a state of calm awareness.

Now, bring your attention to your heart center. Imagine a warm, gentle light growing there. This light represents your capacity for compassion, for yourself and for others. As you focus on this light, allow it to expand, filling your chest, then your whole body.

With this compassionate awareness, begin to reflect on your journey so far. Think of the challenges you've faced, the disappointments, the moments of hope and fear. Acknowledge each experience without judgment, simply observing them as part of your path.

As you recall these moments, you might notice feelings of frustration, anger, or resentment rising. Perhaps towards your own body, medical professionals, or well-meaning but insensitive friends or family. Notice these feelings without getting caught up in them.

Now, imagine each of these difficult experiences or relationships as a heavy stone you've been carrying. One by one, pick up each stone in your mind. Feel its weight, its texture. Recognize how carrying this stone has affected you.

Then, with compassion for yourself and others, decide to set this stone down. As you do, say to yourself, "I release this burden." Feel the lightness that comes as you let each stone go. With every exhale, you are setting the stone down, you are releasing the weight. With every inhale, your body is lighter and brighter.

Some stones might feel too heavy to release just yet. That's okay. Acknowledge them, thank them for their lessons, and know that you can return to them when you're ready.

As you continue this process, become aware of a sense of spaciousness growing within you. Where there was tightness or heaviness, there is now room for new possibilities.

Bring your attention to your lower abdomen. Imagine the warm light of compassion flowing into this area, nurturing and revitalizing your reproductive system. Visualize this area as fertile soil, rich with potential.

Take a moment to set an intention for your fertility journey. It might be something like, "I am open to life's possibilities" or "I trust in my body's wisdom." Whatever feels right for you.

As you sit here, feeling grounded yet open, take in the beauty of your surroundings. The gentle lapping of water at the pond's edge, the soft rustle of leaves in the breeze, the warmth of the sun on your skin. Let these sensations remind you of the constant renewal in nature, the cycles of growth and rest.

When you feel ready, take a deep breath and slowly open your eyes. Carry with you the peace, light, and openness you've cultivated. Remember, you can return to this practice of forgiveness and compassion whenever you need to release, renew, and reconnect with your body's innate wisdom.

This exercise is something I would do whenever I had the time. I focused particularly on light dissolving any endometriosis once I had that diagnosis. Now instead of the "fertility visualization," I usually imagine my body as a thriving machine. Every cell working towards optimal health.

MY MIND-BODY EXERCISE

Preparation:

- Find a quiet, comfortable space where you won't be disturbed.
- Wear loose, comfortable clothing.
- Have a journal or notepad nearby.

Step 1: Grounding and Centering

- Sit or lie in a comfortable position.
- Close your eyes and take three deep, slow breaths.
- Feel your body making contact with the surface beneath you.
- Imagine roots growing from your body into the earth, anchoring you.

Step 2: Body Scan and Relaxation

- Slowly scan your body from head to toe.
- Notice any areas of tension or discomfort.
- As you breathe out, imagine releasing that tension.
- Pay special attention to your abdomen and pelvic area.
- Visualize warm, healing light flowing into these areas.

Step 3: Emotional Awareness

- Tune into your emotions without judgment.
- Acknowledge any feelings of frustration, sadness, or anxiety.
- Place a hand on your heart and offer yourself compassion.
- Silently repeat: "I am worthy of love and support" or "There is nothing wrong with me."

Step 4: Fertility Visualization

- Imagine your reproductive organs as healthy and receptive.
- Visualize them surrounded by a warm, nurturing glow.
- Picture this glow expanding to envelop your whole body.
- Allow yourself to feel hopeful and open to possibilities.

Step 5: Gratitude Practice

- Think of three things you're grateful for in your body.
- Acknowledge the strength and resilience of your body.
- Silently thank your body for all it does for you.

Step 6: Intention Setting

- Set a positive intention for your fertility journey.
- Phrase it in the present tense, such as "I am nurturing my body and mind."
- Repeat this intention three times, feeling it resonate in your body.
- Let the intention move through you without pushing it.

Step 7: Gentle Movement

- Slowly open your eyes and gently stretch your body.
- Pay attention to how each movement feels.
- Move in ways that feel nurturing and supportive to your body.

Step 8: Reflection and Integration

- Take a few moments to journal about your experience.
- Note any insights, sensations, or emotions that arose.
- Write down your intention and how you can carry it into your day.

THE INNER WORK OF HEALING STARTING POINT

Before you dive deeper into breathwork, beliefs, or brain chemistry, pause and check your mental playlist.

Pick one thought or belief from today that made you clench your jaw or ruminate.(You know the one: "I'm behind," "I should've done more," "Why is this happening to everyone else but me?")

Now ask yourself:

- "If my best friend said this about themself, what would I say back?"
- Now say *that* to yourself. Out loud. Yes, even if your dog tilts their head in judgment.

Then consider:

- "Would I talk to a friend the way I talk to myself?"
- "Is this thought helpful or is it hijacking my vibe?"
- "Is this the full story or just the scariest edit?"

Pick one of those questions. Let it interrupt the spiral.
That interruption? That's progress.

Now try this:

Choose a thought that feels slightly better. Not toxic positivity, just one click lighter. If "I'm broken" is too heavy, maybe try, "I'm doing my best, and that matters."

Healing isn't about forcing new thoughts. It's about noticing the old ones and starving them of energy.

That's how neural pruning works: when you stop feeding a thought with repetition, the brain slowly lets that pathway die off.

Pair that lighter thought with a slow, intentional breath.

Then another.

This is how rewiring actually happens.

One breath. One gentler thought. One tiny shift in attention at a time.

In addition to working on my cognitive and emotional state, I knew I needed better answers about my body. It wasn't enough to hope or think positively. I wanted data, clarity, and a deeper understanding of what was happening beneath the surface. That desire led me to the world of functional medicine, where I began exploring the biological foundations of fertility in a whole new way.

CHAPTER 3:

Functional Foundations

FUNCTIONAL HEALTH MEDICINE

By now, I was no stranger to lab work. Infertility had already turned me into a hormone sleuth. But after our failed embryo transfer, I started asking a new question—not *Can I get pregnant?* but *Why don't I feel quite like myself?*

My sleep felt more chaotic than restorative, and despite my best efforts, I couldn't shake the sense that something was off. I'd spent years hyper-focused on reproductive hormones, but now I wanted to understand my whole body. How could I optimize energy, immunity, and mood, and not just fertility?

Enter: labs, functional testing, and the not-so-glamorous world of hormone panels and stool samples. (Yes, really. Nothing says "personal growth" like mailing your gut microbiome, aka poop, to a stranger.)

This time, I was testing not to diagnose, but to optimize. I wanted to know what thriving looked like for me and I was willing to wade through cortisol curves, micronutrient levels, and even peptides to find out.

I found a functional health provider and went all in with blood work, gut analysis, cortisol testing, and more. And while none of it was covered by Tricare (or as I half-jokingly call it, "Try to Care"), I was willing to invest in answers.

Surprisingly, my gut health was excellent with no major red flags, no glaring imbalances. It was a small but satisfying win, like finding out your car's engine is solid even if it's been making weird noises.

I approached my results appointment with an open mind. What we found genuinely surprised both me and the provider. Some of the markers, like DHEA and my cortisol curve, had never been part of my previous lab work. My DHEA levels were practically non-existent, and my cortisol awakening response was severely blunted. DHEA is a hormone produced by the adrenal glands, a sort of master precursor that helps produce estrogen and testosterone. It also plays a role in energy, mood, muscle tone, and immune support. And mine? Tanked.

The provider looked at me seriously. "It looks like you've been under significant stress for quite some time," he said. "So much so that your body isn't producing cortisol or DHEA the way it should." This wasn't "you-need-a-nap" tired, it was cellular exhaustion.

Oddly, that gave me comfort. It validated what I had been feeling. And more importantly, it gave me a direction. Together, we developed a protocol to support recovery with supplements and peptides: DHEA, pregnenolone, epitalon, BPC-157, and CJC/Ipamorelin. I also restarted acupuncture to support stress reprieve and recovery.

It's also worth noting, my primary care manager (PCM) at the Air Force base was outstanding. She was genuinely invested in my health, helped track key labs like AMH during my fertility journey, and truly listened. But like most military providers, she was limited by system constraints and couldn't offer the same in-depth testing or time that functional care did. Still, she was the bright spot in my military healthcare experience.

ANTI-MÜLLERIAN HORMONE (AMH): FERTILITY MARKER AND LONGEVITY COMPASS

I first mentioned AMH back in Part 1, when I was deep in the trenches of fertility treatments, tracking numbers like they were lottery tickets to a baby. But over time, I came to see AMH not just as another lab result, it became a mirror reflecting how my body was still holding potential.

When I started working with my functional health provider and PCM after our last failed egg transfer, we monitored my AMH closely to see how fast it was declining.

Tracking my AMH wasn't about chasing perfection. It was about knowledge. It allowed me to:

1. Make informed decisions about whether IVF was still viable for us.
2. Watch how AMH decline related to the onset of perimenopause.
3. Hold space for hope.

After several months of prioritizing sleep, incorporating targeted supplements, and experimenting with peptide therapy like epitalon, my level nudged up to 3.57. While AMH naturally fluctuates depending on cycle phase, age, and BMI, mine remained consistently above average.

To put that in context: the average AMH at age 42 is around 0.92 ng/mL. By age 43, it drops closer to 0.59. Yet even before I conceived our surprise baby, my AMH was 2.72. After his birth? It was still 2.84.

For me, that number wasn't about bragging rights, it was information. It explained why my body still had the capacity to respond to fertility treatments and, later, conceive naturally. It reminded me that fertility isn't a binary on-off switch; it's a spectrum influenced by genetics, environment, stress, and overall health.

That's why I tell every woman: Track your AMH early and often.

Not to fixate on it, but to understand your personal baseline. A low AMH doesn't mean "no eggs." It can fluctuate with stress, sleep, thyroid issues, inflammation, or birth-control history. But knowing your number helps you ask better questions and make informed choices long before panic sets in.

AMH gave me something many women in their forties are told they no longer have, options. It became my compass, not my verdict. It guided my IVF decisions, helped me monitor early perimenopausal changes, and most importantly, restored my trust in my body's capacity to adapt. As I dug deeper, I was curious about what AMH means for longevity, menopause, and my overall health.

Recent advances in ovarian research are reshaping how we understand fertility and aging. When I first began this journey, the idea of improving or regenerating ovarian function seemed impossible. But new studies have identified stem cells within the ovaries, actual stem cells, which raises the possibility that under certain conditions, women might be able to generate new eggs. While the science is still emerging and actively debated, the implications are profound. It challenges the long-standing belief that women are born with a fixed number of eggs, offering a new perspective on reproductive potential. This is an area worth watching in the years to come.

Right now, there are protocols using a woman's own stem cells or exosomes applied directly to reproductive organs. Some reports claim up to 85 percent success in restoring menstrual cycles, improving endocrine function, and even triggering ovulation, results that can last for up to three years.[21] Ovarian tissue transplants are also being explored as a way to delay menopause, preserve fertility, and extend hormonal health.

One groundbreaking 2024 study mapped how ovaries age. It found changes in cell types, mTOR signaling, and stem cell behavior that could eventually help us slow down or reverse ovarian aging and extend the reproductive lifespan.[22] Additional studies show a positive association between delaying menopause and increased longevity. These fascinating implications for women's overall health suggest the ovaries might hold regenerative potential that extends beyond fertility, into hormone balance, bone health, and even lifespan.

As a woman, can you imagine never hitting menopause? Research consistently links later natural menopause with greater longevity. It makes sense, since hormones like estrogen and DHEA play protective roles far beyond reproduction. Supporting ovarian health, then, isn't just about fertility, it's about vitality and long-term well-being.

So, when people ask if I ever imagined having a baby naturally in my mid-forties, I smile. IVF once sounded impossible too. And yet, here I am, living proof that our bodies are capable of incredible things when supported and understood. What I've learned is that our biology is not fixed; it is responsive, adaptable, and far more resilient than we're often led to believe.

AMH began as a fertility marker but evolved into something more. It became a signal of resilience and, ultimately, an entry point into a much bigger story about women's health, aging, and the possibility of thriving far longer than we've been told to expect. Over time, it transformed from a data point into a compass, guiding me not just through fertility, but toward longevity, vitality, and self-trust. With each lab draw and every new piece of research, I felt more empowered to walk this path with clarity, curiosity, and hope.

FUNCTIONAL FOUNDATIONS STARTING POINT

Start by asking: What is my body trying to tell me?

This chapter wasn't about fixing, it was about listening. Instead of seeing labs as a report card, I started treating them like conversation starters. Here's how you can begin that dialogue:

- **If you are a cycling female, know your AMH:** Ask your provider to run it. Not to obsess; just to understand your baseline and start tracking patterns over time.
- **Cortisol check-in (no lab required):** How do you feel when you wake up? Alert and rested? Or groggy, anxious, or wired? Your energy tells a story.
- **Track one marker with curiosity:** Choose something easy: sleep quality, cycle length, afternoon energy, mood around ovulation. Write it down. Just observe.
- **Reframe your self-talk:** Instead of "What's wrong with me?" try "What's my body asking for today?" This mindset opens the door to self-trust and recovery.

You don't have to optimize everything at once. Just start the conversation. The rest, how you eat, move, and breathe, comes next.

CHAPTER 4:

Food, Movement, and Breath

Who knew fertility could taste like kale one day and feel like a brisk ice plunge the next?

By the time IVF rolled around, I'd tried every trend in the book, raw, keto, juice, gluten-free, you name it. And yet, our success story wasn't one of restriction; it was about resonance.

I discovered that it wasn't about what diet I followed, but how I *listened* to my body. I tracked blood sugar like a detective, fueled myself with protein (and yes, a little...okay, a lot of chocolate!), and tuning into breath and movement. Occasionally I also froze my butt off to reset my nervous system.

So, slow down. Forget the food shaming and diet drama. Instead, let's explore how gentle awareness of what you eat, how you move, and how you breathe can harmonize your fertility, longevity, and everyday energy.

FOOD: PERSONALIZE YOUR PLATE

In the years leading up to our successful IVF, I found myself caught in a cascade of dietary trends, raw, keto, juice cleanses, gluten-free, dairy-free. We tried them all, clinging to each new approach as if it might be the magic ticket. None of them helped us conceive naturally.

Ironically, when we finally conceived our son, I wasn't following any particular diet. What I had been doing, for several years at that point, was tracking my blood sugar. Not because I was prediabetic, but because I was curious. I started with a keto-mojo device and later upgraded to a continuous glucose monitor (CGM), watching how different foods affected my energy and mood. My goal wasn't fertility, it was longevity.

After years of chasing every new diet headline, I finally realized that my body didn't need another trend; it needed consistency and nourishment that supported stable energy and hormonal balance. The more I studied fertility and longevity research, the clearer it became: blood sugar regulation, adequate protein, and micronutrient quality mattered far more than restriction or perfection.

So instead of following someone else's plan, I built a framework that worked for me: simple, sustainable, and science-supported.

My simple framework looked like this:

- **Protein-forward:** ~90g/day to stabilize blood sugar, support hormones, and preserve lean muscle, only about 0.66 grams per pound of body weight.
- **Better basics:** organic when it mattered (Dirty Dozen), 100 percent grass-fed (grass finished) when affordable (thank you, ButcherBox), fruits/vegetables in the Clean Fifteen.
- **Realistic joy:** daily chocolate, balanced meals to blunt glucose spikes and keep the process enjoyable.

This approach wasn't about dieting my way to pregnancy; it was about building a body that felt safe, nourished, and strong enough to sustain new life, and my own life, for the long run.

While I had previously encountered literature on the benefits of blood sugar regulation for conception, my HbA1c levels had never indicated prediabetes or insulin resistance (mine is usually around 5.1). However, I now believe that optimizing my blood sugar played a crucial role in our successful pregnancy, based on emerging research and data.

Several studies underscore the critical role of glycemic control in fertility. A study in Human Reproduction revealed that women with higher insulin resistance faced an increased risk of infertility, suggesting insulin resistance as a potential target for improving fertility outcomes.[23] Research in the Journal of Clinical Endocrinology

& Metabolism demonstrated that women with polycystic ovary syndrome, a condition often linked to insulin resistance, had higher ovulation and pregnancy rates when treated with metformin, a blood sugar-regulating medication, compared to those on placebo.[24]

Furthermore, a study in Fertility and Sterility showed that women with higher fasting blood sugar levels experienced lower rates of embryo implantation and pregnancy after IVF compared to those with lower levels.[25] Adding to this evidence, research in the Journal of Ovarian Research found that elevated blood sugar levels were associated with decreased ovarian reserve, a factor that can significantly impact fertility.[26] These studies collectively suggest that blood sugar regulation may play a more significant role in fertility than previously recognized, even for individuals who are not diagnosed as prediabetic or diabetic.

Rather than prescribing a one-size-fits-all diet, I recommend a personalized approach to understanding your body's glucose responses. Investing in a keto-mojo device or a CGM like the Stelo can provide valuable, personalized insights into how your body reacts to different foods. For about $100 per month, you can collect this data, maintain a detailed food and glucose journal, and pinpoint foods that trigger significant glucose peaks or valleys for you. Stelo now integrates with the Oura ring, allowing you to see how sleep patterns affect your blood sugar.

It's crucial to remember that food combinations play a significant role in blood sugar regulation. Consuming protein, fats, and fiber *before* carbohydrates can help mitigate blood sugar spikes. This strategy is supported by research showing that the order in which you eat different types of food can impact postprandial glucose and insulin levels.[27] So perhaps don't eat dessert first!

More importantly, I began to understand how blood sugar regulation affected egg quality. Elevated glucose can trigger oxidative stress and mitochondrial dysfunction in oocytes, or immature egg cells. A study in *Frontiers in Endocrinology* highlighted how oxidative stress contributes to the age-related decline in egg quality, causing chromosomal abnormalities and lower developmental potential.[28] Another, in the *Journal of Mammalian Ova Research,* showed that high glucose in egg maturation environments led to increased oxidative damage and impaired embryo development.[29]

In the end, no single diet held the answer. What worked was personalized awareness, tuning into how food impacted my blood sugar, stress, and energy. That quiet data-driven approach may not have gone viral on Instagram, but for me, it made all the difference.

IT'S ALL ABOUT THE BREATH

What does breathing possibly have to do with fertility? Breathing is an automatic function of life, yet its depth and quality have profound effects on our overall health, including reproductive wellness. The connection between breath and fertility is often overlooked, but scientific research and ancient wisdom alike recognize its significance. Oxygenating the body, reducing stress, and balancing hormones are just a few ways that intentional breathwork can support conception. By understanding how different breathing techniques influence the nervous system, circulation, and energy flow, we can harness the power of breath to optimize fertility.

Pranayama Breathing

I'd be remiss not to mention pranayama, the centuries-old yogic practice of breath control. When I first started Bikram yoga, pranayama felt almost comical. My shoulders were so tight, I could barely get through a six-second exhale without feeling like I was being tortured! But like most things in yoga (and life), it got easier.

Pranayama is designed to channel prana, or life force energy. For fertility, it offers three big wins: it reduces stress, boosts oxygenation, and supports blood flow to the reproductive organs. Over time, I found that the best results came from practicing it in the morning, on an empty stomach, though it's also a great pre-meditation or pre-bed ritual to downshift the nervous system.

Holotropic Breathing

Holotropic breathwork, developed by psychiatrist Stanislav Grof and his wife Christina in the 1970s, is a powerful technique designed to induce altered states of consciousness through accelerated breathing. The practice emerged as an alternative to psychedelic therapy when LSD was banned in the 1960s, with Grof seeking to replicate the profound experiences he had observed in his earlier work with psychedelics.[30]

Often paired with music, the rapid breathwork allows for intense physical and emotional experiences. Practitioners often report profound insights, emotional releases, and even encounters with birth memories or transpersonal experiences.[31] When our amazing Higher Ground Hot Yoga owners offered a holotropic breath workshop to us instructors, I was all in.

As I settled onto the floor, surrounded by fellow yoga teachers, a mix of anticipation and nervousness fluttered in my stomach. The room, usually filled with jujitsu, was about to become the stage for my first holotropic breathing experience. As we prepared to begin, I speculated, *What secrets will my breath unlock today?*

The facilitator's soothing voice guided us into the practice. "Breathe deeply, let go of your thoughts," she intoned. Easy for her to say, I mused, my mind buzzing with questions. Hours of breathing? Really? I stifled a chuckle, imagining myself turning into some kind of human balloon. As we synchronized our breaths, the room filled with a rhythmic whoosh. In, out. In, out. The air felt electric, charged with possibility and aligned to music.

My chest expanded and contracted, a steady rhythm that soon became my entire world. Time seemed to stretch and warp, minutes blending into what felt like hours. Deeper and deeper we went, and I found myself drifting into a state I'd never experienced before. It was as if my body were dissolving, melting into the mat beneath me. The physical sensations were intense—tingling in my fingers and toes, a warmth spreading through my core. My mind, usually a deluge of thoughts about the Air Force and my impending transition, began to quiet.

And then it happened. From the depths of my consciousness, a single word emerged, clear and powerful: "RISE." The impact was visceral. I felt a surge of energy coursing through me, like a phoenix bursting from the ashes. In that moment, all my anxieties about leaving the Air Force transformed into excitement for the future. It was as if a confirmation that the best part of life was to come.

As we slowly returned to normal breath, I looked around the room, dazed but deeply grounded. I caught the eye of a fellow teacher, and we shared a knowing smile. Whatever had just happened, it was real, and it was powerful. Sitting up, I contemplated the beauty of it all. There I was, on terminal leave, breathing my way into a new chapter.

4-7-8 Breathing

Many have heard of box breathing, a technique often used by military personnel and high performers to maintain composure under pressure. But when it comes to preparing for deep, restorative sleep, I turn to 4-7-8 breathing. Popularized by Dr. Andrew Weil,[32] this simple yet powerful practice is designed to activate the parasympathetic nervous system, shifting the body into a state of relaxation.

I first discovered 4-7-8 breathing in a podcast during a stressful period when sleep felt elusive. My mind would race the moment my head hit the pillow—ruminating, replaying the day's events, planning for tomorrow, and running through mental checklists that seemed never-ending. I needed something to quiet the noise. That's when I committed to trying this breathwork technique with intention.

The process is straightforward: inhale deeply through the nose for four seconds, hold the breath for seven, then exhale slowly through the mouth for a full eight seconds. It sounds simple, but the effects are undeniable. After just a few rounds, I can feel my heart rate slowing, my shoulders dropping, and a sense of calm washing over me. It's as if my body gets the memo: it's time to rest!

Over time, 4-7-8 breathing has become an essential part of my wind-down routine, seamlessly integrated alongside other practices like limiting blue light, stretching gently, and journaling. It's not just about sleep; it's about a routine signaling to my nervous system that it's safe to relax, let go, and recover. A 2022 study examined the effects of controlled breathing techniques like 4-7-8 on sleep quality and stress reduction. The findings suggest that breathwork significantly enhances relaxation, decreases heart rate, and improves overall sleep efficiency, further supporting the benefits of integrating this practice into a nightly routine.[33] The science has caught up to what our bodies have always understood—breath is medicine.

If you find yourself struggling with sleep, anxiety, or just the relentless pace of modern life, I highly recommend incorporating this breath into your evening ritual. Just a few minutes of conscious breathing might be the soft reset your body's been waiting for, a signal that you are safe to let go.

WIM HOF METHOD

Cold exposure has rapidly gained popularity, and much of that momentum is due to the Wim Hof Method,[34] pioneered by extreme athlete Wim Hof. This method combines controlled hyperventilation with cold exposure and meditation, delivering powerful physiological benefits. By increasing oxygen saturation, reducing inflammation, and strengthening the autonomic nervous system, it enhances circulation and lowers cortisol levels. These effects not only promote overall resilience but also create an internal environment more conducive to fertility.

I was first drawn to the Wim Hof Method near the end of my military career. After years of operating in high-stress mode, I could feel the wear on my nervous system. I'd already mastered the heat of Bikram yoga, but I sensed I needed the opposite—something that could strengthen me through stillness and discomfort instead of sweat and motion. During my final squadron command, I was focused on building resiliency tools for our Airmen. That's when I invited a certified Wim Hof facilitator to lead a guided session for our team. I'd dabbled with the Wim Hof app before, but doing it live, in community, with an expert? Game changer.

We started with the science and how deliberate hyperventilation boosts oxygen saturation and strengthens the autonomic nervous system. Then we moved into practice. Within minutes of the rhythmic breathing, a deep inhale, relaxed exhale, I could feel tension melting away. My body grew warm, light, almost buoyant. I was so relaxed, I think I actually nodded off mid-session (that's not a brag, it's just what happens when your nervous system finally unclenches).

Then came the real challenge: the ice plunge. Two full minutes in freezing water about 35–40 degrees Fahrenheit, cold enough to make every cell scream. I stepped in, breath steady, mind focused. My fingers went numb almost instantly but no way was I getting out early. I ended up going just over 3 minutes. Afterward, we did the signature horse stance and breathwork to reheat our bodies. By the end, I felt brand new. Rebooted. Like someone had hit a giant "refresh" button on my nervous system.

A 2022 study examined the effects of the Wim Hof Method on immune system regulation and stress response. The findings suggest that this practice may help mitigate inflammation and enhance overall physiological resilience, further supporting its potential benefits for fertility and overall well-being.[35] The combined practice of breath work and cold exposure stimulates both the sympathetic and parasympathetic systems, helping the body become more adaptable and able to recover faster from physical or emotional stress. In simpler terms: it trains your body to stay steady when life gets cold.

If you're looking for a way to optimize your health, reduce stress, and improve circulation, consider trying cold exposure at home and start gradually. Begin with cool showers before jumping into an ice bath. Focus on calm, controlled breathing and never hyperventilate while submerged. Always listen to your body's cues. The goal isn't to suffer, it's to regulate. Stay in long enough to feel challenged, not overwhelmed, and always have a safe exit strategy before you begin. Over time, your body and breath will acclimate naturally.

MOVE THAT BODY

Movement had always been part of my story. In the early years, I moved in order to pass a military fitness test, manage stress, and prepare my body for pregnancy. Yoga, cardio, even Jillian Michaels-style home workouts were all part of the mix. Back then, my focus was simple: stay in shape, stay ready.

But over time, my relationship with movement evolved. What began as a way to be "healthy to conceive" gradually became something much deeper—a way to stay grounded, resilient, and connected to my body. I started realizing that how I moved mattered as much as how much I moved.

Looking back, I can see how that shift from mostly yoga to a balanced blend of Pilates, bodyweight strength, TRX, cycling, and even walks with a weighted vest prepared me not just for pregnancy and labor, but for longevity. Movement became my medicine, helping me build a body strong enough to carry life, and one I could thrive in long after.

Yoga had always been my main form of exercise and escape, something I wrote about in Part I. It was a way to calm my nervous system, stay flexible, and create a sense of balance amid the chaos of military life and infertility treatments. But as I started diving deeper into longevity research, I realized that while yoga was incredible for stress reduction, flexibility, and mobility, I needed to prioritize building muscle before menopause made it harder to do so.

As women transition into menopause, estrogen, progesterone, and testosterone levels decline, making it significantly more difficult to maintain muscle mass and bone density.[36] Research suggests that women can lose up to 8 percent of muscle mass per decade after 30, and that rate accelerates post-menopause.[37] Sarcopenia, or age-related muscle loss, is associated with increased risk of fractures, metabolic disorders, and overall frailty.[38] That was enough to convince me: if I wanted to age strong and stay healthy, I had to shift how I moved.

I changed my routine. Yoga stayed, but I added reformer Pilates to build strength and mobility, resistance training to boost muscle and bone, and cycling for heart health, without the joint-jarring impact of running. After I retired from the military, you wouldn't catch me jogging unless I was chasing a toddler. Running had its place but so did listening to my body (particularly my knees and hips!).

A 2021 study published in *Fertility and Sterility* found that excessive endurance exercise and overtraining can negatively impact female fertility by increasing cortisol and reducing luteinizing hormone (LH) and progesterone levels.[39] Chronic stress, including excessive exercise, has been linked to disruptions in ovulation, menstrual cycle irregularities, and decreased implantation rates.[40] In contrast, moderate resistance training and low-impact cardio can support metabolic health, insulin sensitivity, and reproductive function.[41]

By avoiding excessive high-intensity exercise and focusing on strength and metabolic health, I believe I created a more balanced internal environment, one that wasn't constantly under stress.

This was a huge shift in my mindset. I had spent years thinking that more was better, pushing myself in intense hot yoga workouts (sometimes 3+ hours in the heat) because that's what I had always done. But as I learned more, I realized that the right kind of exercise, not just exercise itself, mattered for fertility and long-term health benefits.

So, instead of burning myself out, I aimed for five workouts a week, mixing yoga, Pilates, cycling, and strength training for flexibility, power, and restoration. It wasn't about doing the most but about doing what supported my body the best. I truly believe this shift played a role in conceiving our son.

By prioritizing muscle building, metabolic health, and nervous system recovery over constant output and results, I set the foundation for hormonal balance, reduced stress, and improved overall well-being. I believe that balance, of strength and softness, of movement and stillness, became the foundation of my fertility at the age of 45, and will support my long-term vitality for years to come.

Food, Movement, and Breath Starting Point

Let's keep this simple and doable. Before you jump to the next chapter (or to a gluten-free snack), take a minute to check in:

Blood Sugar Moment: What was the last thing you ate? How do you feel? Energized, sleepy, snacky? You don't need a CGM to start noticing patterns. Awareness is step one.

Movement Scan: Have you moved your body today in a way that felt good? A walk counts. So does dancing in the kitchen. So does foam rolling while yelling at your tight IT band. (Just me?)

Breath Check: Take one intentional 4-7-8 breath right now. Yes, even if you're standing in the pantry. Inhale for 4...hold for 7...exhale for 8. Feel that?

This is how it begins: small steps, repeated often. Not another diet or overhaul—just attention, intention, and a little self-compassion, sprinkled in like sea salt. It's not about forcing your body to perform; it's about honoring it. One breath, one bite, one step at a time.

As I refined what fueled me and how I moved, something unexpected happened: I began to notice what no longer belonged. Habits, products, even thought patterns that once felt essential started to feel heavy. Letting go became just as powerful as adding in.

The next chapter is about discernment and the quiet, ongoing process of releasing what drains you while embracing what restores you. Because healing isn't just about doing more; it's about making space for what truly serves.

CHAPTER 5:

What I Let Go and What I Added

This is the part of the story where my Type A soul met her match: the supplement aisle. And the Environmental Working Group (EWG) app. And my Amazon order history. For a while, I treated wellness like a full-time procurement mission. But somewhere between collagen peptides and adaptogenic mushroom powders, I realized that healing wasn't just about what I could add—it was also about what I needed to release. The toxic mascara. The endocrine disruptors. The belief that more was always better.

But here is the real plot twist: I learned that healing wasn't just about piling on new protocols and popping the latest mitochondrial miracle supplement. It was also about letting go. Of chemicals, yes, but also of perfectionism. Of shame. Of the urge to fix everything all at once. Of the belief that I had to earn rest. Of the stories I told myself about time running out or needing to check every box perfectly before I was "ready" for motherhood.

I had already begun unraveling perfectionism in how I lived, but here I saw how deeply it had embedded itself in how I healed. Even my wellness rituals had become another performance, another way to measure worth through effort. Somewhere along the way, I had replaced military-grade discipline with "clean living" checklists, and it still left me depleted.

Releasing those beliefs was just as essential as the supplements. Because sometimes, the heaviest toxins we carry aren't in our mascara or mattress; they're in our minds.

What follows isn't a shopping list or a sales pitch. It's a look at the tools I tried, the habits I shifted, and the sneaky things I let go of to make space—for health, for energy, and eventually… for hope.

Take what resonates. Leave what doesn't. And if you're still using plug-in air fresheners...we can still be friends.

TOXINS: PHTHALATES AND ENDOCRINE DISRUPTERS

I'll admit it: I was already *slightly crunchy* before we even started trying. Years of yoga had nudged me toward cleaner food, natural deodorant, and that vague sense of unease about products with ingredient lists longer than a CVS receipt. I wasn't militant about it, I still wore mascara and lit Yankee candles, but I *thought* I was doing okay.

Then one day, I walked into our fertility clinic and saw a sign that stopped me:

"Please no fragrance. It can harm embryos."

I had already begun cleaning up my personal care routine, not out of paranoia, but with purpose. When you're trying to make IVF work, even small changes feel like a way to regain control. Anything flagged in research, phthalates, parabens, or potential endocrine disruptors, went on my "question first" list.

I swapped in EWG-verified lotion, switched to a zinc-based sunscreen (still a debated topic, but a trade I felt comfortable with), and began reading ingredient labels like they were mission checklists.

I went through every product still lingering in our bathroom and under the kitchen sink. The conventional cleaning sprays? Gone. Even the candles got reevaluated. I kept only the ones made with essential oils and natural wax. I wasn't just dabbling anymore. I was all in.

My approach wasn't perfect, but it was intentional. I committed to doing the research, making informed swaps, and letting both science and intuition guide my choices.

The deeper I dug, the more alarming the science became. Endocrine-disrupting chemicals (EDCs) like phthalates and BPA are *everywhere*: in personal care products, plastics, cleaning supplies, even clothing. And they don't just "maybe" interfere with fertility, they've been linked in study after study to real, measurable harm.

Phthalates, for example, are associated with:[42]

- Disrupted ovarian function and hormone imbalance.
- Reduced sperm quality and motility.
- Increased rates of endometriosis and PCOS.
- Infertility in both men and women.
- Pregnancy loss and complications.
- Abnormal genital development in infants.[43]
- Neurodevelopmental issues in children.

One 2021 study even estimated that pthalate exposure may contribute to over 100,000 premature deaths each year among older Americans, with an economic burden of $40–47 billion annually. That's not a wellness blog talking. That's peer-reviewed, published data.[44]

Given the ubiquity of phthalates and EDCs in everyday products and the environment, these findings underscore the urgent need for stricter regulations and increased public awareness to minimize exposure and protect reproductive health.

Even my yoga pants weren't safe. I learned that clothing, especially anything labeled "wrinkle-free," "stain-resistant," or made from synthetic fabrics, can be full of endocrine-disrupting chemicals like PFAS, BPA, and formaldehyde. These toxins can be absorbed through the skin, inhaled as fibers shed, or even ingested through hand-to-mouth contact. That's especially concerning when you're trying to conceive or already pregnant.

So now, I buy organic cotton when I can. I wash everything before wearing it. I still love a cute pair of leggings, but I read tags like a lawyer reads contracts.

And no, I'm not perfect. I'm not here to win the internet's version of "most non-toxic." I light essential oil candles. I wear cleaner mascara. I eat chocolate that isn't raw, organic, or fair trade. This isn't about rigid purity or performative wellness. It's about intention and making empowered choices where I can, letting go of guilt where I can't, and refusing to let the pursuit of health become another source of stress.

Because at the end of the day, healing isn't a competition. And perfectionism is one toxin I'm no longer willing to carry. When it comes to protecting your body, your fertility, and your long-term health, I'll choose the vinegar spray and fragrance-free shampoo every time.

ELECTROMAGNETIC FREQUENCIES (EMF)

I also became more mindful of electromagnetic frequencies. At first, I dismissed the idea. How could something invisible matter so much? But after diving into the research, I noticed this conversation was happening across both wellness and scientific communities, not in panic, but with genuine curiosity. That was enough to get me reading more.

The research on EMFs is still developing, and not all studies agree. High-intensity electromagnetic radiation, like occupational exposure or medical imaging, is well understood. But the effects of everyday, low-level exposure from phones, Wi-Fi, and wearable tech are still being explored. Some studies suggest potential biological effects, including oxidative stress, changes in sleep quality, and subtle shifts in cellular signaling. Others show no measurable impact. The bottom line? The science isn't conclusive, but paying attention feels reasonable.

What I knew for sure was this: even if EMFs weren't the root cause of anything I was facing, there was enough data to make me reconsider my relationship with constant connectivity. I began making small changes. I switched my phone to airplane mode at night, stopped carrying it directly on my body, unplugged the Wi-Fi when I could, and even experimented with EMF-blocking gear. Whether placebo or not, those actions gave me a sense of calm and control. My sleep felt deeper. My nervous system felt quieter. Whether the reason was physics or psychology didn't matter, what mattered was that I felt better. And sometimes, that's reason enough to listen.

Before we dive into what I added...

I want to be clear: I didn't follow any formal detox protocols. The word "detox" gets thrown around a lot, but I focused on supporting my body's natural detoxification systems, primarily the liver, kidneys, and skin. I did that by adding targeted nutrients like glutathione and alpha-ketoglutarate (AKG). These weren't part of some master plan or rigid routine. They were tools I incorporated gradually, based on research, how my body responded, and what made me feel clearer, more energized, and more consistent in my everyday life.

PHOTOBIOMODULATION AKA RED-LIGHT THERAPY

Red-light therapy might be everywhere now: glowing panels in influencer bathrooms, masks promising eternal youth, even biohacker forums raving about mitochondrial miracles but back in 2013, it was still more of a curiosity than a trend.

I remember when our chiropractor handed me this expensive ($400) little palm-sized device and said, "Try shining it over your ovaries a few times a week, about ten minutes at a time." I nodded, hopeful. Quietly skeptical. At home, I'd lie on the couch with the light pressed against my lower abdomen, wondering if it was even doing anything. It didn't feel warm. I couldn't see a glow. Half the time I wasn't even sure the thing was *on*. (Fun fact: many therapeutic red and near-infrared lights operate between 600–850 nanometers, and some wavelengths are literally invisible to the naked eye. So... yeah. Not reassuring when you're looking for signs it's working.)

There *were* studies out there mostly niche, quietly promising ones buried in obscure journals. But red-light therapy hadn't exploded into the wellness world the way it has today. I didn't have a TikTok video or a podcast host explaining photobiomodulation in everyday terms. I just had a tiny lamp and a stubborn belief that maybe, just maybe, it would help.

Eventually, that first device got tucked into a drawer. But after my second daughter's birth and C-section recovery, I circled back. This time with a bigger, higher-quality red-light panel and Ari Whitten's The Ultimate Guide to Red Light Therapy[45] in hand. I was more consistent. More informed. And this time, I could feel the difference in my energy and recovery.

By the time I conceived Declan, I was combining red-light therapy with low-dose methylene blue, a compound known to enhance mitochondrial efficiency. I was doing everything I could to support my cells, my cycles, and my sanity.

And while I'm not saying red-light therapy is a magic fix, the science is more than just intriguing, it's quietly compelling.

Photobiomodulation uses low-wavelength red or near-infrared light to stimulate mitochondrial activity, improve circulation, and reduce inflammation.[46] It's non-invasive, generally safe, and has become an area of serious study across multiple fields. A 2016 study showed that red light improved muscle performance and recovery.[47] Athletes saw gains in endurance, strength, and rebound times.

And when it comes to fertility?

That's where things get especially interesting.

A 2012 Japanese study followed 70 women with long-term infertility undergoing ART. After adding red-light therapy, 16 became pregnant and 11 of them went on to have live births.[48] Another 2014 study found that women with thin uterine linings had higher pregnancy rates and better endometrial thickness after low-level laser therapy.[49] And a 2018 systematic review concluded that while more research is needed, existing data suggest red light may enhance ovarian function and endometrial receptivity.[50]

As for combining it with methylene blue? One 2015 study showed the pairing enhanced mitochondrial function and helped protect brain cells from degeneration, not directly fertility-focused, but mitochondria matter in every cell, especially in high-energy systems like reproduction.[51]

So no, red light didn't "fix" everything. But it gave me something that's hard to come by on this path: a way to support my body when it felt like nothing else was working. A ritual. A moment of light, literally, in the midst of so much waiting in the dark.

YOU WANT ME TO TAKE WHAT? YOUR MITOCHONDRIA MATTER!

These days, my husband calls me a *drug dealer*. Not because I sell anything illegal, but because the moment someone mentions an ache, fatigue, brain fog, or fertility struggle, I light up like a Christmas tree and start rattling off suggestions: *Have you tried CoQ10? Maybe some NAC? Oh! Magnesium glycinate at bedtime works wonders...*

He is not wrong. Once you go down the rabbit hole of fertility, longevity, and functional wellness, your brain just starts connecting dots. And nearly every time it comes back to one powerhouse word: *mitochondria.* Mitochondria are the cell's energy plants converting nutrients into ATP, the fuel that powers nearly everything your body does. But in fertility, they're more than just powerhouses; they're the spark behind new life.

Mitochondrial health is a major focus in longevity circles; just ask Dr. Mercola or Dave Asprey. But mitochondria aren't just about energy and aging; they're essential for fertility. Mature oocytes (egg cells) contain more mitochondria than any other cell in the human body, hundreds of thousands in a single egg. These energy powerhouses fuel critical processes like egg maturation, fertilization, and early embryo development. Here's the catch: once those mitochondria are formed, they don't divide or regenerate. What your egg starts with is what your future embryo inherits.

When I first stumbled across the CCRM supplement protocol, yes *the* Colorado Center for Reproductive Medicine, it was like a roadmap fell into my lap. I didn't do IVF through them, but their recommendations became my starting point: Melatonin, Ubiquinol, Omega-3s, Vitamin C, Vitamin E, and Pycnogenol. These supplements support mitochondria and reduce oxidative stress.

Before our first IVF, I was cautious. I was already healthy-ish, on a good prenatal, B complex, Omega-3s, and a few antioxidants. I didn't want to overload my system. But after that first failed cycle, my inner Type A took over. I dove into fertility message boards, PubMed, you name it, I probably read it. I wanted to know what I could control. What I could *optimize.*

For round two, I added Pycnogenol (great for endo), bumped up my antioxidants, kept the melatonin. By round three, I had added PQQ and increased my Ubiquinol dose. That third fresh cycle? Our best one yet and I was 39.

After our second child, my energy crashed. I felt like I'd been hit by a truck and left behind on the side of the road. So, I got back on the stack—not necessarily to prep for another baby, but to reclaim my vitality. When baby #3 showed up? Let's just say my mitochondria were ready.

Now, I'm not a doctor, and I don't pretend these supplements are a magic fix. Many of the studies that inform these stacks are small, industry-funded, or based on mice. Some findings are incredibly promising; others, early-stage at best. I'm the first to say: always do your own research and talk to your provider.

But I also knew this: I didn't have much to lose by trying, especially with thoughtful medical oversight. And if the potential payoff was more energy, better clarity, improved hormonal balance, and maybe even a baby, it felt more than worth it.

So yes, I may be a "drug dealer" in my house and to my friends. My cabinet looks like a vitamin aisle exploded. But if something I've learned or experienced can help someone else feel even 10 percent better, I'll happily hand over the bottle (and research link to go with it!).

Alpha-Ketogluterate

I first stumbled across calcium alpha-ketoglutarate (Ca-AKG) while listening to a longevity podcast, the kind where phrases like "mitochondrial biogenesis" and "biological age reversal" are casually tossed around. Ca-AKG is a compound naturally produced during the Krebs cycle, the process your cells use to generate energy (ATP). It's a metabolic multitasker, helping convert food into fuel, supporting collagen production, and keeping mitochondria functioning efficiently. Like many things that support vitality, its levels decline with age. The takeaway? Ca-AKG might promote longevity and improve the quality of eggs or sperm. Intrigued, I started diving into the research.

One study in *Cell Metabolism* (2020) found that Ca-AKG extended the lifespan of mice by 12 percent and boosted their health span, meaning they not only lived longer but felt better doing it.[52] The kind of study that makes you whisper, "Okay, fine, add to cart."

When I dug into the fertility angle, I found even more rabbit holes to explore. A 2023 study showed that Ca-AKG helped aging mice produce healthier sperm by balancing their reproductive environment.[53] Another study suggested Ca-AKG could help improve ovarian reserve in aging female mice.[54] Translation? AKG might give your reproductive cells a little pep talk, regardless of gender.

These rabbit holes led me to NOVOS Core, a supplement designed for cellular longevity. It combined Ca-AKG with several other ingredients I'd already seen floating around the fertility and biohacking communities, many of which were backed by promising animal or early human studies. For someone juggling motherhood, hormones, and mitochondrial wishful thinking, it felt like an efficient, science-forward way to support both fertility and long-term health.

Fisetin, for instance, is like spring cleaning for your cells, clearing out "zombie cells" that linger and cause trouble. In mouse studies, it's even been shown to extend lifespan, especially hopeful when started later in life. Glycine is another gem, known for improving sleep and reducing inflammation (basically the holy grail for anyone over 35). Then there's hyaluronic acid, not just a skincare darling, but a compound shown to support uterine health and potentially boost fertility outcomes. L-Theanine rounds it out, the calm-your-nervous-system amino acid that's essentially yoga in a capsule by boosting alpha brain waves and easing anxiety without the drowsiness. Sure, I could have pieced these together individually, but NOVOS Core felt like a convenient, research-backed way to cast a vote for Future Me (and Future Little Me).

I did consider doing one of those fancy TruAge DNA methylation tests to see if it was actually "working," but toddler chaos plus a low-dollar supplement-testing budget made that a hard pass. At $500 a pop (and double that if I wanted before-and-after data), I went with the highly scientific metric of "How do I feel?" Spoiler: I felt pretty great. If AKG helps keep those mitochondria humming along, I was all in.

This wasn't about chasing some impossible "anti-aging" ideal. It was about energy, vitality, and maybe, just maybe, giving my cells one last pep talk before they pulled off one more little miracle. Did it help? Well...I'm writing this with a baby monitor beside me. So yeah, I think it did.

Spermidine: The Marie Kondo of Supplements

I first came across spermidine in one of Dave Asprey's books. He described it as a way to trigger autophagy, the body's cellular spring cleaning, without having to fast. That sounded like a win. Who wants to skip breakfast when you can just take a supplement?

Spermidine is a naturally occurring polyamine compound found in foods like wheat germ, soy, mushrooms, and aged cheese. Inside the body, it helps maintain cellular renewal by promoting the breakdown and recycling of damaged components. Basically, it tells your cells, "Keep what works, toss what doesn't."

Soon after, I started seeing spermidine everywhere—in podcasts, wellness blogs, even whispered among longevity nerds like it was the next best thing since cold plunges. So, I did what I always do: went full research mode.

A 2019 *Nature Medicine* study showed that aged female mice taking spermidine produced nearly twice as many pups per litter compared to the control group[55]. A 2021 study in *Cell Reports* explained why: spermidine boosted mitochondrial function in aging eggs and reduced chromosomal abnormalities.[56] Translation? Better energy at the cellular level and possibly better outcomes for conception. There was also a *Cells* journal review that talked about spermidine's broader role in clearing out damaged cell parts—great for longevity and fertility alike.[57] Basically, it was the Marie Kondo of supplements.

So, obviously… I bought the most expensive version I could find.

When I saw the options on the SpermidineLife website, my Type A brain locked in: go big or go home. I chose the Pro Strength, $280 for a 30-day supply. Was it a little over the top? Maybe. But I was in full-on optimization mode and willing to try anything that might support fertility.

At first? Nothing magical. No glow. No "aha" moment. But eventually, I noticed better sleep and more stable energy. My Oura ring started giving me tiny high fives. And yes, it matched what a 2018 *Aging Cell* study showed, older adults on spermidine had better cognition and sleep.[58]

Now, let's be clear: the ideal human fertility dose is still a mystery. Most studies hover around 15 mg/day, while mice get mega-doses like 50 mg/kg (lucky rodents). But a 2022 review in *Frontiers in Cell and Developmental Biology* proposed that spermidine could enhance IVF outcomes by improving egg quality and embryo development.[59] That was enough for me to stick with it.

In the months leading up to conceiving my son, I took spermidine daily, usually around 800 mg, sometimes more if I felt like my mitochondria needed a pep talk. I don't know if it was the magic bullet, but it was part of the bigger picture. And given that I was 45 and still had a functioning uterus and a half-decent sleep score, I'll take the win.

Today, I still take it. Not because I'm trying for another baby, but because I like the idea of aging well and remembering where I left my car keys. If you're building your own fertility or longevity stack and your budget allows, spermidine is worth considering. Worst case? You've got clean cells and less money. Best case? Tiny miracles.

DHEA

I wrote about the results of my DHEA-S testing when I went to the functional health provider but let me go into more detail here.

I'd read about DHEA improving IVF outcomes early on, but most of what I found said it was mainly for women with premature ovarian failure or diminished ovarian reserve. Neither applied to me, or so I thought. In hindsight, I *really* wish someone had tested my levels at the beginning of our infertility journey. It might have saved me a lot of guesswork (and maybe a few tears).

Once I started digging deeper, I realized DHEA is kind of a big deal. It's a precursor hormone, which means it helps your body make other essential hormones like estrogen and testosterone.[60]

And as we age, our natural DHEA production drops. Not great news when you're trying to grow a human.

In fertility circles, DHEA is often associated with women who have diminished ovarian reserve,[61] but there's more to the story. Studies have shown it may improve ovarian function and increase both egg and embryo counts during IVF. Some research even links it to better pregnancy rates and reduced miscarriage risk.[62] Pretty compelling stuff.

What really caught my attention was its impact on egg quality. DHEA may help protect eggs from oxidative stress and reduce chromosomal abnormalities, especially important for those of us trying to conceive later in life. It does this, in part, by boosting the body's antioxidant defenses.[63] Think of it like giving your eggs a little armor and pep talk before the big game.

But DHEA doesn't stop at fertility. It's also linked to heart rate variability,[64] specifically, supporting the parasympathetic nervous system (aka your "rest and digest" mode). Higher DHEA levels often mean better stress resilience. And let me tell you, when you're juggling IVF cycles, military life, and a hopeful heart? That *matters.*

There's more: DHEA might help support bone density, lift your mood,[65] improve memory, and even help maintain muscle and skin tone as you age. Basically, it's a quiet multitasker that doesn't get nearly enough credit.

I wish I'd had the resources early on to see a functional health provider and test both my DHEA and cortisol levels. I *felt* the stress but seeing it spelled out in my labs was eye-opening. I pondered: if I had started DHEA sooner, could I have conceived before needing IVF?

When I finally got serious about DHEA, I paired it with a little pregnenolone (another hormone precursor), and that was the combo I was taking when I conceived. Coincidence? Maybe. But let's just say I'm still working to get my levels to "optimal" even now. Because whether it's for fertility, perimenopause, longevity, or just surviving toddlerhood with grace, I'll take all the hormonal support I can get.

Because DHEA and pregnenolone are precursor hormones that influence multiple systems, it's important to work with a functional or integrative provider to monitor levels and determine appropriate dosage.

CoQ10/Ubiquinol

One supplement that caught my attention early on was ubiquinol, the more bioavailable form of Coenzyme Q10 (CoQ10). It was part of the well-known CCRM fertility cocktail, and honestly, anything promising more energy and better IVF outcomes had my attention. When I first added it, I was prepping for our second IVF cycle and just trying to stay upright, tired from hope, from hormones, from all of it.

Ubiquinol is the reduced, active form of CoQ10, which our bodies produce naturally but less so as we age. And let's be real: fertility in your late 30s doesn't exactly come with a surplus of cellular energy. CoQ10 plays a central role in mitochondrial function by helping convert nutrients into ATP, the energy currency of the cell. And since egg cells contain more mitochondria than any other cell in the human body, that energy production is critical. If your mitochondria are underpowered, your eggs are too.

Research backed this up. A 2015 study showed that CoQ10 could help restore mitochondrial function and fertility during reproductive aging. It delayed ovarian reserve depletion, improved mitochondrial activity, and even helped with gene expression in oocytes.[66] Other studies showed CoQ10 acting as an antioxidant—reducing oxidative stress,[67] protecting eggs and sperm from damage, and improving clinical pregnancy rates, especially in women with poor ovarian response or PCOS.[68]

I started with 200 mg of ubiquinol during that second cycle. But by our third IVF, when I was a tired squadron commander juggling long days and longer lists, I doubled the dose. I didn't know if it would be the magic bullet, but I needed every ounce of support I could get. That third cycle? Our best one yet.

After our second daughter was born, I stopped taking ubiquinol, newborn life was overwhelming enough without juggling supplement bottles. But as the months passed and my energy dipped again, I circled back. This time, it wasn't for fertility, but for energy, clarity, and maybe a touch of longevity magic. I didn't expect much, yet I noticed a real difference.

Around the same time, I added PQQ, and that's when things truly shifted. My energy lifted, the mental fog cleared, and I began to feel like myself again. It was subtle but steady, enough to keep both supplements in my routine long after IVF was behind us.

What I realized later was that the things I began for fertility ended up supporting me far beyond it. Ubiquinol and PQQ became part of my bridge from survival mode to genuine vitality.

If mitochondria are the powerhouses of our cells, these nutrients are the quiet spark plugs keeping that power alive and, in hindsight, it felt like my body had been quietly supported all along.

Pyrroloquinoline Quinone (PQQ)

As I dug deeper into ways to support egg quality during our second daughter's IVF cycle, I became a bit of a mitochondria enthusiast. I was already following many of the CCRM supplement suggestions, but I wanted to understand *why* they were recommended and whether there were other tools that might give my aging ovaries a little extra support. That's when I came across PQQ, which I mentioned earlier.

At first, it sounded like just another alphabet-soup supplement, but once I started reading about its role in mitochondrial biogenesis,[69] helping create *new* mitochondria, I was intrigued. Egg cells are notoriously demanding when it comes to energy. They have more mitochondria than any other cell in the female body, and as we age, the performance of those mitochondria naturally declines. The idea of giving them a tune-up (or a full engine replacement, really) made sense.

The more I learned, the more PQQ earned its spot on my supplement shelf. In addition to helping generate new mitochondria, it's also a powerful antioxidant, which meant it could help protect my eggs from oxidative stress, something that's closely linked to age-related fertility issues.[70] That was a big deal for me. At that point, I wasn't trying to be trendy or cutting-edge. I was just a hopeful mom in her late 30s trying to stack the odds.

I also stumbled across early research suggesting that PQQ might support embryo development during in vitro maturation.[71] Granted, these were animal studies, and more human trials are needed, but the direction was promising. One study that stood out showed that PQQ significantly increased both pregnancy rates and litter size in mice with chemically-induced ovarian damage. I wasn't a mouse, but I saw enough overlap to feel like this was worth trying.

Interestingly, while I was mostly focused on my egg quality, I also came across data showing that PQQ might support sperm motility and mitochondrial function.[72] It made me wonder if it could help Matt, too so it became a part of his supplement stack.

I started with 10 to 20 mg daily, which is what many of the studies suggested. And whether it was the PQQ or the whole combination of things I was doing, that third IVF cycle turned out to be our best one. Same protocol as IVF #2. Same doctor. The big difference? This time, we had day-5 blastocysts. And I was two years older. I can't prove it was the PQQ, but it earned my respect. I've taken it ever since.

And here's the thing, I didn't just feel like it helped my fertility. I noticed subtle shifts in my energy and focus, too. Turns out PQQ has been studied for its neuroprotective benefits and potential impact on cognitive function. So even if it hadn't nudged my egg quality in the right direction, it still felt like a win for my overall health.

One of the biggest lessons from IVF #3 was this: my supplements were doing more than just filling in nutritional gaps. They were changing the quality of the eggs I had left, even though I was older. And for that, I'm grateful.

Methylene Blue (MB)

If there's one supplement that blends cutting-edge science with a touch of mystery, it's methylene blue (MB). Originally developed as a dye in the late 1800s, it later became one of medicine's most versatile compounds used to treat infections, improve oxygen delivery, and support mitochondrial health. Today, researchers are revisiting MB for its remarkable effects on energy metabolism, cognition, and cellular resilience.

At low doses, methylene blue acts as an electron carrier within the mitochondrial electron transport chain, the system responsible for producing ATP, the body's primary energy currency. In simple terms, it helps your cells make energy more efficiently while reducing oxidative stress. Studies show that MB can enhance mitochondrial function, increase ATP production, and even restore function in damaged or aging cells.[73]

Its benefits are perhaps most studied in the brain. Low doses of MB have been shown to boost short-term memory, focus, and overall cognitive performance. One human clinical trial found that a single microdose improved memory retrieval accuracy by 7 percent, confirmed by fMRI scans showing greater activity in the prefrontal cortex, parietal lobe, and occipital cortex—the same regions that light up during high-focus mental work.[74] Other research highlights MB's neuroprotective potential, showing it can help reduce the effects of oxidative stress, inflammation, and even early cognitive decline.[75]

Beyond the brain, MB's impact on mitochondrial performance has made it a growing interest in the longevity and fertility space. Healthy mitochondria are vital for egg and sperm quality, and while research on MB's reproductive applications is still early, its role in supporting cellular energy and reducing oxidative damage makes it a promising adjunct for overall reproductive health.

I first came across MB while researching mitochondrial support, but I couldn't try it until after retiring from the Air Force. At the time, it appeared on the "banned substances" list, likely due to its prescription status and pharmacologic effects rather than safety concerns. Once I finally did try it, I immediately felt a difference at only 4mg. My energy and focus spiked, almost too much at first, so I limited it to once or twice a week. I wasn't taking it to boost fertility, but rather to support cognition and cellular energy. Still, knowing how deeply mitochondria influence reproductive health, I can't help but think MB quietly played a supporting role in the background.

Now, let's talk about the fine print (aka the important warnings):

Do Not Take MB If You're on SSRIs: This is a hard no. Methylene blue can dangerously interact with SSRIs, potentially leading to serotonin syndrome, a condition where your serotonin levels go haywire. Symptoms include confusion, rapid heart rate, sky-high blood pressure, and in severe cases, things you definitely don't want to deal with, like seizures or coma.

Skip MB During Pregnancy: If you're already pregnant, MB needs to stay on the shelf. It's been linked to potential risks for fetal development and may contribute to oxidative stress, which isn't baby-friendly.

For me, methylene blue was never about chasing a miracle; rather, it was about optimizing the system that powers everything. Used thoughtfully, it became one of those quiet but powerful tools that helped me feel sharper, calmer, and more energized as I moved through the next chapter of both motherhood and midlife.

Minerals

In my quest to optimize my longevity, I discovered the significant role that essential minerals, particularly magnesium, play in overall well-being and reproductive health. I figured if magnesium could help me sleep at night plus improve my cognitive function, then I was more than willing to take it!

Magnesium, an essential mineral involved in over 300 enzymatic reactions, also plays a vital role in reproductive health. It contributes to muscle and nerve function, blood glucose control, and energy production. Research indicates that magnesium is integral to DNA, RNA, and protein synthesis, as well as the regulation of vascular tone and heart rhythm.[76] These functions are crucial for overall health and may indirectly support reproductive processes. When you think about it, that means magnesium supports almost every system tied to fertility and longevity: metabolic stability, sleep, recovery, and emotional regulation.

I typically took 250 to 500 mg of magnesium at night to promote relaxation and sleep. In the morning, I added essential minerals and a fulvic and humic mineral supplement to my routine. This gave me a broader spectrum of trace minerals that supported hydration, cellular energy, and overall mineral balance. It wasn't just about targeting one nutrient. It was about giving my body the foundational tools it needed to thrive.

Berberine

Who knew that my insatiable love for chocolate would lead me down a path of fertility optimization? Certainly not me! While I've never been pre-diabetic, I found myself on a quest to tame my blood sugar levels, hoping to have my cake and eat it too, all while aiming for longevity. Little did I know that this sugary adventure would introduce me to a powerful ally in the world of fertility: berberine, a compound that would become my unexpected fertility friend.

Berberine, a natural plant alkaloid, has been used in traditional Chinese medicine for centuries.

But it's not just an ancient remedy; modern science has uncovered its impressive effects on metabolic health and, surprisingly, fertility. While I was initially taking berberine (and later, its more bioavailable cousin, dihydroberberine) for blood sugar management, I was unknowingly setting the stage for improved fertility.

The research on berberine's effects on fertility is nothing short of amazing. It's like this little yellow compound decided to become a superhero for ovaries everywhere. Studies suggest that berberine may increase ovulation rates, balance hormones, and improve insulin sensitivity, which are all key factors in reproductive health. One study found that berberine enhanced ovulation and endometrial receptivity, helping to create a more supportive environment for conception.[77] Another systematic review concluded that berberine was effective in improving reproductive and metabolic outcomes in women with PCOS.[78] Finally, berberine has been recognized for its role in weight management, which can further support fertility, particularly for those struggling with metabolic imbalances.

Because I took a few different supplements that included berberine and/or dihydroberberine, my dosing varied. On average, I would say I was getting around 500 mg of berberine or 200 mg of dihydroberberine daily. That said, most clinical studies use 500 mg of berberine taken two to three times a day, especially for metabolic and blood sugar support. If you're just starting out, that's a common dose recommended in the literature.[79] For dihydroberberine, a more bioavailable form, 100–200 mg once or twice daily is often suggested[80].

Always start low and check with a provider if you're unsure, especially if you're taking other medications or managing insulin sensitivity. Personally, I found this supplement helped stabilize my energy and glucose spikes, which, let's be honest, is helpful whether you're trying to conceive or just trying to survive parenting toddlers.

Melatonin

I'll just say it: melatonin gives me nightmares. Especially anything 3 mg or above. That being said, I did use 1 mg melatonin in preparation for our third IVF as well as intermittently before having our son. There must be a reason it is in the CCRM stack, right?

The answer is yes! Melatonin isn't just a sleep hormone; it's also a potent antioxidant. It plays a key role in protecting cells from oxidative stress, which is especially relevant for egg quality and embryo development. Oocytes are particularly vulnerable to oxidative damage, and melatonin helps neutralize free radicals that can compromise their health and viability.

During my never-ending research, I came across several studies that showed promising results, particularly for women undergoing IVF. One study that caught my attention reported a remarkable increase in fertilization rates from 20.2 percent to 50 percent when women took just 3 mg of melatonin daily. Even more encouraging, the same study found an increase in good quality embryos from 48 percent to 65.6 percent.[81] Other studies suggest that melatonin can improve ovarian function and increase pregnancy rates, especially when taken consistently for several months before IVF.

Because of this, many reproductive endocrinologists recommend taking at least 3 mg of melatonin nightly for about 120 days before an IVF cycle to support egg quality and antioxidant defense. It's affordable, accessible, and widely studied, but, as I learned firsthand, it's not one-size-fits-all.

For me, lower doses worked best, around 1 mg, taken a few nights a week. Anything higher and I was starring in my own subconscious thriller. Still, even that small amount seemed to help regulate my sleep, support recovery, and align my body's rhythms in those critical months before conception.

Melatonin may not be for everyone, but it's a reminder that sometimes the most powerful fertility tools are also the simplest in supporting not just our sleep, but the deep cellular repair and renewal that happen while we rest.

NMN and Resveratrol

When David Sinclair's book *Lifespan* came out in 2019, I had a 1-year-old and a 3-year-old and was running low on sleep, energy, and anything that resembled cellular vitality. His deep dive into Nicotinamide Mononucleotide (NMN) and Resveratrol caught my attention, especially the idea that these compounds might improve cellular health, increase energy, and even extend lifespan. Yes, please.

NMN is a precursor to NAD+ (Nicotinamide Adenine Dinucleotide), a molecule that's critical for mitochondrial function, DNA repair, and maintaining healthy circadian rhythms. But NAD+ levels naturally decline with age, and that decline has been linked to fatigue, metabolic dysfunction, and other age-related issues.

Supplementing with NMN has been shown to restore NAD+ levels, potentially reversing some of the effects of aging. Research suggests that NMN may enhance mitochondrial function, improving energy production at the cellular level; support DNA repair mechanisms, reducing oxidative damage; and improve vascular health and blood flow, critical for maintaining organ function.[82]

Then comes Resveratrol, the polyphenol compound famously found in red wine, grapes, and berries. It is known for its antioxidant and anti-inflammatory properties, but its most compelling role in longevity lies in its ability to activate sirtuins. Sirtuins are a family of proteins that play a key role in cellular health, particularly in regulating metabolic processes, stress resistance, and DNA repair. In simple terms, sirtuins are the cell's maintenance crew keeping things clean, efficient, and balanced.

By activating sirtuins, Resveratrol helps to mimic some of the benefits of calorie restriction, a well-documented method for extending lifespan in various organisms. Additional benefits of Resveratrol may include enhancing insulin sensitivity and metabolic health, protecting against neurodegenerative diseases by reducing inflammation and oxidative stress,[83] and supporting cardiovascular health through improved blood vessel function.[84]

NMN and Resveratrol may complement each other's effects, making them a powerful duo for promoting longevity. While NMN works to replenish NAD+ levels, Resveratrol amplifies the activity of sirtuins, which rely on NAD+ to function effectively. This synergy could lead to greater improvements in cellular repair, energy metabolism, and resilience against aging-related diseases.

I also started paying attention to studies linking these compounds with reproductive health. A 2020 study published in *Cell Metabolism* showed that NMN improved egg quality and embryo development in aging mice.[85] In another study in *Aging*, Resveratrol helped increase live birth rates in older mice and improved mitochondrial health in oocytes.[86] Even more exciting, a clinical trial in *Fertility and Sterility* found that Resveratrol improved embryo quality in women undergoing IVF.[87]

That was more than enough for me to try it.

I incorporated this into my routine to boost my energy, support natural fertility, and promote longevity. I noticed the effects almost immediately. Before conceiving my son naturally, I was taking 250 mg of NMN and 500 mg of resveratrol. Although this was way lower than David Sinclair's regimen of 1 gram of NMN and 1 gram of resveratrol, I still felt a difference, which reassured me that it was having a positive impact.

Bioregulators

I first came across bioregulators in a podcast, but at the time, they didn't make much of an impression on me. Later, I began hearing more about them on more podcasts, and it sparked my curiosity. I thought, "Could these tiny peptides actually help the body repair itself at the genetic level?" It sounded like science fiction but compelling enough to explore.

Bioregulators are short-chain peptides, typically just 2–4 amino acids long, that act as epigenetic switches. By interacting with specific regions of DNA, they help turn genes on or off, supporting cellular repair and regeneration. In essence, they remind your cells how to function like they did when you were younger.

Remarkably, bioregulators can cross cellular and nuclear membranes to modulate protein synthesis and influence gene expression. Most of the bioregulator research originates from Russia, in particular from Professor Khavinson who authored more than 700 scientific publications on the subject. Research indicates they may help slow the aging process, enhance DNA methylation, and restore organ function, making them a promising tool for longevity and overall health.

Bioregulators are typically taken in cycles and the aim is to allow the body to regulate naturally without becoming dependent. They generally have no side effects or contraindications. I decided I didn't have anything to lose (except money) so I decided I would cycle with the pineal gland (Endoluten), blood vessel (Ventfort), thymus (Vladonix) and ovary (Zhenoluten). I'll be honest, I did not feel much different other than a slight uptick in some heart rate variability. I mention them only because I did cycle them the year before conception with my son.

Perhaps it was coincidence, subtle cellular support, or just part of a much bigger picture; I can't say for certain. But here's what I've learned: sometimes the body doesn't need fireworks to change course. It just needs quiet reminders—small, molecular nudges that help it remember how to repair, restore, and renew.

Peptides

Increasing in popularity, peptides are more mainstream than ever before! Peptides are short chains of amino acids, the building blocks of proteins, linked together by peptide bonds. Typically, peptides consist of 2 to 50 amino acids, distinguishing them from larger, more complex proteins. Their relatively small size allows them to act as versatile biological messengers, carrying out specialized functions in the body.

Peptides serve a variety of critical functions in the body, acting as messengers to regulate processes such as hormone production, immune response, and tissue repair. They play a key role in skin health by promoting collagen production and improving elasticity, making them valuable in anti-aging skincare. Additionally, peptides aid in muscle growth and recovery, support metabolic functions, and offer natural antimicrobial properties to protect the body from infections.

When I began working with a functional health provider, they prescribed epitalon which is a synthetic peptide modeled after a naturally occurring compound in the pineal gland. Known for its antioxidant properties, epitalon has been shown to protect oocytes (immature egg cells) from post-ovulatory aging by reducing oxidative stress and supporting mitochondrial function. We started with epitalon because it's considered a foundational peptide for anti-aging, cellular repair, and hormonal balance.

In animal studies, Epitalon significantly decreased the frequency of spindle defects and abnormal distribution of cortical granules during oocyte aging, while increasing mitochondrial membrane potential and DNA copy numbers.[88] These protective effects may help preserve oocyte quality and extend the window for successful fertilization. Additionally, Epitalon has been shown to stimulate melatonin production, which can help normalize circadian rhythms crucial for reproductive function.

Earlier I stated that my AMH (albeit minimally) went up after taking epitalon. Was it a coincidence? Maybe. But I also slept better on it and that alone was worth taking it. While I tried other peptides later, I cycled this one every six months and I believe this one had the most impact of the peptides I tried.

Peptides, at their core, aren't about quick fixes or futuristic hacks. They're reminders that the body has built-in intelligence and, given the right signals, it remembers how to heal, rejuvenate, and even surprise you.

Glutathione

As someone living with endometriosis, I'm always on the lookout for natural ways to manage my symptoms and support my body's detoxification processes. When I learned about glutathione, I was drawn to its potential to address both of these concerns, and even more encouraged when I discovered its potential benefits for fertility.

Glutathione, often called the body's master antioxidant, plays a crucial role in detoxification as well as in combating oxidative stress. I discovered that women with endometriosis often have lower levels of antioxidants, including glutathione, in their bodies. This deficiency can contribute to the inflammation and oxidative damage associated with the condition.[89]

One study that caught my attention examined oxidative stress in endometriosis patients. The researchers found that glutathione peroxidase, an enzyme that uses glutathione to neutralize harmful peroxides, was expressed at higher levels in endometriotic cells compared to healthy controls.[90] This suggested to me that my body might be trying to compensate for increased oxidative stress by ramping up its glutathione-dependent defenses.

I was particularly interested in glutathione's detoxification properties. Research has shown that glutathione helps eliminate environmental toxins like dioxins and PCBs, which have been linked to endometriosis development. Given my exposure to various environmental pollutants while being in the Air Force, supporting my body's natural detox pathways seemed like a smart strategy.

But what really caught my attention was glutathione's potential impact on fertility. As someone hoping to start a family despite my endometriosis diagnosis, I was excited to learn about its benefits for reproductive health. Studies have shown that glutathione can improve egg quality by protecting oocytes from oxidative damage during their development.[91] This is crucial because egg quality is one of the factors most affected by aging, and it's particularly relevant for women with endometriosis who may already face fertility challenges.

I was fascinated to discover that higher levels of glutathione in follicular fluid have been associated with increased fertilization rates during IVF procedures. This gave me hope that supporting my glutathione levels might improve my chances of conception, whether naturally or through assisted reproductive technologies.

Moreover, I learned that glutathione plays a vital role in early embryo development and implantation. It's involved in forming the male pronucleus after fertilization, meaning it helps those first critical cellular steps that develop a fertilized egg into a viable embryo. This made me think about how glutathione might not only help me conceive but also support a healthy pregnancy.

While investigating glutathione supplementation, I learned that oral glutathione can be difficult for the body to absorb. However, I came across a study that used liposomal glutathione, a more bioavailable form. The researchers found that taking 500 mg or 1000 mg of liposomal glutathione daily for four weeks increased glutathione levels in various body compartments and improved markers of oxidative stress.

Another approach I used was supplementing with N-acetylcysteine (NAC), a precursor to glutathione. Some endometriosis patients have reported benefits from NAC supplementation, though individual results can vary. NAC not only supports glutathione production but also has its own anti-inflammatory properties that could potentially help with endometriosis symptoms and fertility.[92] I found myself cycling between 500 mg glutathione and 600 mg NAC to see which would help with ovulation and menstrual pain the most (it seemed to be a tie!).

Whether for managing endometriosis, improving egg quality, or simply aging a little more gracefully, glutathione became one of the quiet foundations of my routine.

Vitamin D

As I was going through all my medical records to write this book, I noticed that my vitamin D levels were never tested (perhaps REs test them now?). Having been deficient in the past, and after years of hearing wellness experts emphasize its importance, I had my levels tested and tracked.

While I was already taking vitamin D, I hadn't fully appreciated its critical role in fertility. Often called the "sunshine vitamin," I initially thought of it as mainly supporting bone health, immunity, and muscle and brain function. But I came to learn that vitamin D behaves more like a hormone than a traditional vitamin, with receptors found throughout the reproductive system to include the ovaries, uterus, and even sperm cells. This hormonal action is essential for key reproductive processes like steroidogenesis, follicle maturation, endometrial receptivity, and sperm development. One study that caught my attention found that women with sufficient vitamin D levels were nearly twice as likely to conceive through IVF compared to those with a deficiency.[93] This statistic gave me hope that addressing any potential vitamin D issues could improve my chances of success.

I also learned about vitamin D's role in egg quality and development. Apparently, it helps regulate anti-Müllerian hormone (AMH) production.[94] Some research even suggests that vitamin D supplementation can improve AMH levels and antral follicle count in women with deficiencies.

Beyond conception, I was intrigued to find out that vitamin D may play a role in supporting early pregnancy. It seems to be important for proper implantation and placental function. This made me grateful that I was already taking this important supplement. I keep my levels between 50–70 ng/mL.

SLEEP, WEARABLES, AND WHY MY SCREENS GLOW RED

After diving deep into the world of mitochondria, fertility, and longevity supplements, one truth became crystal clear: you can't out-supplement bad sleep. That's a tough pill to swallow when you've got little ones waking up at 2 a.m. asking for snacks, but I tried my best.

When our second daughter, Aliana, was born, I bought my first Oura ring. It quickly confirmed what I already suspected: newborn sleep equals zero readiness. Ha! Still, I loved being able to track my data: heart rate variability (HRV), deep sleep, body temperature trends, and more. It gave me insight and agency at a time when everything else felt like chaos.

Over time, sleep optimization became nonnegotiable. It didn't cost me much, mostly a little discipline and intention. I tried sleep medications and supplements over the years, but nothing restored my sleep like good sleep hygiene. Stress had made my sleep terrible (probably due to the cortisol), and when I retired, it definitely improved with these simple low-cost or free habits:

- Consistent sleep and wake times (even on weekends).
- No screens at least an hour before bed if possible. If not, I use blue light blocker glasses and I turn my screens to red.
- Bedroom temp cooled to 65–69°F.
- Blackout curtains and white noise.
- Magnesium before bed.

While serving as commander of the 649th Munitions Squadron at Hill Air Force Base, I had the opportunity to merge my personal passion with professional innovation. I procured wearables and supported a study called RATE: Rapid Analysis of Threat Exposure. The study explored whether smartwatches and rings could detect COVID.[95] Additionally, my team and I used wearable data to start conversations about health, not punishments, not extra workouts, but support. The big idea? Preventive, personalized wellness that could eventually replace outdated models like the annual fitness test. We were one of the first units to test the concept through the Air Force Research Lab's Beta Test initiative for the Space Force and while we didn't solve everything, I like to think we laid some groundwork for better, tech-driven health support in the military (not spying!). And recognition that sleep and recovery are just as important as exercise.

Sleep, it turns out, is a force multiplier. It's one of the cheapest, most potent tools for recovery, hormone balance, rebuilding muscles, immune resilience, and yes, fertility.

These days, my screens glow red after sunset and I have installed lights to mimic sundown. Red-light filters block blue wavelengths that suppress melatonin, the hormone that cues sleep and regulates reproductive rhythms. Swapping harsh blue light for warm amber tones helps my body wind down naturally, syncing my circadian rhythm with the same system that governs hormone balance, ovulation, and rest. It's a small shift with a big payoff: deeper sleep, steadier energy, and calmer evenings.

You can track your HRV, stack your supplements, and optimize your mitochondria, but in the end?

Nothing replaces good sleep.

Trust me. I've tried.

WHAT I LET GO AND WHAT I ADDED STARTING POINT

You just read about a *lot*. Take a breath and ask:

Based on what I know about my body, labs, symptoms, energy, what's the one thing I could do today that would likely move the needle the most?

Need a nudge? Start small, stay curious, and consider these evidence-backed, low-lift, high-return starting points:

- **Vitamin D**
  Haven't tested lately? Start here. Most people are deficient, and optimizing levels (50–70 ng/mL) supports everything from fertility to mood to immune resilience.
- **Magnesium at Night**
  Improves sleep, reduces stress, supports hormone function. Easy win. Start with 250–400 mg of magnesium glycinate or threonate.
- **Ubiquinol (CoQ10)**
  Especially if you're 35+, this supports mitochondrial health and egg quality. Dose: 200–600 mg/day.
- **Swap One Endocrine Disruptor.**
  Just one. Maybe the mascara. Maybe the "fresh linen" plug-in. You don't have to do it all today; just remove one known toxin or stressor from your environment.

Choose the one that feels most aligned with *your* story, not someone else's. Because the best supplement stack is the one your body actually responds to and your brain can keep track of. If you only remember one thing from this chapter, let it be this: healing isn't about adding more. It's about listening more.

EPILOGUE:

The Journey Continues

I recently came across a concept on a podcast that truly resonated with me: *Freudenspanne*, a term that captures "the joy in your life," especially as it relates to longevity and the quality of our experiences. The moment I heard it, something clicked. I couldn't stop thinking about it.

Freudenspanne reminded me of *eudaimonia*, the ancient Greek idea I mentioned earlier in living a life of fulfillment, virtue, and purpose, rather than simply chasing pleasure. Both center around what truly gives life meaning and what I have been learning all along: that longevity isn't about adding years to life, it's about adding life to our years.

As I reflect on my own journey, I see how these concepts have taken root in my life. I wouldn't trade a single step along our path, not the setbacks, the late nights, the research rabbit holes, or even the heartbreaks. Because all of it led us to our children. It gave us a deeper understanding of our biology. And it helped us align our lives with what we value most.

And here's what I hope you take away: you don't have to do everything. You just have to start, by letting go of one thing, or adding one aligned choice. That could be switching off your phone at night, pausing for a few minutes of intentional breath, or simply becoming more aware of what fuels or drains you. You don't have to buy expensive supplements or completely overhaul your life to move toward joy, healing, or wholeness. Alignment doesn't require a budget, it requires intention.

Also know this: this didn't happen overnight. My transformation, our transformation, was years in the making. One shift, one question, one insight at a time. Give yourself permission to go slow.

Finally, be willing to question the beliefs that quietly shape your life. Many of us carry invisible scripts, stories we've absorbed over time about what we're capable of, what we deserve, or what's possible. These aren't facts; they're often outdated ideas that no longer align with who we actually are. Letting go of even one limiting belief can open up space for something new: a fuller breath, a more grounded step, a clearer connection to joy.

Through it all, we've found ourselves living not just longer, but fuller, anchored in purpose and joy. The struggles, the triumphs, the doubts, and the breakthroughs have all contributed to our *Freudenspanne*, our "span of joy," and the pursuit of something much more lasting than comfort: *eudaimonia*.

If our story has inspired you, touched something within you, or helped you reflect on your own joy span, then sharing it will have been worth it. Because life isn't only about how long we live but how deeply we feel, love, and find meaning along the way.

Gratitude

To my husband, Matt,
The rock to my roll. The almond butter to my hormonal jelly. The man who never flinched, not even when giving me those first progesterone shots, back when I couldn't do it myself. You lived this journey with me...every crazy, miraculous moment. Our family exists because of your steady love, tireless perfectionism, and that uncanny ability to function on even less sleep than when you were pulling alert duty. LUM.

To Avery, Aliana, and Declan,
You are the impossible made manifest. Proof that miracles are real and that the universe has a wicked sense of timing. Thank you for choosing us. (Now please go to bed on time and sleep all night.)

To my amazing circle of friends and family,
While I could not name every parent, sibling, or loved one in these pages, please know this story does not exist without you. Your prayers, patience, presence, and quiet faith held us and kept us sane. Thank you for your unrelenting support and patience, and for pretending to understand acronyms like FSH, TWW, and POAS.

Nicole and Abby, my brutally honest beta readers, I both love you and mildly resent you. You made this book better and would not let it be less than it could be.

Thank you for listening to my endless wellness learnings, rants, and lectures, and for letting me lovingly push supplements, tinctures, and bizarre teas into your lives. Gifts of love are my love language. You just happen to receive yours in capsule form.

To my colleagues and fellow veterans,
I could not have asked for better people to work with in my second act, whom I honestly consider friends more than coworkers. Especially to those who found the courage to write and share their own stories, you reminded me that our words matter.

To my book coach, Zach, and book designer, Mel,
You kept me accountable, encouraged me when I was overwhelmed, and gently reminded me that done is better than perfect.

To my yoga family,
Thank you for sweating it out beside me, listening without judgment, and holding space on and off the mat. Your presence kept me grounded, literally and spiritually, even when I was upside down in life.

To my fellow infertility warriors,
For every appointment, injection, heartbreak, and moment of fierce, quiet hope, you are not alone. You are brave, resilient, and stronger than you realize. May your story unfold with its own miracle, whether it looks exactly as you dreamed or nothing like you imagined (both things can be true).

About the Author

Naomi Franchetti is a retired U.S. Air Force officer, two-time commander, yoga teacher and pilates instructor, and ICF-certified Human Potential Coach. Her infertility journey led her to explore the science of longevity, the power of mindset, and the surprising role of surrender.

Today, she serves as Director of Coaching at The Arbinger Institute. She also helps others protect their fertility and longevity, optimize energy, and reclaim what feels out of reach, whether that is parenthood or peak performance.

From Waiting to Wonder is her first book and the story she never expected to live, let alone tell.

www.chettilifeelevated.com

Endnotes

1 This definition comes from Dave Asprey. It generally refers to a broad range of practices aimed at enhancing physical and mental performance, often through science-based interventions, self-experimentation, or lifestyle optimization. It can include everything from taking supplements and tracking sleep to using wearable tech, red-light therapy, or nootropics aka brain supplements.

2 Bruce H. Lipton. *The Biology of Belief: Unleashing the Power of Consciousness, Matter & Miracles* (Carlsbad, CA: Hay House, 2005).

3 Randine A. Lewis. *The Infertility Cure: The Ancient Chinese Wellness Program for Getting Pregnant and Having Healthy Babies* (New York: Little, Brown, 2008).

4 Coyle, Daniel. *The Culture Code: The Secrets of Highly Successful Groups*. New York: Bantam Books, 2018.

5 "Military Women: On the Hook for Infertility?" IVF Minnesota. Accessed October 12 and 19. https://ivfminnesota.com/military-women/.

6 Service Women's Action Network. 2018. *Survey of Active-Duty, Guard, and Reserve Servicewomen and Female Veterans on Women's Health and Wellness*. https://www.military.com/daily-news/2018/12/13/

-nearly-40-percent-active-duty-women-report-fertility-problems.html.

7 Hillcoat, Alexandra, Jaya Prakash, Leah Martin, Yu Zhang, Gabriela Rosa, Henning Tiemeier, Nicole Torres, Vicente Mustieles, Charleen D. Adams, and Carmen Messerlian. 2023. "Trauma and Female Reproductive Health Across the Lifecourse: Motivating a Research Agenda for the Future of Women's Health." *Human Reproduction* 38 (8): 1429–1444. https://doi.org/10.1093/humrep/dead087.

8 Lucy E. Stirland, Biniyam A. Ayele, Catherine CorreaLopera, and Virginia E. Sturm.*"Authenticity and Brain Health: A ValuesBased Perspective and Cultural Education Approach,"*
Frontiers in Neurology 14 (2023): Article 1206142. https://doi.org/10.3389/fneur.2023.1206142.

9 Stirland, Lucy E., Biniyam A. Ayele, Catherine Correa-Lopera, and Virginia E. Sturm. 2023. "Authenticity and Brain Health: A Values-Based Perspective and Cultural Education Approach." *Frontiers in Neurology* 14:1206142. https://doi.org/10.3389/fneur.2023.1206142.

10 Rahm, T., et al. "Measuring the frequency of emotions—validation of the Scale of Positive and Negative Experience." *PLoS ONE* (2017).

Stirland, L. E. et al. "Authenticity and Brain Health: A Values-Based Perspective and Cultural Education Approach." *Frontiers in Neurology* 14:1206142.(August 1, 2023).

11 Mayo Clinic. "Chronic stress puts your health at risk." Last modified July 31, 2023. https://www.mayoclinic.org/healthy-lifestyle/stress-management/in-depth/stress/art-20046037

12 "Female Infertility as a Result of Stress-Related Hormonal Changes." *GREM Journal*. Accessed October 12 and 19. https://gremjournal.com/journal/0203-2022/female-infertility-as-a-result-of-stress-related-hormonal-changes/.

13 Sara Szal Gottfried and Nancy Wu, *The Autoimmune Cure: Healing the Trauma and Other Triggers That Have Turned Your Body Against You* (New York: HarperCollins, 2024).

14 Hillcoat, Alexandra, Jaya Prakash, Leah Martin, Yu Zhang, Gabriela Rosa, Henning Tiemeier, Nicole Torres, Vicente Mustieles, Charleen D. Adams, and Carmen Messerlian. 2023. "Trauma and Female Reproductive Health Across the Lifecourse: Motivating a Research Agenda for the Future of Women's Health." *Human Reproduction* 38 (8): 1429–1444. https://doi.org/10.1093/humrep/dead087.

15 Namazi, Mahin, Ebrahim Ghazanfarpour, Marziyeh Mirzaii Najmabadi, and Mamak Shams. "The Effectiveness of Cognitive Behavioral Therapy on Depression, Anxiety, and Quality of Life in Women with Infertility: A Systematic Review and Meta-Analysis." *Journal of Affective Disorders Reports* 9 (2022): 100363. https://pubmed.ncbi.nlm.nih.gov/36239578/

16 Li, Xue, Lei Tang, and Xiaohui Jiang. "The Effect of Mindfulness-Based Stress Reduction on Anxiety and Depression in Women with Infertility: A Meta-Analysis." *Journal of Affective Disorders* 310 (2022): 168–177. https://pmc.ncbi.nlm.nih.gov/articles/PMC10498716/

17 Chan, Cecilia Lai Wan, Dennis Yuk Ming Lo, and Fiona Ka Wai Ngai. "A Randomized Controlled Trial of a Body–Mind–Spirit Intervention for Fertility Patients." *Frontiers in Psychology* 12 (2021): 643395. https://www.frontiersin.org/journals/psychology/articles/10.3389/fpsyg.2021.643395/full

18 Ricciardi, Emiliano, et al. "How the Brain Heals Emotional Wounds: The Functional Neuroanatomy of Forgiveness." *Frontiers in Human Neuroscience* 7 (2013): 839. https://pmc.ncbi.nlm.nih.gov/articles/PMC3856773/

19 Pan, Xiaohong, et al. "The Neural Basis of Forgiveness: A Voxel-Based Morphometry Study." *Scientific Reports* 7, no. 1 (2017): 16868. https://www.nature.com/articles/s41598-017-16868-3

20 Johns Hopkins Medicine. "Forgiveness: Your Health Depends on It." Published April 2020. https://www.hopkinsmedicine.org/health/wellness-and-prevention/forgiveness-your-health-depends-on-it

21 Austin Biotec. "Fitness Function Foundation: For a Fully Extended Life." Accessed December 1, 2024. https://www.austinbiotec.com.

22 Jin, Xiaojin, Yujie Wang, Jingyi Zhang, Yilin Wang, Yue Yin, Yingying Qin, and Zi-Jiang Chen. "Molecular and Genetic Insights into Human Ovarian Aging from Single-Nuclei Multi-Omics Analyses." Nature Aging 4, no. 11 (2024): 1214-1231.

23 Chavarro, Jorge E., Janet W. Rich-Edwards, Bernard A. Rosner, and Walter C. Willett. "Diet and Lifestyle in the Prevention of Ovulatory Disorder Infertility." *Obstetrics & Gynecology* 110, no. 5 (2007): 1050-1058

24 Palomba, Stefano, Angela Falbo, Fulvio Zullo, and Fortunato Orio. "Evidence-Based and Potential Benefits of Metformin in the Polycystic Ovary Syndrome: A Comprehensive Review." *Endocrine Reviews* 30, no. 1 (2009): 1-50.

25 Jungheim, Emily S., and Kelle H. Moley. "Current Knowledge of Obesity's Effects in the Pre- and Periconceptional Periods and Avenues for Future Research." *American Journal of Obstetrics and Gynecology* 203, no. 6 (2010): 525-530.

26 Tatone, Carla, Francesco Amicarelli, Maria C. Carbone, Paolo Monteleone, Daniela Caserta, Raffaele Marci, and Roberto Colonna. "Cellular and Molecular Aspects of Ovarian Follicle Ageing." *Human Reproduction Update* 14, no. 2 (2008): 131-142.

27 Shukla, Alpana P., Roxana G. Iliescu, Christine E. Thomas, and Louis J. Aronne. "Food Order Has a Significant Impact on Postprandial Glucose and Insulin Levels." *Diabetes Care* 38, no. 7 (2015): e98-e99.

28 Agarwal, Ashok, Anamar Aponte-Mellado, Beena J. Premkumar, Amani Shaman, and Sajal Gupta. "The Effects of Oxidative Stress on Female Reproduction: A Review." *Reproductive Biology and Endocrinology* 10, no. 1 (2012): 49.

Sutton-McDowall, Melanie L., Robert B. Gilchrist, and Jeremy G. Thompson. "The Pivotal Role of Glucose Metabolism in Determining Oocyte Developmental Competence." Reproduction 139, no. 4 (2010): 685-695.

29 Zhang, Xiao-Yang, Xiao-Hua Wu, Shu-Fang Zhou, Yan-Ling Wang, Jie Xu, and Xiao-Ming Liang. "Deficit of Mitochondria-Derived ATP During Oxidative Stress Impairs Mouse MII Oocyte Spindles." *Cell Research* 16, no. 10 (2006): 841-850.

30 "Should You Try Holotropic Breathwork? Here's What It

Does." *Cleveland Clinic.* Accessed October 12 and 19. https://health.clevelandclinic.org/should-you-try-holotropic-breathwork-heres-what-it-does.

"The History of Breathwork: Origins of This Ancient Healing Practice." *Breathless Expeditions.* Accessed October 12 and 19. https://breathlessexpeditions.com/origins-history-of-breathwork/.

31 "What Is Holotropic Breathwork And Can You Get High From It?" *VICE.* Accessed October 12 and 19. https://www.vice.com/en/article/what-is-holotropic-breathwork-and-can-you-get-high-from-it/.

32 Weil, Andrew. "Breathing Exercises: 4-7-8 Breath." Video. Dr. Weil. September 9, 2024. https://www.drweil.com/videos-features/videos/breathing-exercises-4-7-8-breath/.

33 Zaccaro, Andrea, Antonio Piarulli, Gabriele Laurino, Giacomo Garbella, and Giuseppe Barbieri. "How Breath-Control Can Change Your Life: A Systematic Review on Psycho-Physiological Correlates of Slow Breathing." *Frontiers in Psychology* 13 (2022): 927751. https://doi.org/10.3389/fpsyg.2022.927751.

34 Almahayni, Omar, and Louise Hammond. "Does the Wim Hof Method have a beneficial impact on physiological and psychological health-related outcomes?" PLOS ONE 19, no. 3 (March 13, 2024): e0286933. https://doi.org/10.1371/journal.pone.0286933.

35 Kopplin, Cristopher Siegfried, and Louisa Rosenthal. "The Positive Effects of Combined Breathing Techniques and Cold Exposure on Perceived Stress: A Randomized Trial." *Current Psychology*, October 7, 2022. https://doi.org/10.1007/s12144-022-03739-y.

36 Faulkner, John A., Lisa K. Larkin, and Christopher R. Claflin. "Age-Related Changes in the Structure and Function of Skeletal Muscles." *Journal of Applied Physiology* 95, no. 4 (2013): 1527-1537.

37 Iannuzzi-Sucich, Michele, Richard J. Prestwood, and Anne M. Kenny. "Prevalence of Sarcopenia and Predictors of Skeletal Muscle Mass in Healthy, Older Men and Women." *Journals of Gerontology* 57, no. 12 (2002): M772-M777.

38 Janssen, Ian, Steven B. Heymsfield, and Robert Ross. "Low Relative Skeletal Muscle Mass (Sarcopenia) in Older Persons is Associated with Functional Impairment and Physical Disability." *Journal of the American Geriatrics Society* 50, no. 5 (2002): 889-896.

39 De Souza, Mary Jane, et al. "Excessive Exercise and Female Reproductive Health: The Role of Energy Availability and Hormonal Adaptations." *Fertility and Sterility* 115, no. 3 (2021): 552-563.

40 Rickenlund, Anette, et al. "Amenorrhea in Female Athletes is Associated with Leptin and Energy Availability." *Journal of Clinical*

Endocrinology & Metabolism 89, no. 2 (2004): 793-798.

41 West, Daniel W. D., et al. "Effects of Resistance Training on Female Metabolic Health: A Systematic Review." *Sports Medicine* 49, no. 3 (2019): 437-450.

42 Jin, Xiaojin, Yujie Wang, Jingyi Zhang, Yilin Wang, Yue Yin, Yingying Qin, and Zi-Jiang Chen. "Molecular and Genetic Insights into Human Ovarian Aging from Single-Nuclei Multi-Omics Analyses." Nature Aging 4, no. 11 (2024): 1214-1231.

43 "Endocrine Disrupting Chemicals Research." *National Institutes of Health.* Accessed October 12 and 19. https://pmc.ncbi.nlm.nih.gov/articles/PMC2726844/.

"Phthalates and Human Health." *Nature.* Accessed October 12 and 19. https://www.nature.com/articles/s41370-022-00517-7.

"Endocrine Disruptors and Reproductive Health." *Frontiers in Endocrinology.* Accessed October 26. https://www.frontiersin.org/journals/endocrinology/articles/10.3389/fendo.2024.1478655/full.

44 "Six Tips to Avoid Phthalates After Study Highlights Health Harms." *Environmental Working Group.* Accessed October 12 and 19. https://www.ewg.org/news-insights/news/2021/10/six-tips-avoid-phthalates-after-study-highlights-health-harms-billion.

45 Whitten, Ari. The Ultimate Guide to Red Light Therapy: How to Use Red and Near-Infrared Light Therapy for Anti-Aging, Fat Loss, Muscle Gain, Performance Enhancement, and Brain Optimization. CreateSpace Independent Publishing Platform, 2018.

46 Hamblin, Michael R. "Photobiomodulation or Low-Level Laser Therapy." *BBA Clinical* 5 (2013): 159-174.

47 Ferraresi, Cleber, Michael R. Hamblin, and Vanderlei S. Bagnato. "Low-Level Laser (Light) Therapy on Muscle Tissue: Performance, Fatigue and Repair Benefited by the Power of Light." *Photonics & Lasers in Medicine* 4, no. 3 (2016): 231-244.

48 Sato, K., et al. "Efficacy of 830-nm Light Therapy for Assisted Reproductive Technology Patients with Long-Term Infertility." *Laser Therapy* 21, no. 1 (2012): 27-30.

49 Abdel-Salam, Z., et al. "Effects of Low-Level Laser Therapy on Endometrial Thickness and Pregnancy Rates in Infertile Women." *Fertility and Sterility* 101, no. 5 (2014): 1186-1191.

50 Vladoiu, S., et al. "Low-Level Laser Therapy and Its Impact on Female Infertility: A Systematic Review." *Journal of Reproductive Medicine* 63, no. 2 (2018): 123-135.

51 Gonzalez-Lima, F., and A. Auchter. "Protection Against

Neurodegeneration with Low-Dose Methylene Blue and Near-Infrared Light." *Neurobiology of Aging* 36, no. 2 (2015): 210-222.

52 Asadi Shahmirzadi, Azar, Daniel Edgar, Chen-Yu Liao, Yueh-Mei Hsu, Michael Lucanic, Azar Asadi Shahmirzadi, Colin D. Wiley, et al. "AlphaKetoglutarate, an Endogenous Metabolite, Extends Lifespan and Compresses Morbidity in Aging Mice." *Cell Metabolism* 32, no. 3 (September 1, 2020): 447–456.e6. https://doi.org/10.1016/j.cmet.2020.08.004.

53 Xu, Chang, Yexian Yuan, and Cha Zhang, et al. "Smooth Muscle AKG/OXGR1 Signaling Regulates Epididymal Fluid AcidBase Balance and Sperm Maturation." *Life Metabolism* 1, no. 1 (2022): 67. https://doi.org/10.1093/lifemeta/lsac005.

54 Sui, Qi, Panpan Chen, Xuejing Fang, Li Liu, Mei Lin, Weiwei Wang, and Qian Zhao. "AlphaKetoglutarate Supplementation Ameliorates Ovarian Reserve and Oocyte Quality Decline with Aging in Mice." *Cell Reports* (2023). https://pubmed.ncbi.nlm.nih.gov/37098377.

55 Eisenberg, Tobias, et al. "Cardioprotection and lifespan extension by the natural polyamine spermidine." *Nature Medicine* 22, no. 12 (2016): 1428–1438.

56 Schroeder, Sabrina, et al. "Dietary spermidine improves cognitive function." *Cell Reports* 32, no. 5 (2020): 108078.

57 Madeo, Frank, et al. "Spermidine in health and disease." *Science* 359, no. 6374 (2018): eaan2788.

58 Wirth, Michael, et al. "The effect of spermidine on memory performance in older adults at risk for dementia: A randomized controlled trial." Aging 10, no. 19 (2018): 3810–3827.

59 Wang, Tian, et al. "Polyamine metabolite spermidine rejuvenates oocyte quality by enhancing mitophagy during female reproductive aging." *Frontiers in Cell and Developmental Biology* 10 (2022): 813652.

60 "DHEA and Fertility." *Fertility Pregnancy Acupuncture Clinic.* Accessed September 14, 2024. https://fertilitypregnancyacupunctureclinic.com.au/dhea-to-improve-fertility/.

"Low Levels of Dehydroepiandrosterone Sulfate Are Associated with Infertility." *National Institutes of Health.* Accessed September 14, 2024. https://pmc.ncbi.nlm.nih.gov/articles/PMC10118840/.

61 "Effects of Dehydroepiandrosterone (DHEA) Supplementation on Fertility." *National Institutes of Health.* Accessed September 14, 2024. https://pmc.ncbi.nlm.nih.gov/articles/PMC10304479/.

62 "Effect of Dehydroepiandrosterone on Oocyte and Embryo Yields." *Human Reproduction.* Accessed September 14, 2024. https://academic.oup.com/humrep/article-abstract/21/11/2845/2939179?login=f

alse&redirectedFrom=fulltext.

63 "The Benefits of DHEA Supplements for Fertility." *Rescripted.* Accessed September 14, 2024. https://rescripted.com/posts/what-are-the-benefits-of-dhea-supplements-for-fertility.

64 "Low Levels of Dehydroepiandrosterone Sulfate Are Associated with Infertility." *National Institutes of Health.* Accessed September 14, 2024. https://pmc.ncbi.nlm.nih.gov/articles/PMC10118840/.

65 "Dehydroepiandrosterone: A Panacea for the Ageing Ovary?" *National Institutes of Health.* Accessed September 14, 2024. https://pmc.ncbi.nlm.nih.gov/articles/PMC4534532/.

66 "Coenzyme Q10 Restores Oocyte Mitochondrial Function and Fertility During Reproductive Aging." *National Institutes of Health.* Accessed September 21, 2024. https://pmc.ncbi.nlm.nih.gov/articles/PMC4568976/.

67 Coenzyme Q10, α-Tocopherol, and Oxidative Stress Could Be Key Factors in Improving Female Fertility." *Wiley Online Library.* Accessed September 21, 2024. https://onlinelibrary.wiley.com/doi/10.1155/2015/827941.

68 "CoQ10 for Fertility: How This Antioxidant Can Help Improve Egg Quality." *Illume Fertility.* Accessed September 21, 2024. https://www.illumefertility.com/fertility-blog/coq10-for-fertility-improve-egg-quality.

69 "Pyrroloquinoline Quinone Stimulates Mitochondrial Biogenesis Through cAMP Response Element-Binding Protein Phosphorylation and Increased PGC-1α Expression." *National Institutes of Health.* Accessed September 21, 2024. https://pmc.ncbi.nlm.nih.gov/articles/PMC2804159/.

70 "Pyrroloquinoline Quinone (PQQ) Protects Mitochondrial Function of HEI-OC1 Cells Under Premature Senescence." *npj Aging.* Accessed September 21, 2024. https://www.nature.com/articles/s41514-022-00083-0.

"Pyrroloquinoline Quinone Promotes Human Mesenchymal Stem Cell Proliferation." *Stem Cell Research & Therapy.* Accessed September 21, 2024. https://stemcellres.biomedcentral.com/articles/10.1186/s13287-024-03705-4.

71 "PQQ Dietary Supplementation Prevents Alkylating Agent-Induced Damage." *National Institutes of Health.* Accessed September 21, 2024. https://pmc.ncbi.nlm.nih.gov/articles/PMC8948422/.

72 "Pyrroloquinoline-Quinone to Reduce Fat Accumulation and Ameliorate Metabolic Dysfunction." *Frontiers in Molecular Biosciences.* Accessed September 21, 2024. https://www.frontiersin.org/journals/molecular-biosciences/articles/10.3389/fmolb.2023.1200025/full.

73 "Protection Against Neurodegeneration With Low-Dose Methylene Blue." *Frontiers in Cellular Neuroscience.* Accessed September 21, 2024. https://www.frontiersin.org/journals/cellular-neuroscience/articles/10.3389/fncel.2015.00179/full.

"From Mitochondrial Function to Neuroprotection—An Emerging Role for Methylene Blue." *PubMed.* Accessed September 21, 2024. https://pubmed.ncbi.nlm.nih.gov/28840449/.

74 "Methylene Blue Shows Promise for Improving Short-Term Memory: Study in Humans." *ScienceDaily.* Accessed September 21, 2024. https://www.sciencedaily.com/releases/2016/06/160628072028.htm.

75 "Methylene Blue Preserves Cytochrome Oxidase Activity." *Frontiers in Cellular Neuroscience.* Accessed September 21, 2024. https://www.frontiersin.org/journals/cellular-neuroscience/articles/10.3389/fncel.2020.00130/full.

"Therapeutic Benefits of Methylene Blue on Cognitive Impairment." *PubMed.* Accessed September 21, 2024. https://pubmed.ncbi.nlm.nih.gov/25079810/.

76 Schwalfenberg, Gerry K., and Stephen J. Genuis. "The Importance of Magnesium in Clinical Healthcare." *Scientifica* 2017 (2017): 4179326. https://doi.org/10.1155/2017/4179326.

77 Wang, Z., et al. "Berberine Improves Ovulation and Endometrial Receptivity in Polycystic Ovary Syndrome." *Journal of Clinical Endocrinology & Metabolism* 106, no. 10 (2021): 2825–2838.

78 Xie, L., et al. "Berberine for Reproductive and Metabolic Outcomes in Women with Polycystic Ovary Syndrome: A Systematic Review and Meta-Analysis." *Medicine* 98, no. 8 (2019): e14962.

Di Pierro, F., et al. "Clinical Efficacy, Safety, and Tolerability of a New Formulation of Berberine Phytosome in Polycystic Ovary Syndrome: A Randomized, Double-Blind, Placebo-Controlled Clinical Trial." *Phytotherapy Research* 37, no. 1 (2023): 123–131.

79 Gunnars, K. "Berberine — A Powerful Supplement with Many Benefits." *Healthline*, June 29, 2023. https://www.healthline.com/nutrition/berberine-diabetes.

80 Endurance Research. "Compared to Oral Berberine, Oral Dihydroberberine Achieves a Higher Blood Berberine Level at a Lower Dose, Study Shows." *Endurance Research*, February 16, 2021. https://enduranceresearch.com/blogs/news/compared-to-oral-berberine-oral-dihydroberberine-achieves-a-higher-blood-berberine-level-at-a-lower-dose-study-shows.

81 Tamura, Hiroshi, et al. "Melatonin and Female Reproduction." *Journal of Obstetrics and Gynaecology Research* 40, no. 1 (2014): 1-11. Accessed September 21, 2024. https://pubmed.ncbi.nlm.nih.gov/24628045/.

82 Yamamoto, T., et al. "Nicotinamide Mononucleotide (NMN) Restores Fertility in Aging Mice through Improvement of Oocyte Quality." *Cell Reports* 33, no. 4 (2020): 108423.

83 Khavinson, Vladimir Kh., and Sergey D. Trofimova. "Peptide Bioregulators as a New Strategy for Healthy Aging." *Biogerontology* 13, no. 3 (2012): 219–223. Accessed September 21, 2024. https://link.springer.com/article/10.1134/S2079057012040091.

84 Liu, M., et al. "Resveratrol Rescues Oocyte Mitochondrial Function and Fertility in Mice with Maternal Aging." *Aging* 10, no. 9 (2018): 2386–2397.

85 Bertoldo, Michael J., Diah R. Listijono, Wei Jun Ho, et al. "NAD Repletion Rescues Female Fertility during Reproductive Aging." *Cell Metabolism* 32, no. 4 (2020): 1–16.

86 Takeo, Shun, Dai Sato, Kosuke Kimura, et al. "Short-Term Resveratrol Treatment Restored the Quality of Oocytes in Aging Mice." *Aging (Albany NY)* 14, no. 13 (2022): 10340–10359.

87 Xu, Y., et al. "Resveratrol Supplementation Improves Ovarian Stimulation Response and Outcome of in Vitro Fertilization-Embryo Transfer in Older Women: A Randomized Controlled Trial." *Fertility and Sterility* 112, no. 5 (2019): 928–935.

88 Ivanov, D. S., et al. "Epitalon Protects Against Post-Ovulatory Aging-Related Damage of Mouse Oocytes In Vitro." *Aging* 14, no. 7 (2022): 3147-3162. Accessed September 21, 2024. https://www.researchgate.net/publication/359930041_Epitalon_protects_against_post-ovulatory_aging-related_damage_of_mouse_oocytes_in_vitro.

89 Mukherjee, S., Sharma, S., and Agarwal, A. "Review on the Role of Glutathione on Oxidative Stress and Infertility." *JBRA Assisted Reproduction* 22, no. 1 (2018): 61–66.

90 Porpora, M. G., Brunelli, R., Costa, G., Imperiale, L., Krasnowska, E. K., Lisi, L., and Sangiuliano, C. "A Promising Medical Treatment for Endometriosis: An Observational Cohort Study on N-Acetylcysteine." *Gynecological Endocrinology* 29, no. 8 (2013): 733–736.

Anastasi, E., Granato, T., Marconi, M., Manganaro, L., Tomei, F., and Fuggetta, E. "The Effect of N-Acetylcysteine on Endometriosis-Related Pain and Quality of Life: A Randomized Controlled Trial." *Journal of Endometriosis and Pelvic Pain Disorders* 15, no. 1 (2023): 29–35.

91 Singh, A. K., Chattopadhyay, R., Chakravarty, B., and Chaudhury, K. "Markers of Oxidative Stress in Follicular Fluid of Women with Endometriosis and Tubal Infertility Undergoing IVF." *Reproductive Toxicology* 29, no. 1 (2010): 136–142.

92 Porpora, M. G., Brunelli, R., Costa, G., Imperiale, L., Krasnowska, E. K., Lisi, L., and Sangiuliano, C. "A Promising Medical

Treatment for Endometriosis: An Observational Cohort Study on N-Acetylcysteine." *Gynecological Endocrinology* 29, no. 8 (2013): 733–736.

93 Aleyasin, A., Hosseini, M. A., Mahdavi, A., Safdarian, L., Fallahi, P., Mohajeri, M. R., Abbasi, M., & Esfahani, F. (2011). Predictive value of the level of vitamin D in follicular fluid on the outcome of assisted reproductive technology. *European Journal of Obstetrics & Gynecology and Reproductive Biology*, 159(1), 132–137.

Chu, J., Gallos, I., Tobias, A., Tan, B., Eapen, A., Coomarasamy, A., & Wong, W. (2018). Vitamin D and assisted reproductive treatment outcome: a systematic review and meta-analysis. *Human Reproduction*, 33(1), 65–80.

Rudick, B., Ingles, S., Chung, K., Stanczyk, F., Paulson, R., & Bendikson, K. (2012). Characterizing the influence of vitamin D levels on IVF outcomes. *Human Reproduction*, 27(11), 3321–3327.

94 Irani, M., Minkoff, H., Seifer, D. B., Merhi, Z., & Maclin, V. (2015). Vitamin D supplementation significantly increases serum anti-Müllerian hormone levels in infertile women. *Endocrinology*, 156(8), 2808–2814.

95 Todd Cromar, "649th MUNS Tests Wearables to Detect COVID-19," *Hill Air Force Base*, December 1, 2020, https://www.hill.af.mil/News/Article-Display/Article/2439001/649th-muns-tests-wearables-to-detect-covid-19/.

www.ingramcontent.com/pod-product-compliance
Lightning Source LLC
Chambersburg PA
CBHW060414130626
46555CB00005B/2066
* 9 7 9 8 9 9 4 4 0 7 7 1 4 *